DATE DUE

FEB 10 1994			

INTEGRATION AND COMMUNITY BUILDING
IN EASTERN EUROPE

INTEGRATION AND COMMUNITY BUILDING
IN EASTERN EUROPE

Jan F. Triska, series editor

The German Democratic Republic
Arthur M. Hanhardt, Jr.

The Polish People's Republic
James F. Morrison

The Development of Socialist Yugoslavia
M. George Zaninovich

The People's Republic of Albania
Nicholas C. Pano

The Czechoslovak Socialist Republic
Zdenek Suda

The Socialist Republic of Rumania
Stephen Fischer-Galati

The Hungarian People's Republic
Bennett Kovrig

Revolution Administered:
Agrarianism and Communism in Bulgaria
Nissan Oren

REVOLUTION ADMINISTERED

AGRARIANISM AND COMMUNISM IN BULGARIA

NISSAN OREN

THE JOHNS HOPKINS UNIVERSITY PRESS

Baltimore and London

The Johns Hopkins University Press, Baltimore, Maryland 21218
The Johns Hopkins University Press Ltd., London

Library of Congress Catalog Card Number 72-8831
ISBN 0-8018-1209-7 (clothbound edition)
ISBN 0-8018-1210-0 (paperback edition)
Manufactured in the United States of America

Originally published, 1973
Johns Hopkins Paperbacks edition, 1973

Library of Congress Cataloging in Publication Data will be found on the last printed page of this book.

In Memory of

GICHEV, MUSHANOV, and PASTUKHOV,

Men of Politics and Courage

CONTENTS

FOREWORD

This study of the People's Republic of Bulgaria is the eighth and last of a series of monographs dealing with integration and community building among the Communist party states of Eastern Europe. These studies of East European countries are part of a larger program of studies of the Communist systems sponsored by Stanford University.

It seems appropriate here to outline the theoretical and methodological concepts that were developed for the series as a whole. The focus has been on the world Communist movement as a system. The major underlying assumption is that each Communist party state has characteristics peculiar to it which predispose it toward varying degrees of cooperation, coordination, and integration with the others. We think that the present behavioral characteristics of the system can be traced to environmental, attitudinal, and systemic factors, and that we can learn a great deal from a comparative analysis of the process and degree of integration of each member state into the system of Communist party states—whether, for example, the process involves force or consent, similar or shared institutions and codes of behavior, or whether integration is effective at elite levels and/or lower levels as well, and so on.

The concept of political integration and community formation and maintenance is, as a focus of intellectual curiosity and investigation, as old as the study of politics. The mushrooming of supranational integration movements since World War II has given a considerable new impetus to the old curiosity and has changed the emphasis of the investigations. Social scientists who in the last two decades have been building a general theory of political integration—whether on a subnational, national, or supranational level—have been perhaps less concerned with the philosophical content of the concept of integration than with discovering operational indicators that would endow the concept with empirical meaning and allow the theory to be tested for validity and reliability. The principal centers of their inquiry have been two broad, independent variables, *interaction* and *attitude*. Although in most cases investigated separately, interaction and attitude are assumed to combine to constitute a *community*, the *objective* of the *process* of integration.

The principal subjects of inquiry have been *transactions* across the boundaries of state units and *attitude formation* within the states. The theorists stipulate that numerous transactions are necessary for political integration and they postulate that the density of transactions among the units indicates their relationship to one another. The flow of mail and telephone traffic; trade; aid; exchange of tourists, officials, and migrants; cultural exchange of persons and communications; newspapers, periodicals, and book sales and translations; radio, TV, and motion picture exchange; mutual treaties and agreements; common organizations and conferences—these are the kinds of indicators that, measured and plotted over time, should demonstrate the direction of integrational trends and developments.

With reference to *attitude formation,* theorists have been more concerned with the process of integration than with its results (conditions) within the individual states. The pertinent literature yields relatively little on this subject. In *Nationalism and Social Communication,* Karl Deutsch argues that it may be fruitful to study two sets of persons within a unit of analysis: those "mobilized" for integrational communications and those "assimilated" into the new and larger unit. If those assimilated multiply at a more rapid rate than those mobilized, then "assimilation" is gaining and "community is growing faster than society."

At present, enormous problems are involved in studying the *results* of the integration process in Communist countries. It is difficult to assess attitudes, because of the great sensitivity of officials and decision-makers, and it is either difficult or impossible to get reliable aggregate and survey data. This informational problem makes it correspondingly difficult to develop a general theory of integration or to make systematic comparative analyses. We have therefore been compelled to rely on indicators of degrees and trends, indicators which depend considerably on subjective judgment and inference.

Although the data available are uneven in quality and quantity, our approach has been rigorous and systematic. Each author was asked to examine the country under review with reference to five historical periods: (1) the pre-Communist stage before the country became a party state and hence a member of the system; (2) the period of the Communists' consolidation of power after World War II, when the states of Eastern Europe entered the system; (3) the subsequent era of repression and rigid controls; (4) the period of relaxed controls following Stalin's death; (5) the last ten years. For each of these periods, as appropriate, each author was asked to identify and analyze the phenomena relevant to that country's integration into the system, its ecological-physical features, its demographic structure, belief system, social system, degree of autonomy, its dependence on other states, and its hopes, needs, and expectations with regard to integration and development. Within these broad confines, each author was asked to emphasize the periods and events having the greatest significance for the integrational development of the country in question. It is our feeling that a more rigid set of prescriptions would have been self-defeating, in view of our objectives and the exploratory nature of our undertaking.

The present study by Nissan Oren examines those aspects of behavior of the People's Republic of Bulgaria which are significant in terms of integration and community formation with its socialist neighbors and allies. But again, and to an even greater extent than was the case in the other studies in this series, the real issue is the Soviet-Bulgarian relationship. As Professor Oren puts it, with a touch of sad irony: "Having preserved for Bulgaria her prewar frontiers, the Communists proceeded to reduce the country to the level of yet another Soviet socialist republic, along with Armenia, Georgia, Estonia, and the remaining components of the enormous Great Russian domain. As a result, politics was converted into mere public administration, and international politics has all but lost its meaning in the process. Rather than turn it into a Soviet regional subsystem, the Communists effectively integrated the land of this once unruly people into the Soviet in-system. Bulgaria's present-day statesmen—if such they be—act more like Soviet regional governors than like Russian imperial viceroys. The absurd charges brought by Stalin's secret agents against the Bulgarian Communist émigrés in the thirties, accusing them of conspiracy to annex the Ukraine to Bulgaria, have, in the reverse situation, proved not so absurd. For all practical purposes, the Soviet Union annexed Bulgaria, despite the absence of land contiguity."

The present study is divided into seven historical parts. Each period is discussed in terms of the changes that took place in the environment of the Bulgarian socio-economic-political system—both in other parts of the Communist system and in the rest of the world—and is analyzed for the most significant domestic changes relevant to Bulgaria's integration into the system. In addition, there is a discussion in each period of the changes that took place in the form and degree of Bulgaria's integration into the system, the costs and benefits for various segments of the Bulgarian population, and the major conflicts between Bulgaria and the rest of the system resulting from the nature of the integration during the given period.

The series is an intellectual product of many creative minds. In addition to the authors of the individual monographs—in this case, Professor Nissan Oren—I would like to thank especially Professor David D. Finley of The Colorado College for his original contribution and assistance.

JAN F. TRISKA

Institute of Political Studies
Stanford University

PREFACE

Bulgaria lies in the shadows of European politics. Developments of the last generation have left her in a state of immobility on the international scene. This explains but does not justify the absence of sustained scholarly effort. The country remains the cornerstone of the Soviet presence in the Balkans today, just as the German Third Reich cultivated Bulgaria as its main bastion in the center of the Balkan peninsula. While dominion over Bulgaria has never provided sufficient guarantee of the consolidation of the entire region by a Great Power, primacy over Southeastern Europe cannot be effected without control over the land of the Bulgarians. This truism was first perceived by the Russians and the Germans. The real significance of Bulgaria has not come to be appreciated by the West, however. This has worked to the detriment of Western interests in Europe, of the Balkan region as a whole, and, not least of all, of the Bulgarian people themselves.

In the main, Bulgaria is important not for her geostrategic position but for her people, her society, and her politics. In no other land in contemporary Europe has the clash between agrarianism and communism—Marx against the peasant—been more vividly manifested. For a time, the peasantry attained not only a position in politics but a comprehensive, homebred ideology as well. The antecedents of Bulgarian communism contained a measure of originality of their own which was only gradually lost to the preponderance of Russian communism.

The present work endeavors to serve as an outline of the major trends and political sequences in the development of Bulgaria from the end of the First World War to the present. The intention has been to provide the reader with an overview, rather than with a detailed survey, of chronological events. Politics, domestic and international, has been given precedence over economics. Similarly, the basic positions of the various political groupings have been given preference over the roles of individual leaders. This is reflected in the references and in the bibliography. The latter, although moderately extensive, contains only a few of the published political biographies and autobiographies and omits periodic literature altogether. Only a few of the more important articles appear in the footnotes. Statistical data have been kept to the minimum. They are readily available in works already published in Western languages.

The brief Introduction of the present study endeavors to bring together some of the major phenomena which have converged on Bulgaria. Chapters 1 and 2 provide a general survey of the interwar years. The first deals with the domestic political scene, while the second is devoted to Bulgaria's foreign affairs. Chapter 3 centers on the Second World War. The attention here has been given to Great Power diplomacy as well as to the distribution of power within the country. Chapter 4 covers the first years of sovietization. It opens with the entry of the Red Army into the country and closes with the destruction of the anti-Communist opposition. Chapter 5 is devoted to the years of the greatest terror, which coincided with the rule of Chervenkov. The more significant developments from the mid-fifties through the late sixties are traced in Chapter 6. Chapter 7 is organized in the form of a vertical incision of the contemporary scene, with a discussion of the new Constitution and the Tenth Communist Party Congress held in the spring of 1971.

The very real hardships faced by the student of East European politics can hardly be overstated. Communist-produced histories, as well as histories written by non-Communists, have their own biases. The scholar is forced to steer his way through these unchartered waters as best he can. Certainly, there are no set rules for the attainment of objectivity, which, in any case, the present author does not dare claim. Despite the great out-pouring of printed materials from Bulgaria, a great many valu-able monographs and personal accounts have remained in manuscript form on deposit with the Bulgarian Academy of Sciences or with the Institute for Party History; these are avail-able only to the official Bulgarian historians. Unfortunately, Bulgarian political exiles forced out of the country by the Communist regime have so far produced little or nothing. They carry an obligation which they must fulfill soon, for time is running short.

I am thankful to Jan F. Triska, the series editor, for having invited me to write this volume. Mr. John G. Gallman of the Indiana University Press was the first to suggest to me that I undertake the preparation of this volume. I am particularly grateful to Mr. J. G. Goellner of The Johns Hopkins University Press for his advice and great patience. My gratitude goes as well to Penny James, of the Hopkins Press, who edited the final manuscript, and to Susan Kerman, who prepared the index. While working on the book, I was aided by a research grant awarded to me by The Eliezer Kaplan School of Economics and Social Sciences of The Hebrew University of Jerusalem. I would like to express my special appreciation to Miss Rivka Dyckman for her invaluable assistance in editing and typing the various drafts. Finally, as ever, my thanks go to Hannah, my wife, for her wisdom and patience.

NISSAN OREN

The Hebrew University of Jerusalem

REVOLUTION ADMINISTERED

INTRODUCTION

The time span of this study is very wide. The period covered is dealt with in two almost equal parts, each stretching over a full generation: the first half surveys developments from the end of World War I until the end of World War II; the second half opens with the entry of the Red Army into Bulgaria and closes with the present day.

If spontaneity were to be applied as the test for revolutionary change, 1918 and the years that followed could be said to have witnessed a revolutionary upheaval more genuine than that of the early years of sovietization. The first transformation came in the aftermath of a crushing defeat on the battlefield which generated the rage of the masses and gave rise to violent resentments which subsided only gradually. The coup d'état of September 9, 1944, carried out immediately after contingents of the Red Army had started crossing the Danube, came about in a context of less upheaval. In the First World War, the Bulgarian people invested all they had. In the main, Bulgaria remained aloof from the fighting in the Second World War. With its defeat, the Bulgarian army of 1918 turned its back to the fighting front and marched on the capital, seeking revenge from its own leaders. In September, 1944, the Germans withdrew from Bulgaria and were replaced by the armies of Soviet Russia. The country was impoverished but not devastated. Although demoralized, the Bulgarian army remained intact. There was dissatisfaction as well as hope for a better future. Except for an extremist fringe, however, the people at large showed little inclination for revolutionary change.

Yet, 1944 opened an entirely new era in Bulgarian history, in the course of which the country underwent a fundamental transformation. On the other hand, the flames of 1918 and after were gradually extinguished. From the mid-twenties on, Bulgaria settled down to a state of affairs which, although far from being harmonious, came to approximate the traditionalist past. In all respects, interwar Bulgaria remained more akin to the Bulgaria of the decade preceding the outbreak of World War I than to post-1944 Bulgaria.

The victorious Allies of 1918 imposed their terms on the country and brought about a new political settlement. At the same time, except for a token number of Allied troops, Bulgaria was not occupied. From September, 1944, until the fall of 1947, Bulgaria remained under the massive physical occupation of the Red Army. The imposition of Soviet might on the land assured the rule of Russia's favorites. Thus, the Bulgarian Communist party became the transmission belt by means of which Moscow conveyed and imposed its will. The insufficiency of revolutionary spontaneity from below was compensated for by Russia's determination to remake the country in her own image. A new social ordering was brought about by a revolution administered from the top. And yet, the transformation of the society and its economy did not take place in a vacuum. The process of sovietization could not develop independently of Bulgaria's specific conditions. Bulgaria's historic heritage and recent past made their own claims on the future development of the country. The use of violence did not, and could not, totally obliterate the force of continuity.

The Bulgarians were relatively late in succumbing to the forces of modern nationalism. Their national awakening came well after the sovereign nation-state had become a reality in Western Europe. More significantly, modern national consciousness struck root in Bulgaria after the Greeks, the Serbs, and the Rumanians had become politically independent or were well on their way to doing so. The reasons for this retarded nationalist development were manifold. The Turks, who had ruled Bulgaria for centuries, were eager to retain their grip on this, their last European dominion, to the end. They were not interested in seeing the small Slavic community gain a nationalist identity of its own, and they did all they could to suppress the early political symptoms of the impulse for freedom.

More fundamentally, however, the Bulgarians were peasant people who for the most part did not populate the urban centers of their country. The towns, such as they were, were inhabited overwhelmingly by Turks, Greeks, Jews, and other minorities. In the countryside, the Bulgarians retained their tongue, their religion, and their mores. In the main, the villages in which they lived were small and isolated. They did not constitute an easy base on which modern nationalist ideas could develop. An overwhelmingly rural Bulgaria was late in developing its own intelligentsia. Thus, the modern nationalism which had swept Europe was slow in gathering momentum on Bulgaria's soil. The spirit of the new ideas filtered in only gradually. The sons of the well-to-do peasants, who traveled for their studies to Europe and even more so to Russia, became the chief propagators of the new concepts. Gradually, Bulgaria's forgotten history became a reality. The Bulgarians turned back to the grandeur of the medieval Bulgarian kingdom for inspiration. Reality and the myth of the past mingled to make the present and, especially, the future.

The Bulgarians did not escape the fate of other small peoples. Ultimately, political independence was contingent upon the rise of nationalist consciousness at home, as it was linked with the European Great Power configurations. Even though independence was inevitable, its timing was determined by the outcome of the struggle for power in the Balkans, in which a number of European countries engaged throughout the nineteenth century. There was, in addition, one more dimension to Bulgaria's international position: the relations of the Bulgarians with the other peoples in the region. After gaining its independence, sovereign Bulgaria faced an equation which it found difficult to resolve. Relations with the Great Powers could not easily be squared with the inevitable regional conflicts. In the first decades, Austro-Hungary and Russia presented themselves as potential backers. The constant rivalry between the two gave Bulgaria some room to maneuver. In her dealings with the larger world

Bulgaria could alternate her diplomatic orientations. Her regional neighbors, however, were fixed and given. Her national designs stood in conflict with the interests of the Serbs, Greeks, Turks, and Rumanians. Particularly after the disastrous outcome of the Balkan wars and of the First World War, Bulgaria's regional conflicts became perpetual. Her regional battles precluded the possibility of total disengagement from the Great Powers. Cast in a revisionist role from the outset, Bulgaria required the active support of at least one European Great Power at all times. This need was, and remains, a fixture of Bulgarian diplomacy.

The fundamental reason for this dependence was Bulgaria's unfulfilled national aspirations. Repeatedly, the Bulgarians tried but failed to enclose within their political boundaries the areas and peoples whom they considered to be integral parts of the "Bulgarian tribe." In the early years, the choice alternated between Vienna and Saint Petersburg. In the twenties, when Austria had become irrelevant, Germany lay prostrate, and Russia had succumbed to Bolshevik rule, the Bulgarians tried their hand at maintaining an entente with Mussolini's Italy. France and the West were committed to Bulgaria's rivals and thus were irrelevant. In the thirties, Germany became the only acceptable alternative. After Germany's defeat in the Second World War, only Soviet Russia was available as a successor.

The desire to see Macedonia and Thrace as integral parts of the Bulgarian state mobilized and committed the better part of the nation's energies. Since Bulgaria's national designs were always larger than her true capabilities, her endeavors met with failure. The net results were detrimental to Bulgaria as well as to her neighbors. One cannot place the blame on Bulgaria's leaders alone, as some historians do. The sentiments which moved the people to take up arms repeatedly were genuine and profound rather than the product of political manipulation. It is much too early to determine whether or not the sovietization of Bulgaria, which has lasted a full generation, has in any way mitigated these same national impulses.

1: THE INTERWAR: FROM TURMOIL TO AUTHORITARIANISM

The political events in interwar Bulgaria centered on three major cataclysms. The first was the military defeat suffered at the end of the First World War. The second was the forceful elimination of the Agrarian regime at the hands of a military-political coalition. The third was the military *Putsch* of 1934. These events cut across the twenty-year period of relative peace. They, more than any other single factor, shaped the domestic scene, repeatedly bringing about a new distribution of power.

The defeat in war gave rise to a revolutionary wave nourished by popular suffering and a crushing national disappointment. Unable to sustain the stresses of modern war, the Bulgarians bore the major brunt of the fighting in the southeast. The country's meager resources were devoted to the support of a peasant army which, in material terms, stood little chance of containing, for any length of time, the Anglo-French expeditionary force on the Salonika front.

Yet, the revolutionary energies released by the general military collapse were deflected and temporarily contained by the forces of peasant populism. Although poor, the Bulgarian peasants possessed the land they tilled. They had appropriated their small plots of land immediately after their liberation from the Turks. As a class, the peasants constituted an egalitarian society. Moreover, they had acquired the rudiments of a political organization long before the war. The Bulgarian Agrarian Union represented the peasants in politics.

Once defeat had become a reality, the Agrarian Union stepped in and undertook to change the sociopolitical destiny of the country. For a time, the Agrarians succeeded in stabilizing the revolutionary potential in midcourse, thus preventing a deterioration to the extreme left. The Agrarian Union saw itself not as the carrier of a counterrevolution but as the architect of a revolution of its own. The Agrarians endeavored to establish their own political hegemony in the face of antagonism from both rightists and leftists. They developed new forms of political action and introduced a new style of political dominion. They presented the country with a comprehensive program which proposed to answer both the national and the socioeconomic problems. The first postwar years, therefore, represented the Agrarian era.

Ultimately, the Agrarians were not permitted to bring their consolidation of power to fruition. The old middle-class formations, aided by representatives of the professional military corps, combined to cut short their reign. In this process the extreme left, in the form of the Communist party, played no significant independent role. The rightist coalition was powerful enough to tackle its Agrarian rivals by utilizing its own resources. While this was being done, the Communists remained aloof. They were dealt with after the Agrarians had been deposed. The consolidation of power by the middle-class factions was to prove more successful than the earlier Agrarian attempt. However, the establishment of middle-class hegemony during the mid-twenties brought the country to a state of civil war. The process necessitated the employment of massive repression directed equally against the forces of populism and communism.

By the late twenties, a new equilibrium had emerged. Gradually, the more moderate elements among the Agrarians were reintegrated into the new political system. In 1931, a coalition of the moderate middle-class factions combined with the recently resurrected Agrarian Union to fight and win an electoral victory. This opened the way for the establishment of a new regime based on an urban-peasant alliance. For a brief time during the early thirties, Bulgaria appeared to have discovered the ways and means to a pluralistic political structure based on a free, if undisciplined, interaction of the major forces at work. The new political processes would have proved more successful in introducing some sanity to the Bulgarian body politic had they not been curtailed once again by the intervention of the army, this time acting by itself.

The *Putsch* of May, 1934, was a capricious political act. The military was powerful enough to move in and disestablish constitutional rule, but proved powerless to consolidate political power. Its stated intention was to place Bulgaria on a new road to modernization. In reality, the consequence of its intervention was to open the way for the rise of a one-man authoritarianism exercised by the king. In the second half of the thirties, Bulgaria was ruled by the king's autocracy in the absence of meaningful countervailing forces. Political pluralism was all but stifled, and the country came to be administered by decree. Parliament became a shadow and the country's political groupings were reduced to little more than ghost parties. The military, which had unwittingly made the king's personal supremacy possible, was dealt with in turn. This was the last twist in the complicated sequence of events in which the defeat in 1918 was only the first act.

In mid-September, 1918, the Allied forces in the south opened their final and decisive offensive against the Bulgarian army. The Bulgarian front at Dobro Pole was broken through on September 18. Despite desperate efforts, the Bulgarians were unable to hold their lines of defense. Large contingents of the army were encircled, and some 100,000 soldiers were taken prisoner. At the time of the debacle the Bulgarians had penetrated deep into occupied territory and were far removed from their old boundaries. Their retreat soon turned into a rout. The fleeing soldiers cast aside their commanders and began to converge on the capital, where they sought revenge. On September 25, the cabinet decided to declare an immediate armistice. That same day, on the initiative of the war minister, Alexander Stamboliiski, the leader of the Agrarian Union who had been in prison because of his opposition to the war, was freed. He was asked to go to the army in an attempt to appease the rebellious soldiers. Because of the high esteem in which he was held by the peasants, it was hoped that his personal intervention would help stem the rising revolutionary wave. At this crucial juncture Stamboliiski wavered. His fiery oratory failed to dissuade the rebellious soldiers, who proceeded to proclaim the so-called Radomir Republic. At the insistence of some of his lieutenants, Stamboliiski decided to join in the rebellion, becoming its nominal head.

The reckoning came in the last days of September. The government in Sofia dispatched several units of officer cadets from the military academy who, supported by a number of German military units, fought and ultimately decimated the rebellious contingents at the very gates of the capital. By October 2, the soldiers' rebellion had been put down. In the meantime, a Bulgarian delegation had reached Salonika, where, on September 29, an armistice agreement was signed. It provided for the immediate withdrawal of all Bulgarian army units from territories occupied during the war, as well as the withdrawal from Bulgarian territory of all the military contingents of the Central Powers. On October 3, Ferdinand abdicated and was succeeded to the throne by his son Boris.[1]

Although the rebellion had been suppressed, Bulgaria lingered on the brink of revolution. On October 17, 1918, representatives of the Agrarian Union were brought into a newly formed coalition government. This was a significant development, for it indicated the growing dependence upon the Agrarians for the maintenance of stability. With every successive government, the relative weight of the Agrarians increased. In the general elections of August, 1919, the Agrarian Union

[1] The literature dealing with Bulgaria's experiences during the two Balkan wars and the First World War is very large indeed. The most detailed and extensive accounts are given in Girginov's four volumes—namely, *Narodnata katastrofa: Voinite, 1912–1913; Bulgariia pred Velikata voina; Izpitaniata v voinata, 1915–1918;* and *Ot voinata kum mir.* Wartime politics and the stands of Bulgaria's politicians are dealt with in Omarachevski, *Bulgarskite upravnitsi prez Svetovnata voina: Fakti i dokumenti,* while the aftermath of the war is traced in Tsankov, *Posledstvie ot voinata.* Khristov's *Revoliutsionnata kriza v Bulgariia prez 1918–1919* represents a detailed monograph on the soldiers' rebellion which has a pro-Communist bias. For an objective view of the short-lived Radomir Republic, see Rothschild, *The Communist Party of Bulgaria,* Chap. 4.

emerged with the largest plurality, followed by the Communists, who became the second largest political force in Bulgaria. On October 6 of the same year, Stamboliiski became premier of his first coalition government. He led the Bulgarian delegation to Paris, where the peace treaty with Bulgaria was signed on November 27, 1919.

The terms imposed on the country were harsh, both politically and economically. Bulgaria lost western Thrace, which she had gained in the Balkan wars and which had given her access to the Aegean. She was forced to surrender territory to the newly constituted Yugoslav kingdom as well. Faced with imminent bankruptcy, the country was required to pay substantial reparations to the victorious Allies. The impact of the imposed peace was to accentuate the process of political polarization. As the strength of the Agrarians steadily increased, so did the influence and power of the Communists. The Agrarians disbanded Parliament in February, 1920, and organized new general elections in the following month which led to the formation of the first all-Agrarian government in May. The Communists received 20 percent of the popular vote. The growth of populism, on the one hand, and the threat from the extreme left, on the other, forced the leaders of the traditional political groups to unite.[2]

The Bulgarian political scene in the early twenties showed unique characteristics that were unmatched in any other country in Eastern Europe. The assumption of power by the Agrarians was made possible by the particular circumstances which arose at the end of the war. Although the Agrarians were ill-prepared for power, and the major role they were required to play was to contain the revolutionary upsurge, they were unwilling to become the stooges of anyone. They possessed an ideology of their own which, although simplistic in its content, gave them the self-assurance necessary to perceive themselves as the masters of Bulgaria's destiny.

Since the peasants constituted the overwhelming majority of the populace, it was for them to decide how the national wealth

[2] On the growing powers of the Agrarian Union and the successive postwar coalition cabinets leading to the establishment of an all-Agrarian cabinet, see *Istoriia na Bulgariia*, 2nd ed., 3: 48–78.

was to be distributed. The Agrarian regime was determined to ensure that the countryside received a proportionate share of the public expenditure. This constituted a radical departure from the past, when the countryside had been kept subservient to the interests of the small but growing towns. The determination of the Agrarians to remake the country in accordance with the will of the villages placed them in an anomalous position. To fortify their position within the state bureaucracy they were forced to bring their peasant followers into the government administration. This threatened the very existence of the civil servants and outraged the urban intelligentsia.

Stamboliiski's patriotism was never in question. The premier was convinced, however, that Bulgaria had to shed her national obsession over Macedonia if she were to recover from the crippling effects of the war and defeat. His attitude toward the national problem found no acceptance among the professional military class, and his policies aroused the determined enmity of the many displaced Macedonians who had found their way into Bulgaria proper. The Agrarian leadership was anti-monarchist as well. Although this did not make them doctrinaire republicans, the court remained suspicious and readily inclined to extend a helping hand to any and all of Stamboliiski's enemies.[3]

The small working class was equally divided between the Social Democrats and the Communists. The latter enjoyed substantial influence in the countryside as well. The Social Democrats saw the Agrarians as the spearhead of the village reaction, with which they would not collaborate.[4] The leaders of the

[3] The literature on the Bulgarian Agrarian movement is extensive. Yet, a definitive history of the political and socioeconomic views of the Agrarians during the first two decades of this century, and of Stamboliiski, their most outstanding leader, has not appeared. The following is but a sample of the most important available sources: Stamboliiski, *Politicheski partii ili suslovni organizatsii?* Petkov, *Aleksandur Stamboliiski: Lichnost i idei;* Spisarevski, *Zemedelskoto dvizhenie v Bulgariia: Poteklo i razvitie;* Kozhukharov, *Alaeksandur Stamboliiski: Biograficheski ocherk.* For a somewhat later statement of the major principles of Agrarian ideology in English, see the article by Dr. G. M. Dimitrov in Gross, ed., *European Ideologies.*

[4] On the Social Democrats' attitudes toward Stamboliiski as expressed by their leader, Krustiu Pastukhov, see Swire, *Bulgarian Conspiracy,* p. 156; see also various parts of Kazasov, *Burni godini.* The Communist position is fully documented in Rothschild, *The Communist Party of Bulgaria,* as well as in the immediately following references. ⟨

Communist party were too firmly set in an orthodox Marxist cast to appreciate the potential revolutionary energies encased within the ranks of the Agrarian Union. From a purely doctrinal viewpoint, the intellectuals of the Communist party preferred the middle class to the unruly peasant. Thus, the political spectrum was divided in three major ways. The political wars were to be fought on the basis of all against all. The path to temporary alignment between any two of the three major political constellations remained firmly blocked.

In the early spring of 1923, Stamboliiski moved to solidify his newly achieved hegemony. Relying on their advantage as the only ruling political party in the country, the Agrarians undertook yet another general election, which was to give them a clear-cut majority. The elections were held on April 22. Stamboliiski received almost 53 percent of the popular vote, the Communists almost 19 percent, with the remaining votes being divided among all other political factions.[5] The convincing victory of the party in power intensified the process of unification of the parties within the middle-class camp and hastened the development of an anti-Agrarian political conspiracy which had already been hatched.

The coup against the Stamboliiski regime was carried out in June. The undertaking was the collective effort of the military, the great majority of the traditional political leaders, the Macedonians, and the court itself. Politically, the coup was well prepared and proved an immediate success, even though it required bloodshed. Stamboliiski was apprehended and murdered. The capital was occupied and subdued with relative ease. The sporadic and unorganized opposition in the countryside was put down by the force of arms. Despite the rapidity with which the conspiracy prevailed, Stamboliiski enjoyed a powerful allegiance among the peasantry. The diffusion of the political organization in the villages, however, placed the countryside at a disadvantage vis-à-vis the centralized state machinery, whose upper levels were captured by the putschists.[6]

---

[5] The Agrarian Union received 569,139 votes, the Communists 203,972, the Center parties 166,909, the Social Democrats 27,816, with the remaining votes going to the various other political groups; the figures are taken from Kazasov, *Burni godini*, p. 127.

[6] Mitev, *Fashistkiiat prevrat na Deveti iuni 1923 godina* is the single most detailed account of the anti-Stamboliiski *Putsch*. It suffers, however, from an ob-

Peasant populism, as a maximalist political phenomenon, was thus stifled. Stamboliiski's experiment in politics became a powerful mythos and has remained so to the present. As a political force, agrarianism preserved much of its appeal, although its resurrection required a thoroughgoing reform from within.

The conspirators who carried out the anti-Stamboliiski coup constituted a political coalition known as the People's Alliance. Its core consisted of representatives of the Military League. On the civilian side, the People's Alliance was headed by Professor Alexander Tsankov and included leaders from the National Liberal party, the Progressive party, the Democrats, the Radicals, and one representative of the Social Democratic party. The premiership was assumed by Professor Tsankov. In August, 1923, he undertook to enlarge the People's Alliance with the aim of transforming it into the widest possible national coalition. His efforts were only partly successful. The new formation, called the Democratic Alliance, emerged as an enlargement of the original coalition. A number of minor splinter groups were added, as was the Populist party, headed by Atanas Burov. A segment of the Democrats, headed by Malinov, and a section of the Radicals, under Stoian Kosturkov, refused to join the new group. But the majority of Democrats, headed by Andrei Liapchev, stayed within the alliance.

As finally constituted, the coalition was a substantial cluster of forces which dominated Bulgarian politics until 1931. The Democratic Alliance enjoyed the confidence of the army, which contributed the substance of authority. It was and remained devoid of any ideological coloring. A desire to stay in power and a sense of disgust toward the appeals of agrarianism and communism were all that kept the otherwise heterogeneous faction together. The civilian leadership of the alliance was exercised by Tsankov, Liapchev, and Burov, who together formed the working triumvirate of the new regime. It was always possible

---

vious pro-Communist bias. Kazasov's *V tumninite na zagovora*, published in 1925, is an important personal account by a major participant in the anti-Agrarian conspiracy. Agrarian-Communist relations before and during the *Putsch* are traced in detail and analyzed in Rothschild, *The Communist Party of Bulgaria,* pp. 117–32.

to reshuffle the composition of the government without changing the coalition on which it was based. Indeed, in January, 1926, Tsankov surrendered the premiership to Liapchev, who continued to hold office until the general elections of 1931.

Liapchev's premiership, which was the longest in interwar Bulgaria, was characterized by the gradual recovery of Bulgarian politics. The prerogatives of parliamentarianism were slowly expanded, and recourse to arbitrary administrative and police measures was limited. In the late twenties, Bulgaria enjoyed a free press which allowed the open expression of oppositionist views. The rule of law was applied generally, even though the regime demonstrated almost unlimited permissiveness toward the arbitrary political actions of the various Macedonian groups, on the one hand, and a firmly managed antagonism toward the Communists and a few of the more extremist followers of Stamboliiski's doctrines, on the other.[7]

Ultimately, the Democratic Alliance submitted to the test of free elections. In June of 1931, it was defeated on a free ballot by a left-of-center coalition which included the moderate wing of the reconstituted Agrarian Union. This was the last free electoral contest that Bulgaria would have. The regime was turned over to the People's Bloc, which consisted of four parties: the Agrarian Union, and the wings of the Democrats, Radicals, and Liberals which had stayed out of the Democratic Alliance. The Radicals and the Liberals were politically insignificant, for they were minor factions. The Agrarians and the Democrats formed the main axis of the People's Bloc. The principal portfolios went to the Democrats, with Malinov as premier. The Agrarians, headed by Dimitur Gichev, took over the ministries of secondary importance.

The internal distribution of the new government did not reflect the respective electoral might of the Democrats and the

[7] The rule of the Democratic Alliance has never been given fair treatment. It was hated by the Communists (a fact which has been consistently reflected in the post-1944 literature), disliked by the Agrarians, and opposed by the Social Democrats and the more liberal wings of Malinov's Democrats and Kosturkov's Radicals. The assessment offered above is the author's. The moderately favorable view taken is influenced in no small measure by the significant fact that, despite its many defects, ultimately, the Democratic Alliance opened the way to free elections and the restoration of full-fledged free party politics.

Agrarians. While the former had a total of forty-three deputies in the new Parliament, the Agrarians had seventy-two. Despite their numerical superiority, it was understood by everyone that the Agrarians could not head the new government so short a time after the anti-Stamboliiski coup and the repressions against his Agrarian followers, which had lasted through the mid-twenties. Furthermore, although the political might of the Democrats was limited, Malinov and his followers possessed a high degree of respectability and political acceptability which helped legitimize the People's Bloc as a whole. In this sense, the Democrats and the Agrarians complemented each other. As long as it lasted, the alliance between these two principal partners was profoundly significant for the Bulgarian body politic. Malinov's party spoke for the middle and lower-middle urban classes, as well as for some of the well-to-do elements in the countryside. The Democrats were both monarchists and extreme nationalists. Thus, they were well liked by the court as well as by the apolitical elements within the professional army. The Democrats were enlightened and politically experienced. These attributes compensated for the Agrarians' deficiencies, real or imaginary. Even though Gichev did not represent the entire spectrum of the Agrarian Union's following, he enjoyed the confidence and trust of the great majority of them in the countryside. Thus, at long last, Bulgaria appeared to have achieved an equilibrium between urban and rural interests.

Gichev's rise to prominence and his particular outlook on Bulgaria's political and socioeconomic problems are of interest and should be briefly traced. From their political inception the Agrarians had perceived themselves not as a political party but as a movement representing the entire countryside. Although the Bulgarian peasantry was structured along more egalitarian lines than that of any other country in Europe, as a class, the peasants were economically differentiated to a degree, and were becoming more so with the lapse of time. These distinctions were inevitably reflected within the Agrarian Union in the form of internal political factionalism. Factionalism had been a fact of life during Stamboliiski's time as well. Stamboliiski's charisma and prestige, as well as his centrist position, had given the Agrarian Union outward cohesiveness. His departure from the scene removed the underpinnings of the party's organizational unity and led to the formation of several Agrarian wings and winglets into formal factions, each claiming to represent the true disciple of the great master. After 1923 the extreme left joined hands with the Communists and was politically decimated. Some of the rightist factions survived in political limbo after having come to terms with the regime. A number of Stamboliiski's closest collaborators fled the country and found political asylum in Yugoslavia. They were joined by several thousand rank-and-file Agrarians forced out of the country by police repressions during the Tsankov regime.[8]

Gichev came from the second echelon of the Agrarian political hierarchy. A man of great native intelligence, Gichev possessed political integrity as well. His powerful oratory, devoid of political demagoguery, and his organizational abilities combined to give him a large measure of popularity and acceptability in the countryside. From a left-of-center position on the Agrarian political spectrum at the time of the coup, Gichev gradually moved to a right-of-center position in the late twenties. Although not an ideologist, he reformulated some of the basic tenets of agrarianism in terms of practical application. Stamboliiski's more extreme rhetoric on national and foreign-policy questions was dropped. As far as Gichev could see, Yugoslavia was not in a compromising mood and, therefore, the only way Bulgaria could hope to regain possession of Macedonia was by means of a revisionist foreign policy. Essentially, the difference between his stand and that taken by Stamboliiski in the past was more one of style and expression than one of substance. Gichev was not a visionary, nor was he a man of political expediency. As a realist and a man of wisdom, he was determined to see to it that the peasants' demand for political influ-

[8] The internal politics of the Agrarians in the period between the overthrow of Stamboliiski and the coming of the People's Bloc is utterly confused. Nikola Petkov's brother, Petko Petkov, emerged as the leader of the left-wing Agrarians, who, after the coup of 1923, collaborated with the Communists. He was soon murdered, however. The memoirs of Kosta Todorov (*Balkan Firebrand*), written during the Second World War, remain valuable on Agrarian factionalism and particularly on the politics of the Agrarian émigrés. Various sections of Rothschild, *The Communist Party of Bulgaria,* are invaluable. The intricate relations between Moscow and peasant politics in Eastern Europe throughout the twenties are covered by George D. Jackson, Jr., in *Comintern and Peasant in East Europe.*

ence be upheld in the actual bargaining process. To do so, he was prepared to cooperate with the spokesmen for the urban sectors. His willingness to share political power, rather than monopolize it, contributed to the restoration of the Agrarian Union as a legitimate political force.[9]

While Gichev's accommodative policies made him acceptable to the various power establishments in the country, he was open to attacks from the more radical quarters of the Agrarian movement. More specifically, he was made the target of criticism by the Agrarian émigrés and their collaborators at home. The latter split off and established an Agrarian Union of their own, popularly known as the Pladne group. In the early thirties, the Pladnists formed an organized opposition to the Gichev Agrarians. Following the return of the exiled Agrarian leaders to Bulgaria, the schism between the two deepened. The quarrel continued unabated until well into the first stage of sovietization after the Second World War. It consumed the better part of the political energies on both sides. Gichev's authority was thus impaired by forces which sprang from within the peasant movement. Still, he continued to command the support of what was probably the overwhelming majority of the politically minded peasants.[10]

[9] It is difficult to document objectively Gichev's career and his political ideas. One of the most influential and powerful men in Bulgaria's interwar period, he remains obscure and little appreciated except among those intimately familiar with Bulgarian politics. In retrospect, he is best judged by his deeds rather than by his speeches, which remain scattered in the Agrarian newspaper and periodical literature of the time and in the parliamentary minutes of the Bulgarian *Subranie* from 1923 to 1940. From the mid-twenties until his trial at the hands of the Communists in 1948, Gichev enjoyed—and deserved—a greater degree of popularity and mass support than any other leader in Bulgaria.

[10] On the formation of Pladne, formally known as "The Agrarian Union—A. Stamboliiski" (as distinguished from "The Agrarian Union—Vrabcha 1," which was the more formal name of the Gichev wing), see Oren, *Bulgarian Communism*, pp. 21–24, 26, and the various sections dealing with later developments. The single most important source on the conflicts between the Gichev and the Pladne Agrarians is *Narodno subranie: Stenografski dnevnitsi*, debates of December 7–9, 1938, pp. 289–366. Petrova, *BZNS i narodniiat front, 1934–1939*, is an important recent monograph devoted to Agrarian-Communist relations as well as to intra-Agrarian conflicts in the thirties. Despite its pro-Communist bias, the monograph contains otherwise unavailable important factual information. Todorov, *Balkan Firebrand*, remains of interest, largely because of Todorov's personal accounts as the outstanding leader of the Pladne group.

The regime of the People's Bloc lasted less than three years. Its short tenure of power commenced after the outbreak of the world's economic crisis. Even though Bulgaria escaped the worst of the depression, the crisis left its marks on the country's economy and on its society. The political partnership between Agrarians and Democrats was not given enough time to mature. The Agrarian politicians resented their underrepresentation in the government. Much of the government's time and energy was taken up by political trifles rather than by the great issues at stake. It was never able to create sufficient discipline, without which neither progress nor meaningful reform were possible. The state bureaucracy and local governments underwent extreme politicization. This strained the meager resources of the country to the utmost.

The fundamental ills of the country were not caused by the regime, however; rather, they were reflected by it. To emerge from her stagnation, Bulgaria required capital, domestic and foreign. The People's Bloc government was not able to generate such capital at home, nor was it able to import it from abroad in sufficient quantities. Economically and politically, the times were against the regime. Authoritarianism was fast becoming the new order of the day for much of Europe. Those countries in Eastern Europe which had not as yet become dictatorships were rapidly succumbing. Thus, the People's Bloc regime found itself in an anomalous position from the very day it assumed power. From the start, the government undertook to diminish the enormous domestic debt. Concrete measures were adopted to encourage the development of industry.[11]

[11] The state of the economy is best reflected in the official economic yearbook for 1940, *Statisticheski godishnik na tsarstvo Bulgariia*. Zagoroff, *The Economy of Bulgaria*, and Zagoroff et al., *The Agricultural Economy of the Danubian Countries, 1935–45*, provide a good analysis of major economic trends in the thirties. Zagoroff's main contention is that the depression affected but did not disrupt Bulgaria's economy for any length of time. A clear trend toward economic recovery had already set in by the mid-thirties. Bulgaria's rapid integration within the new German economic system helped agricultural exports. As in other peasant countries, much of the urban unemployment remained invisible largely because of the shift of workers in industry back to the countryside, where they subsisted for a time. The prognosis of Communist economic historians is much graver. Natan, *Ikonomicheska istoriia na Bulgariia*, is the most outstanding work by a Communist. Its value is greater for the statistics reproduced than for

In the latter part of its tenure, the regime endeavored to restrain the unruly Macedonian groups which fought each other in the streets of Sofia and kept the country in a constant state of terror. While it continued to maintain a firm anti-Communist posture at home, the government initiated a cautious policy of rapprochement with the Soviet Union, the purpose of which was to estabilsh normal diplomatic relations. Although it remained committed to a policy of revisionism on the international scene, after 1933 the regime sought to relax somewhat Bulgaria's overwhelming dependence on Mussolini's Italy in matters of foreign policy. All these were constructive moves. The fact that they were made while the country preserved its essential political pluralism was to the credit of the People's Bloc regime. None of the new approaches could be brought to fruition, however, because of the sudden intervention of irresponsible political groups from the antidemocratic camp.

Following the elections of 1931, the Democratic Alliance fell apart. The leadership of those Democrats who had participated in the alliance fell to insignificant men following the death of Liapchev. The remaining groups deteriorated as well, working themselves into political irrelevance. Professor Tsankov struck out on his own. He used his substantial political abilities to organize a cryptofascist party, popularly known as the Tsankov movement. Tsankov's personal influence on many prominent Bulgarians, including large segments of the urban intelligentsia, was substantial. Although he insisted throughout on the originality of his social and political ideas, the influence of Italian fascism and German national socialism on his movement was unmistakable. He was aided by the spirit of the times. With anti-Bolshevik slogans high on the lists of almost all political

---

the analysis offered. The relative position of foreign capital in the economy is analyzed in Natan and Berov, *Monopolisticheskiiat kapitalizum v Bulgariia.* Although significant in relative terms, foreign capital investments in Bulgaria remained small in absolute terms. Chakalov's *Formi, razmer i deinost na chuzhdiia kapital v Bulgariia, 1878–1944,* and *Natsionalniiat dokhod i razkhod na Bulgariia, 1924–1945,* are the most significant contributions to the economic history of Bulgaria. Khadzhiiliev's *Natrupvaneto i potreblenieto v ikonomikata na Bulgariia pri kapitalizma* and Grigorov's *Razvitie na burzhoaznata ikonomicheska misul v Bulgariia mezhdu dvete Svetovni voini* are instructive and important.

parties and with fascist successes mounting in Europe, Tsankov was quick to capitalize on the disillusionment which had overcome many elements in the country. His appeal, however, was almost entirely restricted to the urban population. By the majority of peasants he was called "Bloody Tsankov," for he had murdered Stamboliiski.

Tsankov's political formulations were complex and somewhat vague. He opposed political parties because they were based on class distinctions. Nazism and bolshevism, he believed, would eventually converge into what he termed "social nationalism." Tsankov was aware of the peculiarities of what he called the "Slav temperament" and insisted that Bulgaria could not import a ready-made political system from the outside. During the early thirties, there was a degree of freshness in Tsankov's neofascist demagoguery. He made a special effort to attract the laboring masses to his movement. Tsankov was decisively opposed to the class struggle and insisted that employers had to make concessions to the working class in order to arrest the radicalization process among the destitute. Even though several other pro-Nazi and profascist political groups emerged in the thirties, the Tsankov movement remained the most powerful among them. His oratory and the noisy campaigns of his followers did much to subvert the authority of the People's Bloc regime. Although he was not to attain power himself, his political activities contributed greatly to the general demoralization which made the rise of authoritarianism possible.[12]

Whereas Tsankov and his followers represented a fascist-like movement grown on Bulgarian soil, interwar Bulgarian politics gave rise to yet another political formation which, from the start, evolved as a unique Bulgarian creation. This was the Zveno group, formally known as the Political Circle Zveno. In one way or another, the great majority of Zveno's leaders were political disciples of Tsankov. In fact, until 1934 and beyond, most of them remained affiliated with Tsankov while belonging to the Zveno group as well. Since the Zveno group claimed not to be a political party as such, but a political consortium of

---

[12] His political and socioeconomic views are explained in Tsankov, *Trite stopanski sistemi*. His theoretical formulations only occasionally coincided with his actions.

persons from the various parties in the country, dual affiliations were compatible.

Zveno grew out of a publication by the same name which first appeared in 1928 under the editorship of Dimo Kazasov. In his earlier days, Kazasov had been a prominent member of the Bulgarian Social Democratic party. He was initiated into the anti-Stamboliiski conspiracy at an early stage and served as a minister of communications after the *Putsch* of 1923. His connection with the Social Democrats was finally severed in 1926, whereupon he entered the political arena on his own. In large measure, his ability as a journalist helped make *Zveno* (the publication) into a journal of some distinction.

The Zveno group attained its political prominence during the regime of the People's Bloc. Unlike the Tsankov movement, the Zveno group did not develop a comprehensive political ideology. Nor did the group endeavor to incorporate within its ranks a large number of followers. Zveno's followers perceived themselves as an elitist group set on modernizing Bulgaria by means of political guidance from above. They were averse to mass action and remained committed to the concept of direct political intervention by the enlightened few. In their estimation, parliamentarianism, as well as the role of the political parties, was withering away. Bulgaria's fundamental ills were not related to the maldistribution of her wealth but to the economic scarcities of the country and the underdevelopment of her economic resources. The only way the country could be modernized was by means of an efficient technocracy accountable to itself. The top-heavy state bureaucracy had to be streamlined and rationalized. Zveno took a minimalist position on the national issue. Even though all the Macedonians were full-fledged Bulgarians in the eyes of the Zveno faithful, Bulgaria could not afford to waste her energies on an irredentist foreign policy which bore little promise of success in the immediate future. The eternal infighting of the various Macedonian émigré factions had brought the country to a state of political paralysis which the Zveno people considered impermissible. The Zveno group was neither pro-German nor pro-Soviet. If anything, it was pro-West by inclination. The group believed that Bulgaria should foster a balanced foreign policy, re-establish diplomatic relations with the Soviet Union, and remain nominally noncommittal in the face of Franco-German rivalries.[13]

While the above represents a fair outline of the Zveno political program, the true significance of the group lies not in its programmatic commitments but in its intimate links with various elements within the Bulgarian army. Specifically, the leadership of the Zveno group included a number of influential retired army officers who commanded substantial influence in parts of the Military League. The Military League dated back to the Balkan wars. It was an informal, yet crucially influential, organization within the professional army. The league did not have a fixed political philosophy. It considered itself the depository of Bulgaria's national interest and acted accordingly. The *Putsch* of 1923 would have been unthinkable without the active support of the Military League. Invariably, the minister of war was the league's nominee.

Despite its presumed internal discipline, the Military League was and remained faction-ridden. In the second half of the twenties, the league was reorganized under the leadership of Colonel Damian Velchev. Velchev was instrumental in carrying out the 1923 coup. It was he who took control of the army in Sofia in June of that year. During the next five years he served as the commandant of the Military College, a position he used to build a personal following among the young officer cadres. Although he was retired from the army in 1928, he continued to maintain his great personal influence on many young officers. Velchev was a man of limited political outlook. For his politics he depended on Kimon Georgiev, who, as a retired colonel, had participated in the anti-Stamboliiski coup as well. Georgiev associated himself with the Zveno group from the beginning. This association marked the "marriage" between the intellectuals and the military within the group, a combination which lasted until the eve of the May, 1934, coup.[14]

The Socialist left remained in opposition throughout the

[13] The outstanding raconteur of the formation and development of Zveno is Dimo Kazasov, the group's own ideologist. All of Kazasov's many writings (listed in part in the bibliography) have a bearing on Zveno's history. Zveno receives a favorable account in Swire, *Bulgarian Conspiracy*, which is instructive.

[14] A definitive history of the Military League is yet to be written. The works of Kazasov, Pundeff, and Swire are important sources on the subject.

years of the People's Bloc rule. Unlike the situation in most other European countries, the Bulgarian Socialists had split into a reformist and an orthodox wing a full decade before the outbreak of World War I. The former, known as the "broad" Socialists, ultimately evolved into the Bulgarian Social Democratic party, while the orthodox Marxist faction, known as the "narrows," formed the Bulgarian Communist party at the end of World War I. In 1919, the Social Democrats were the third largest political party after the Agrarians and the Communists. In the course of the twenties, however, their power diminished radically. Still, the influence of the Social Democratic party was greater than its size would indicate. This was largely the result of the prestige its leaders, Sakuzov, Pastukhov, and Cheshmedzhiev, commanded among the urban working-class circles, as well as among middle-class elements in general. Two other factors added to the political stature of the Social Democrats. The first was the economic base on which the party rested: a small but well-organized trade-union movement and various cooperative credit associations. Second, the Social Democrats maintained close connections with the Second International, a fact which helped enhance the prestige of its leaders at home.

In the aftermath of World War I, the Social Democrats participated in the first two coalition governments. After 1919, they withdrew into opposition and stayed there throughout the interwar years. The Social Democrats disliked Stamboliiski's regime intensely, but they did not take part in the conspiracy against him, with one exception—Kazasov. Although the party did not authorize Kazasov's participation in the June, 1923, coup, once involved, he was supported by the party and remained among its leadership until the mid-twenties. In the general elections held in November, 1923, the Social Democrats elected an unprecedented number of deputies (twenty-nine). This success was never to be repeated. In the elections of 1927, th Social Democrats joined hands with the Gichev Agrarians in the so-called Iron Bloc and gained eleven deputies. In the elections of 1931, which brought the People's Bloc to power, the Social Democrats participated without allies. The results were devastating. They received a total of 25,000 votes, which gave them five seats in Parliament.

Despite their declining political fortunes, the Social Democrats continued to be a factor in national politics, thanks largely to the caliber of their leaders. In terms of rank-and-file support, they were strongest among the teachers, the skilled laborers, and the artisans of the lower middle class. Their political presence in the countryside remained limited and always uncertain. On the whole, they preserved their good political name. As far as the left was concerned, the Social Democrats were in a position akin to that of the Malinov Democrats among the rightist groups. In a country as poor and underdeveloped as Bulgaria, the Social Democrats' reformism could have but limited appeal. They were effectively cut off from the prevalent Slavophile popular sentiment by their stringent doctrinal opposition to bolshevism. The ultimate defeat of socialism in Germany at the hands of the Nazis left the Bulgarian Social Democrats in a state of isolation from which they could not break away without compromising their fundamental beliefs. In the thirties, effective party control passed entirely into the hands of Pastukhov, a man of character and limitless political courage.[15]

The early antecedents of Bulgarian communism can be traced back to the 1890s. Led by Dimitur Blagoev, a Russian-educated Bulgarian intellectual, the more doctrinaire elements among the early Socialists congregated within the "narrow" faction, which became organizationally independent as early as 1903. Politically intransigent, Blagoev's adherents had, at first, a smaller popular following than did the "broad" Socialists. This power relationship was reversed at the end of World War I, when, having renamed themselves the Bulgarian Communist

[15] The early history of Bulgarian Social Democracy and the schisms between the "broad" and "narrow" factions are masterfully traced in Rothschild, *The Communist Party of Bulgaria*. Sakuzov's *Bulgariia v svoiata istoriia*, published in 1918, is still of interest. Tchitchovski, *The Socialist Movement in Bulgaria;* Lambrev, *Polozhenieto na rabotnicheskata klasa ot Osvobozhdenieto do nachaloto na XX vek;* Kosev, *Kum istoriiata na revoliutsionnota dvizhenie v Bulgariia prez 1867–1871;* Klincharov, *Istoriia na rabotnicheskoto dvizhenie v Bulgariia, 1882–1903;* and Natan, *Bulgarskoto vuzrazhdane,* are all important, although of varying quality and interpretation, for the early history of the working class and the beginnings of socialism in Bulgaria. *Ianko Sakuzov iubileen sbornik* (Sofia, 1930) contains valuable information on the life and thought of the founder of "broad" socialism. The position of the Social Democrats throughout the thirties and the war years is traced in various parts of Oren, *Bulgarian Communism.*

party, the "narrows" became the second-strongest political force in the country after the Agrarian Union.

At the time of the anti-Stamboliiski coup, the Communists proclaimed their political neutrality on the ground that the conflict between the "rural and urban bourgeoisie" did not concern them. Thus, the conspirators tackled their Agrarian rivals without facing up to their enemies on the extreme left. Moscow and the Comintern were outraged by the passivity of their Bulgarian comrades and insisted that they vindicate bolshevism by staging—albeit belatedly—their own insurrection. Moscow's decree was obeyed. In September, 1923, the Bulgarian Communists took up arms against the Tsankov regime. The desperate endeavor was supported by only one part of the established Communist leadership. The outcome of the insurrection was as disastrous as could be expected under the circumstances. In Sofia and most of the other larger towns the Communist rebellion fizzled out before it even started. In a number of outlying provinces, where the Communist cadres were initially more successful, the regime was compelled to use its armed forces. The uprising was bloodily suppressed in a matter of days. From Moscow, Zinoviev proudly pointed to yet another revolutionary outburst symptomatic of the coming world revolution. At home, the consequences of political adventurism were, as always, borne by the people at large.[16]

For the Bulgarian Communists the abortive uprising of 1923 constituted the single most important event in the party's history. The movement split apart. While the majority of the rank and file remained in the country, a great many emigrated to the Soviet Union. The more prominent Communist leaders found themselves in Soviet exile as well. This physical schism within the party persisted until the entry of the Red Army into Bulgaria in 1944, when the surviving exiles returned to their homeland. The Communist party at home and the Communist party in exile formed the two axes around which the intricate history

[16] Rothschild, *The Communist Party of Bulgaria*, remains the best source on the formative years of the party as well as on the September, 1923, uprising. Kosev, *Septemvriiskoto vustanie v 1923 godina*, is the single most comprehensive Communist monograph on the abortive uprising. Kuncheva, ed., *Septemvriiskoto vustanie, 1923*, is yet another important source in a huge literature on the subject produced mainly after 1944.

of Bulgarian communism unfolded. Above and beyond the physical schism sustained by the Bulgarian Communists, there were the inevitable doctrinal splits generated by the disaster of 1923, which transected the ranks at home and in exile.

In the twenties, the Bulgarian Communist emigration in the Soviet Union constituted the second-largest group of political exiles, the largest being the Poles. Neither the Bulgarians nor the Russians have ever revealed the size of the emigration. Though their numbers fluctuated because of the two-way traffic which continued until the outbreak of World War II, there were several thousand Bulgarian Communists on Soviet soil at any given time after 1923. Most arrived in several waves during the period 1923–27. The great majority crossed into Yugoslavia and gradually reached the Soviet Union via Austria. Some crossed into Greece, where they were first imprisoned and then gradually released following the intervention of the various leftist international committees operating in Western Europe. A few reached the Crimea via the Black Sea route. In the thirties, immigration to Russia from Bulgaria was made possible by legal means and involved, in particular, the families of émigrés already in Soviet Russia. Most of the Bulgarian Communist exiles were settled in the southern Ukraine, where they were put to work as party functionaries among the so-called Bessarabian Bulgarians, who had made their way to Bessarabia and ultimately the southern Ukraine a century earlier. Those of more advanced political standing were sent to the various party schools and military academies for intensive training. The leaders found their way into the Comintern apparatus.[17]

For the time being, the cadres at home were less fortunate. Those who survived the police repressions of the mid-twenties found themselves in Bulgarian jails, where many were to spend a decade or more. After 1924, the Communist party was declared illegal. Yet, the Communists showed a remarkable buoyancy and adaptability. In 1927, the Bulgarian Workers party was established as a Communist front organization and was allowed to operate openly. The Communist Youth Organization reap-

[17] All aspects pertaining to the formation of the Bulgarian Communist emigration in Soviet Russia are dealt with in some detail in Oren, *Bulgarian Communism*, pp. 35–64.

peared also, under a different name. The Communists sponsored their own trade-union organizations, as well as various voluntary associations for university students, to compete with the Social Democrats and the Agrarians. In the general elections of 1931, the Workers party elected thirty-one deputies. This was an outstanding achievement. In the Sofia municipal elections of 1932, the Workers party received a clear plurality, which gave it the right to select its own mayor. The municipal elections were ultimately abrogated by court action, however, which robbed the Communists of their victory. In 1933, the deputies of the Workers party were evicted from Parliament by a special decree sponsored by the government of the People's Bloc.

The staying power of communism in Bulgaria was remarkable, particularly in view of the inner schisms and endless intra-party struggles. The rise of factionalism within Communist ranks was the inevitable result of the 1923 debacle. Following the disaster, rightist, centrist, and leftist groupings sprang up. The strategies and tactics of 1923 were reanalyzed and replayed at party forums held either in Vienna or in Berlin and attended by representatives of the party at home and the cadres in Soviet exile. The Old Guard, headed by Kolarov and Dimitrov, the men responsible for the attitude of neutrality in June, 1923, and for the abortive uprising of September of the same year, was called to task by both the right and the left. They were accused of irresponsibility and adventurism by the former, and of anti-bolshevism and revolutionary liquidationism by the latter.

Victory came to the faction best adapted to the Comintern's general line of the moment. In the mid-twenties, the Old Guard combined with the leftists to combat the rightists. By 1926, this was indeed accomplished. At home, the more moderate elements were either expelled from the party or left the Communist fold of their own volition. While some left the political scene altogether, others traveled all the way to the center and, occasionally, to the extreme right of the Bulgarian political spectrum. Having no place to go, the rightists in Soviet exile sought to survive as best they could.

The temporary alliance between the Old Guard and the leftists broke down in the latter part of the twenties. The adoption by the Comintern of an extreme left orientation after 1927 gave the leftists within Bulgarian Communist ranks their great political opportunity. Consisting primarily of the younger elements within the party, the leftists prevailed over the Old Guard and consolidated their grip on the party apparatus at home as well as in the Soviet Union. Kolarov's and Dimitrov's followers were pushed to the background. They were relieved of their positions within the party hierarchy and replaced by younger militants. Kolarov and Dimitrov themselves lost much of their influence within the Bulgarian party-in-exile. Within the Comintern they succeeded in salvaging some of their political prestige thanks only to their revolutionary reputations of the past and their personal connections with the Soviet leadership. On the insistence of the Bulgarian section within the Comintern, now firmly controlled by spokesmen for the leftist faction, Dimitrov was removed from Moscow and dispatched to head the Comintern's Western Buro in Berlin. For him, this was an exile within an exile. Only after the famous Leipzig trial, and especially after the switch to the right by Moscow and the Comintern, was Dimitrov able to stage a comeback and re-establish his authority over his Bulgarian detractors. By that time, conditions in Bulgaria, as well as those in the Soviet Union, had undergone a radical transformation. While politics in Bulgaria had become more and more authoritarian following the coup of May, 1934, the Soviet Union was succumbing to the first convulsions of the Great Purge.[18]

Seldom did the interests of the Comintern coincide with those of the Bulgarian Communists. The fact that a sizable portion of the Bulgarian Communist cadres resided in the Soviet Union reinforced the dependence of the Bulgarian party on Moscow's political designs and hampered the evolution of a more autonomous political outlook by the cadres at home. This trend was further strengthened by the presence in the Soviet Union of the majority of the Bulgarian Communist high command. Factionalism was not lacking, however, within the party. In operational

---

[18] The full spectrum of "left" and "right" factionalism within the Communist ranks is covered in detail from various angles in the following works: *ibid.*, pp. 49–72; Rothschild, *The Communist Party of Bulgaria*, pp. 287–94; Barov, *BKP v noviia podem na antifashistkoto dvizhenie, 1929–1935*; Kolarov, *Protiv liiavoto sektantstvo i trotskizma v Bulgariia*.

terms, the faction whose tendencies corresponded most to the Comintern's orientations at any given moment received Moscow's support and approval, which sufficed to assure its domination over the entire party. With every passing year, the Communists within Bulgaria became more dependent on financial support from Moscow. Without the constant flow of funds from the Soviet Union, the organizational and propaganda activities of the party could not have been maintained at the level on which they were indeed carried out. The Comintern provided the training ground for the younger functionaries, who were sent to the various Comintern schools.

Still, outside support could not explain the appeal of communism in Bulgaria or the political power of the party. Nor could the impact of communism be attributed to the class struggle as such. The great majority of party members came from the rural countryside. The intelligentsia, made up of the free professions, and especially of schoolteachers, constituted the second-largest contingent. In terms of socioeconomic origin, the industrial working class stood in third place. The Communist leadership was never satisfied with the social composition of the party. Their endeavors to increase the working-class content continued throughout the interwar years and beyond, but bore little success. The appeals of Slavophilism, the frustrations generated by unresolved national questions, and the lingering rebellious traditions in Bulgarian politics accounted for the appeal of communism more than did the economic determinants of class dissatisfaction. The Communists benefited from the popular admiration of Russia, which was stronger in Bulgaria than in any other country in Europe. The Bolshevik prescription for the resolution of national problems attracted many who were inclined to place their trust in Soviet power rather than in the nation's resources. Finally, the unsettled character of the Bulgarian political processes owed much to the rebellious temperament of these peasant people, who were late in acquiring their own national consciousness. For many a Bulgarian, Soviet Russia loomed as the brave new world and the land of promise. Russia was the only country where Bulgarians could and did attain high rank and realize political careers that were more promising than those found in any other foreign land or even at home. This placed Bulgaria and the Bulgarian Communist party in a unique position relative to the Communist movements in much of Eastern and Central Europe.[19]

While communism represented a point of convergence for varying sociopolitical motives, the power of the heterogeneous Macedonian movement derived from the burning desire of its disciples to see the Macedonian question resolved once and for all. The Communists concentrated their efforts on bringing about revolution along Marxist-Leninist lines; the party constituted the only organizational instrumentality for the attainment of this goal. The Macedonians in politics, on the other hand, spread their efforts along the entire political spectrum. Those who perceived themselves as the guardians of Macedonia's interests populated all the political parties and factions on the Bulgarian scene, as well as the purely Macedonian organizations. Their unfailing devotion to the cause brought about what could be termed the Macedonization of Bulgarian politics in the interwar years. This is not to suggest that the issue of Macedonia was forced on the non-Macedonian majority. The overwhelming majority of Bulgarians responded willingly to the Macedonian problem, in which they saw the very essence of the Bulgarian nation. Often, political leaders made use of the Macedonian issue to foster their own interests and those of the factions they represented. Their cynical preoccupation brought about exaggerations. It could be claimed, as was done by Bulgaria's enemies, that the Macedonian question brought about a distortion in the Bulgarians' own definition of their national interest. The question was much too important to have been invented, however.

The several hundreds of thousands of Macedonians in Bulgaria were not of one stripe. Some had become thoroughly Bulgarized and could make only a vague claim to Macedonian origin. The great majority were well on their way to becoming so. A great many were recently arrived refugees who had found

[19] Burks, *The Dynamics of Communism in Eastern Europe,* presents interesting evidence on the appeals of communism and the socioeconomic composition of the group of Bulgarians who joined the party or were attracted to communism. For an orthodox Communist view of the political orientation of the working class in Bulgaria in the pre-1944 period, see Berov, *Polozhenieto na rabotnicheskata klasa v Bulgariia pri kapitalizma.*

their way into Bulgaria proper in the aftermath of the Balkan wars. Finally, there were Macedonians from the Petrich District, which lay in Bulgaria proper. As an ethnic minority, the Macedonians were more political than the Bulgarians. Some had prospered, while others had remained destitute. From the extreme right all the way to the extreme left, Macedonians had acquired positions of prominence. From 1926 to 1931 the Bulgarian government was headed by Liapchev, a Macedonian. Blagoev, the founder of the "narrow" Socialists; Dimitrov; Kostov, who was to become the general secretary of the Communist party during the first stage of sovietization; Yugov, the minister of interior of the first Fatherland Front government; and many more of the top echelon of the Communist party were of Macedonian origin. While Macedonians could and did achieve top-ranking careers in the world of Bulgarian politics, the Yugoslav political hierarchy, dominated as it was by Serbs, remained strikingly devoid of persons of Macedonian origin. This asymmetry in the distribution of political powers among the ethnic Macedonians was of crucial importance. While Serbia dominated the heartland of Macedonia, Serb politicians effectively repulsed the ethnic Macedonians, whom they considered to be no more than southern Serbs. At the same time, Bulgaria was eager to absorb, assimilate, and open itself to the influence of Macedonian particularism.

In many ways there was an element of duplicity in the Bulgarian position. While all Bulgarians cared about the destiny of Macedonia, the Bulgarians of Macedonian origin cared more. The official consensus within Bulgaria was that there were no differences between Bulgarians and Macedonians and that the two were one and the same people. The maxim claiming the existence of a single people did not fit existing realities, however. While outwardly the Bulgarians maintained a monolithic position on the question of Macedonia, within Bulgaria, and specifically within the Macedonian community, schisms were inevitable. Those Macedonians who had prospered in Bulgaria were suspect in the eyes of their less successful Macedonian brothers. The process of assimilation produced varying shades of Bulgarization among the Macedonians, which in turn gave rise to sharp political divergences in their midst.

The story of the Internal Macedonian Revolutionary Organization (IMRO), founded as early as 1893 to fight for the liberation of Macedonia, need not be retraced here. The crosscurrents within the organization were many and often conflicted. The stream of opinion which believed that the future of Macedonia lay in Bulgaria's outright annexation of the region was opposed by the federalists within IMRO. Resort to armed violence brought to the fore those persons best suited to conduct terrorist activities. Although the underlying devotion to the Macedonian cause was never in question, manifestations of plain banditry became an integral part of IMRO politics. Sofia, Belgrade, Rome, and Moscow all mingled in the affairs of the Macedonian revolutionaries, each sponsoring and manipulating one or more factions for its own political purposes. The need for outside allies was a constant requirement of the IMRO chieftains. Political liaisons were established and disestablished, depending on the immediate circumstances. In the years before the First World War the hand of the Bulgarian court was probably uppermost in the affairs of IMRO.

The Macedonians in their overwhelming majority supported the Bulgarian military effort during the First World War. Bulgaria's defeat and the rise of Stamboliiski brought disenchantment with the Bulgarian political stance regarding Macedonia's future. In the early twenties, IMRO's leadership vacillated between a revolutionary orientation linked to Moscow and an alliance with Stamboliiski's domestic enemies. Even though a formal understanding with the Comintern was reached, Moscow's grip on IMRO did not last long. The few who put their trust in Moscow went over to the Communists, reinforcing the party within Bulgaria as well as the Bulgarian Communist emigration in the Soviet Union. The latter faced yet another dilemma when the Red Army marched into the Balkans in 1944 and they were once again called upon to choose between Sofia and Belgrade. The great majority of IMRO, however, operated within the non-Communist sphere of Bulgarian politics. They joined the Tsankov conspiracy of 1923, lending their gunmen to the anti-Agrarian, and, later, anti-Communist, terror which followed the *Putsch*.

During the decade following 1923 the power of IMRO grew

immensely. In effect, IMRO created a state within a state. The governments in power had only nominal control over the Petrich District, which was governed and administered directly by IMRO. The large monetary subsidies received by the Macedonians from the Italian government were augmented by IMRO's own domestic taxation in the form of "protection money," which its gunmen extorted from bankers and merchants all over the country. Having sustained the tribulations resulting from military defeat, the Bulgarian citizenry was compelled to pay further tribute because of its failure to resolve the national question. While IMRO was allowed to achieve its political and economic demands through the use of terror, the army and police were held in abeyance by the ruling governments. Throughout the regime of the Democratic Alliance, IMRO was perceived as a counterbalance to the radical left. With this in mind, the governments of Tsankov and Liapchev tolerated the Macedonians' encroachments on their sovereignty.

Ultimately, IMRO's power was constrained from within rather than from without. The Macedonians were unable to maintain political discipline within their own ranks. The bulk of their energies were expended in internal factional warfare, in the course of which the great majority of Macedonian leaders lost their lives at the hands of their own compatriots. Gradually, popular resentment rose against the Macedonians' use of arbitrary force. After its first year in power, the People's Bloc government felt strong enough to initiate a few tentative measures against IMRO. By 1933, this newly assumed firmness had become more pronounced. Once again, however, the promise remained unfulfilled, for the *Putsch* of 1934 cut short the tenure of the People's Bloc.[20]

On May 19, 1934, the Military League took power by means of a coup d'état. The transfer of power occurred without bloodshed. The army's occupation of the capital took place without

[20] Kiosev, *Istoriia na Makedonskoto natsionalno revoliutsionno dvizhenie;* Lambrev, *Makedonskiiat vupros i balkanskoto edinstvo;* Mihailoff, *Macedonia: A Switzerland of the Balkans;* Anastasoff, *The Tragic Peninsula: A History of the Macedonian Movement for Independence Since 1878;* Kofos, *Nationalism and Communism in Macedonia;* Swire, *Bulgarian Conspiracy;* and *Istoriia na Bulgariia,* 2nd ed., vol. 3, are only a small sample of the enormous literature, none of which is very objective, devoted to the Macedonian problem.

resistance or civil strife. The provinces followed suit obediently. The king was presented with a list of the new government's members, which he duly approved. Headed by Kimon Georgiev, the new government proceeded to rule by decree. The Constitution was suspended, Parliament was dissolved, and all political parties were abolished. Party publications were declared illegal and the property of all political parties was confiscated. Political meetings were banned and strict censorship was imposed. Local self-government, which had survived through the years, was abolished as the Ministry of Interior took over most of the functions of local administration. State administration was streamlined and centralized. The new government disbanded the various Macedonian organizations, thus ending the rule of IMRO. Sofia reclaimed its authority over the Petrich District by reinstituting a regular civil administration. A state-controlled labor syndicate replaced the autonomous trade unions. As an institution, the monarchy was not tampered with, even though, for the time being, the king was left with only nominal powers. Outwardly, at least, the country was to be depoliticized. Party rule would be replaced by a new technocracy determined to bring about a new order of efficiency.

Although the leaders of the May coup had participated in the anti-Stamboliiski assault of 1923, the differences between the two acts were fundamental. In the first place, the 1923 coup was conceived of as an antirevolutionary act aimed against the Agrarian monopoly of power. The conspiracy was the end result of a widely based agreement among various political forces. In the second place, the prime movers in the 1923 undertaking did not claim for themselves a cohesive political outlook above and beyond their determination to disestablish the rule of peasant populism by reintroducing traditional political pluralism.

The May coup was preceded by little political preparation. From November, 1933, when the conspiracy was first hatched, until its successful execution six months later, the energies of the Military League were expended in forging an internal majority rather than in recruiting outside allies. The fact was that the military was no less faction-ridden than the political parties it despised so completely. First, there were the military elements which stayed outside the Military League. Second, there were the military elements which belonged to the league but favored the king and the monarchic institution. Third, there were the league members who inclined toward republicanism. Finally, there were the officers who, although members of the league, were neither monarchist nor republican but essentially non-political.

In view of this diversity, common action required compromise. The man who undertook to create a majority and who, in May, emerged as the strongman of the new regime was retired Colonel Damian Velchev. Velchev's personal authority rested on the younger, vaguely republican members of the Military League. They combined with the neutral elements within the league to form a temporary majority. On the basis of this unstable alliance, Velchev attained momentary control over the league, which he employed to carry out the coup. Having attained power, Velchev chose to remain in the shadows of the new regime, which was nominally headed by his old-time Zvenoist friend Georgiev. Thus, in effect, the coup of May 19 was a double coup: a wholly successful coup against the regime of the People's Bloc, and a coup by Velchev's followers against their opponents within the Military League, which was only temporarily successful.

What was true of the Military League was true of the Zveno group as well. Only a small fraction of the Zveno leadership was initiated into the conspiracy by Georgiev. This reflected Georgiev's basic distrust of his political friends, whom he suspected of personal ties with the court. Once in power, Velchev and Georgiev rushed to broaden their political base by including individual political figures in the new government. They tried but, despite the generous promises with which he was lured, failed to secure the cooperation of Gichev. Their only success was in drawing a number of second-rate politicians into the government. Very soon, however, it became obvious that the shiny armor of the new military regime enclosed a political vacuum. The process of disintegration from within began immediately after the new government formally assumed power. Within a very short period of time, Velchev found himself in a voting minority within the Military League councils. While determined to impose his will on the country, he was unwilling, and possibly unable, to discipline his fellow officers by the use of strong-arm methods.[21]

The coup of May, 1934, successfully shattered the political institutions of Bulgaria. The country was served with a stream of decrees which reflected the basic tenets of the Zveno program. Despite the visible élan with which the new people in power tackled the Bulgarian body politic, their political muscle did not suffice to consolidate the new order they envisaged. The dismantled state machinery was reassembled by the king to fit his own concept of how Bulgaria should be governed. Although isolated, Boris remained well informed of existing realities within the regime thanks to his personal liaison with the monarchist elements of the new military elite.

It took eighteen months and four cabinets for the king to emerge supreme. The Georgiev government fell in January, 1935, and was succeeded by the transitional cabinet of General Pencho Zlatev, which gave way, in April, to yet a new government headed by Andrei Toshev. In October, 1935, Velchev engineered a countercoup which proved abortive. In November, the king called upon Kioseivanov, a career diplomat, to head the new government. With this change, Bulgaria entered a new political era characterized by the concentration of real power in the hands of the king. Boris proceeded to avenge himself with an iron fist against the politically oriented military officers. The Military League was disbanded and purged. Velchev was tried and sentenced to prison. The army could not withstand the test of the strict discipline with which it was inculcated or the principles of honor and comradeship on which its excellence presumably rested. Career pursuits and petty jealousies revealed themselves in a measure which exceeded that of the traditional political parties. By holding out the promise of promotion, the king exploited individual officers for his own purposes.

Although the coup of May, 1934, was effectively overturned, the old regime was never again to be restored. As political engineers, the Military League and the Zveno group had proven their utter ineptness. All they had accomplished was a lowering

---

[21] *Istoriia na Bulgariia*, 2nd ed., 3: 279–96; Kazasov, *Burni godini*, pp. 497–537; and Swire, *Bulgarian Conspiracy*, constitute three divergent interpretations of the 1934 coup.

of the barriers over which the powers of the king flowed without an effective check or restraint. This was not the last time the Zveno group and the military served the interest of others in politics. In 1944, under different circumstances, yet in a similar way, they once again performed the role of stooge in the interest of the Communists and Soviet Russia.

The true nature of Bulgarian politics in the second half of the thirties is not easily definable. Bulgaria did not become a totalitarian state, nor did it turn fascist in the true meaning of the term. Although banned, political parties continued to lead a shadowy existence. In this sense, party politics remained significant, although strictly limited in scope and depth. While refusing to acknowledge the existence of formally organized political parties, in 1938 Boris decided to restore Parliament for the sake of political expediency. When consulted, the voters gave their votes to the men of their choice, and many politicians thus found their way into the new Parliament, where they spoke out freely. Officially, they were not allowed to refer to their past party affiliations, but, in the public mind, these were both remembered and acknowledged. Parliament was reduced from being an organ of government to acting as merely a consultative instrument. Nevertheless, the house served as a meaningful public forum and a vent for the expression of public opinion.

In view of the general ban on organized party activities, it was only natural that those political groups best suited to perform under illegal conditions would find their relative weight in the political arena enhanced. Thus, the Bulgarian Communist party gained an advantageous position which it retained until 1944. The Communists would have done even better but for the internal upheavals which they experienced.

At the time of the May, 1934, coup, the leadership of the party was in the hands of leftist militants who had gained control in the late twenties. Their prognosis for the May events was based on an orthodox interpretation which saw the changeover as just one more convulsion within the Bulgarian bourgeoisie. This evaluation was akin to that of their German comrades, who judged the rise of nazism in Germany as a symptom of decay in the development of capitalism. If anything, the Zveno group and the Military League were to be preferred to the regime of the People's Bloc, for the new rule could be expected to advance Bulgaria on the road to revolution by sharpening the inner contradictions in the system. Thus, as in 1923, the Communists decided on strict neutrality, which they adhered to during the coup and after. Once again, their stand was deemed wrong by Moscow. The Comintern had just switched its signals and was reversing its orientation from left to right. What the Bulgarian Communists should have done, Moscow reiterated, was to help fortify the democratic camp, not enhance revolution.

A few months before the coup, Dimitrov had returned from imprisonment in Germany and had been received enthusiastically by the leadership in Moscow. His new fame harmonized perfectly with Soviet foreign-policy reformulations. Dimitrov's political career had been launched on a plane far above the context of Bulgarian communism. In the face of Moscow's warm embrace, it was inconceivable that he would continue to be rejected by his own comrades.

Dimitrov's determination to force himself on his compatriots and restore his lost authority became his one compulsion. Employing Kolarov as his henchman, he proceeded to purge the Bulgarian Communist emigration of his leftist detractors. The latter were criticized in a series of meetings held in Moscow during 1934–35. The Bulgarian Communist emigration's wheel of fortune made one more turn. The Bulgarian "left sectarians," as they were now termed by the Dimitrov-Kolarov forces, were pushed out of all positions of authority. In no time, the tag of Trotskyism was affixed to them by the new victors. This effectively sealed their personal fates. Soon, the minor purge of the Bulgarian emigration merged into the mighty stream of Stalin's Great Purge. The anti-Dimitrov opposition was implicated in a number of gruesome conspiracies concocted for that purpose. The Bulgarian Communists working in the Ukraine were accused of no less a crime than that of having conspired to annex the southern Ukraine to Bulgaria! As a result, several hundred of the cadres were arrested. Those not immediately dealt with by the Soviet secret police perished in Stalin's concentration camps. The central leadership of the "left sectarians" was charged with espionage on behalf of Nazi Germany. They, too, were shot or sent to the Kolyma camps. Only a few survived to return to their homeland after 1944.

The purge and massacre of the Bulgarian Communist emigration in Soviet Russia went largely unnoticed by other foreign Communists in exile in the Soviet Union. In fact, only a few knew or understood the intricate inner workings of the conflicts and antagonisms within Bulgarian Communist circles. Since a number of Bulgarian Communist functionaries were given important positions within the Comintern apparatus, now headed by Dimitrov as the Comintern's general secretary, the prevalent contention at the time was that Dimitrov had, in fact, helped spare his Bulgarian comrades. The tragic irony in this miscomprehension was not dispelled until many years later.[22]

While Stalin's secret police could be depended on to deal with the unreliable elements in the Bulgarian emigration, no such easy resort was available within Bulgaria itself. Soon after the May coup, emissaries were dispatched to Bulgaria by Dimitrov for the purpose of purging the home party. They found their task formidable because of the underground and illegal conditions under which they had to work and, more so, because of the stubborn refusal on the part of the leftist militants to surrender control of the party. The purge degenerated into a series of protracted engagements which lasted well into the late thirties.

Soon after the May coup, the leftist Communist leadership decided to dissolve the Workers party. At that time, the decision was as logical as it was practical. Since all political parties were banned, there was no reason for the Communists to continue to maintain a separate Workers party alongside the Communist party, both of which were illegal. Upon their arrival, Dimitrov's emissaries determined to reverse this decision. On the theory that the Workers party, with its parliamentary experience, would be better suited to seeking political allies in the democratic camp, they decided that it should be re-established. At the same time, they were unable to dissolve the illegal Communist

[22] A full account of the purge of the Bulgarian Communist exiles in Russia is available in Oren, *Bulgarian Communism*, pp. 83–100. In the course of time, the Bulgarians had developed a genuine Trotskyite group, but it never became truly significant (*ibid.*, pp. 54, 181–82). The same was true of the Bulgarian Anarchist movement. See *ibid.*, pp. 137, 215; and Rothschild, *The Communist Party of Bulgaria*, p. 143n.

party, which they considered to have become superfluous under the existing political circumstances. This party had become the bastion of leftist elements, who found themselves fighting for political survival. Thus, for almost five years, the Communist underground within Bulgaria clustered around two separate, illegal organizations. Seated in Moscow, Dimitrov's collaborators were apprehensive but could do little more than strengthen their contingent within Bulgaria by increasing their financial assistance and dispatching more emissaries. They resorted to the well-known Communist technique of recalling some of the doubtful Communist functionaries to Moscow for an accounting. In the majority of cases, those who were thus lured perished in the course of the Great Purge.

The cadres at home knew little or nothing of the great disaster that befell their comrades in the Soviet Union. Although the leftist elements fought back against Dimitrov's purgers, they never rebelled against Moscow's authority. To the last, they remained loyal to the Comintern and its dictates. In this sense, they were not Communist deviationists, as they were later accused of being. Their opposition was based on a firm conviction that they alone represented the core of true militants who could best serve the interests of communism in Bulgaria. Ultimately, they were overwhelmed and decimated. A few dropped out of the party altogether. Others succeeded in working their way back into the party's good graces through active participation in the resistance during the war. Because of the dire need for trustworthy cadres, persons whose past record was leftist were allowed to rejoin the Communist party during the first stage of sovietization, and to lend a hand in crushing the anti-Communist opposition. Their political sins, however, were never forgotten. In the late forties and early fifties, when Bulgaria underwent a period of Stalinist extremism, most of them paid dearly for their deviations, as did many others who could not be accused of even these errors of Communist scholasticism.[23]

In the mid-thirties, however, while the party was being purged, the Bulgarian Communists were called upon to direct their efforts toward establishing a popular front in Bulgaria.

[23] On the purge of the leftist opposition within Bulgaria, see Oren, *Bulgarian Communism*, pp. 72–83.

This new line set by the Comintern posed an almost impossible task for the Communists. Had the call come two years earlier, when parliamentarianism was still viable, the undertaking would have had a better chance of succeeding. The May coup and the ban imposed on the formal existence of political parties, however, made interaction between the forces of the center and those of the left largely futile. At best, as of the mid-thirties, popular frontism could be carried out in a semilegal fashion.

Despite the inner stresses which the Communist party was undergoing, select functionaries opened negotiations with leaders of the democratic camp. In view of the sudden change in Communist orientation and the distrust that had accumulated through the years, success was not easily forthcoming. To make any progress, it was necessary for the Communists to reduce their demands to the bare minimum. This they proceeded to do. The sum of their proposals amounted only to a call for the restoration of parliamentary democracy. To be sure, the leaders of the democratic camp did not need to be taught a lesson in democracy by their Communist countrymen. Indeed, the former proceeded to establish a popular front of their own. Led by Pastukhov from the Social Democrats and Gichev from the Agrarian Union, a grouping of five political factions was organized. This was the so-called quintet (*petorka*) set up in 1936, which undertook to issue appeals to the king calling on him and his government to re-establish party rule forthwith. The Communists were thus outmaneuvered. They had no choice but to agree to add their forces to those of the quintet. This led to the establishment of the People's Constitutional Bloc, a temporary political confederation which included the Communists and the five democratic groups.

The pressure from below forced Boris to make political concessions. As a first step, the government decided to hold local elections to be conducted on the basis of individual candidates rather than political parties. The special electoral law which the government promulgated was cast in the most rigid fashion. Following consultations, participants within the People's Constitutional Bloc decided to boycott the elections. The populace was urged to manifest its dissatisfaction with the ruling regime by dropping into the ballot boxes write-in slogans calling for the restoration of the Constitution. The write-in campaign did not prove very effective. The ballots thus cast, which constituted about 20 percent of the popular vote, were invalidated. Without exception, the regime elected its own nominees. Once again, the Comintern in Moscow was dissatisfied with the Bulgarian Communist tactics. Moscow's contention was that the struggle for popular frontism should be undertaken by positive measures rather than by negative ones, and that the invalidation of the ballots served no useful purpose whatsoever.

Following the 1937 local elections, the regime felt confident enough to undertake yet another step in the direction of "guided democracy." Later in the year, it decided to hold a new general election, the first since 1931. A special electoral law was promulgated. This proved to be a reactionary document designed to fit Boris' own political interests. The elections were to be held on the principle of nonpartisanship, as were the 1937 local elections. Individual nominees would be required to sign written depositions to the effect that they had never been Communists. Special boards were to be appointed to decide on the eligibility of every would-be candidate. Those features of proportionate representation which had been retained in the 1931 electoral law were now dropped. The country was divided into 160 single-member constituencies. This opened the way to wide-scale gerrymandering. In determining the size and geographic confines of the individual constituencies, the government did all it could to secure for itself the largest number of safe electoral localities. Finally, the elections would be held on different dates in different places. This was a device the government engineered in order to concentrate the police force in each locality on its day of balloting.

The negative tactics pursued by the opposition during the local elections were not repeated. The various groups decided to participate by placing in nomination their own followers as best they could. The Communists did the same, even though they had to resort to the nomination of persons of only nominal association with communism. This meant that the Communists entered the pre-electoral interparty negotiations with a much-reduced bargaining posture. On the whole, the principles of common action were sustained. Agreement between the Communists and the remaining opposition groups, particularly the Gichev Agrarians and the followers of Pladne, remained informal. In a great many cases, representatives of the democratic factions agreed among themselves, as well as with the local Communist representatives, not to oppose one another's candidates but to concentrate on defeating those of the government. There was no formal electoral platform for the antiregime forces as a whole. In most cases, pro-Communist nominees found it difficult, and often impossible, to establish their eligibility as candidates in the eyes of the government's special boards.

The general election was held during March of 1938. When Parliament convened on May 22, 1938, the opposition counted among its ranks 32 Agrarians, 8 Social Democrats, 5 Communists, and an unspecified number of deputies from the other democratic groups. This gave the government a clear majority of between 93 and 95 candidates out of a total of 160. The delineation between the government camp and the opposition was never clear-cut. The regime used flattery, threats, and promises of all kinds, with the result that a number of nominal oppositionists were drawn into the government camp. In June, to further improve its standing, the regime expelled the 5 nominal Communist deputies from Parliament. In December, 1938, 6 Agrarian oppositionists from the Pladne wing also were expelled. The charges against them were that they had engaged in party parliamentary activities in violation of the standing rules. By resorting to such methods, the government could eventually count on 120 of the 160 votes.

The 1938 elections marked the high point of a unified opposition which included the Communists. Bulgaria's move into the German camp was slowed down but not checked by the opposition's relatively good show of electoral might. Relations between Communist and non-Communist oppositionists, which never were harmonious, deteriorated further following the Munich agreement. Thus, the popular front effort had a limited impact on Bulgaria's political realities.[24]

[24] Oren, *ibid.*, pp. 101–32, traces the popular front effort through the 1938 general election; see also Oren, "Popular Front in the Balkans: Bulgaria," *Journal of Contemporary History*, 5, no. 3 (1970): 69–82. Kolev, *Borbata na BKP za Naroden front, 1935–1939*, presents the Communist view on the same subject.

2: A SMALL-POWER IMPASSE

The breakup of the Austro-Hungarian and Ottoman empires and the forced withdrawal of Germany and Russia from active participation in international affairs created a situation without precedent in the politics of Eastern Europe. The fact that neither Germany nor Russia could play a dominant role in the affairs of Eastern Europe for more than a decade after the end of the First World War produced unique circumstances which can hardly be too strongly emphasized. The countries in the winning camp grew in size beyond their wildest expectations. Their safety was guaranteed by the weakness of the two giants of the East and the West, as well as by the readiness of France to underwrite the new status quo. In the midst of this political abundance, Hungary, Bulgaria, and, to a certain extent, tiny Austria stood out as foci of dissatisfaction. Italy hastened to provide these revisionist states with political shelter which was never too secure. Her expressed ambitions were never matched by her insufficient resources. Italy held the stage as long as the Weimar Republic survived. After 1935, she was forced to give way to Nazi Germany.

For a brief period under the Stamboliiski regime, Bulgaria's foreign policy manifested a degree of originality. Stamboliiski's experimentation in the foreign as well as the domestic domain was cut short, however, by the coup of June, 1923. In the twenties and early thirties, the foreign policies of the regimes of the Democratic Alliance and the People's Bloc were largely linked to Mussolini's international designs. The foreign-policy conceptions of Zveno and the Military League remained stillborn chiefly because of the brevity of their tenure of power. Under Boris, Bulgaria glided smoothly into the German camp. The country's over-all orientation was never in doubt. In the second half of the thirties, Bulgarian diplomats were preoccupied mainly with the price they hoped to extract from the rulers in Berlin.

Bulgaria dropped out of the First World War in September, 1918. At the end of September a Bulgarian delegation signed an armistice agreement with the commander-in-chief of the Anglo-French forces on the southern front. The agreement provided for the immediate evacuation of the Bulgarian army from all territory it had occupied in Greece and Serbia. The army was to be demobilized forthwith, with the exception of three infantry divisions and a small number of specialized units, which were retained for the preservation of domestic order. The weapons and equipment of the demobilized units were to be handed over to military representatives of the Entente. Bulgarian army units west of the Skoplje meridian would be made prisoners of war. The Bulgarian government would be responsible for ensuring that all armed units of the Central Powers withdrew from Bulgarian territory within four weeks of the signing of the armistice. On October 8, military units of the French army encamped in Sofia. They were followed by English and Italian contingents which entered the country and occupied strategic points. The railroads, seaports, and coal mining industry were placed under the direct control of the military occupation authorities.[1]

The Bulgarian delegation to the Paris Peace Conference found itself in complete isolation. Bulgaria was now made to pay dearly for having backed the wrong side in 1916. Rumania's claim to southern Dobruja, which she had occupied in 1913, was confirmed. This was done in total defiance of ethnic considerations and the principle of self-determination. The division of Macedonia, effected in 1913, also was confirmed. Bulgaria was allowed to retain only the smallest portion of the disputed

[1] The terms of the armistice are summarized in *Istoriia na Bulgariia,* 2nd ed., 3: 29–30.

land. Furthermore, the Serbs were awarded three border areas along their frontier with Bulgaria, and these were occupied by the Serb army in the fall of 1918. In territorial terms, the severest blow to Bulgaria was the loss of western Thrace and, with it, Bulgaria's access to the Aegean Sea. This step was taken on strategic grounds which harmonized with the victors' determination to see to it that the ever-growing appetite of the Greeks was satisfied. The peace treaty was signed at Neuilly in November, 1919, by Stamboliiski, who had in the meantime become Bulgaria's premier. The economic sanctions which the peace imposed on Bulgaria were no less severe. The country was to pay a total of $2\frac{1}{4}$ billion gold francs over a period of thirty-seven years. Furthermore, her neighbors were to receive large numbers of livestock as immediate reparations in kind.[2]

The terms of the peace created formidable tasks for the Agrarian regime, which were compounded by the inflow of refugees from the lost territories. Bulgaria was gripped by spiraling inflation and severe food shortages. While protesting the harshness of the imposed conditions, Stamboliiski committed himself and his Agrarian Union to observance of the treaty. The foreign policy that Stamboliiski produced was molded to fit what he considered to be Bulgaria's immediate needs as well as her long-range requirements. The answers that he supplied for Bulgaria's foreign problems were an imaginative mixture of political pragmatism and Agrarian ideology.

Obviously, the era of grand designs and Machiavellian schemes, the era in which King Ferdinand had excelled so brilliantly but with disastrous results, had passed. In earlier years, the rivalry between Petrograd, on the one hand, and Vienna and Berlin, on the other, had given the Balkan states room in which to maneuver. This bipolar structure had given the regional conflicts scope as well as restraint. The outcome of World War I had removed the roof from which the foreign policies of the Balkan countries were suspended and had thereby accentuated the conflict between victors and revisionists.

On the plane of European politics, Stamboliiski endeavored to convince France and Britain that, under his leadership, Bul-

[2] On the treaty of peace, see *ibid.*, pp. 50–54; see also Macartney and Palmer, *Independent Eastern Europe*, pp. 132–33.

garia had broken forever with her heritage and was seeking the beginning of an era of accommodation. His political credentials and those of the Agrarian Union were without taint. Under Agrarian rule, Stamboliiski contended, Bulgarian politics had been transformed. His coming to power represented not merely a change of government but the commencement of a basic transformation. A few of the more perceptive Entente statesmen realized fully that the Agrarians would serve as a barrier to the rise of bolshevism in defeated Bulgaria. Here and there, Stamboliiski's rhetoric generated a degree of good will. However, the basic outlines of the Entente's East European and Balkan policies were not affected. France was determined to see to it that those countries she perceived to be her potential allies gained the most from their victory. Because this was a basic tenet in the defense system which France was enacting in Eastern Europe, no tangible concessions were made to the Bulgarians.

Bulgaria's relations with the new Soviet regime were more significant in terms of their domestic impact than in terms of Bulgaria's international position. In the course of the civil war in Russia and the war of intervention, several thousand White Russians had found their way into Bulgaria. There they enjoyed the protection and good will of the Entente's military occupation authorities. In due course, these émigré contingents became politically organized and came to constitute a factor in Bulgaria's domestic politics. Counterposed to this development was the rise of the Bulgarian Communist party as the second-largest political movement in the country. Taking account of these two factors, Stamboliiski struck a balance in his relations with the new Soviet regime. In his public utterances, he consistently opposed Western intervention in Russia's affairs. As a minor gesture of good will, the Agrarian regime assisted the various voluntary committees which were organized to collect food and donations for famine-stricken Russia. Yet, the Agrarian government refused to establish diplomatic relations with Soviet Russia as long as the Western powers had not done so. On December 11, 1920, the Soviet government officially proposed to Sofia the opening of formal negotiations aimed at the establishment of normal relations between the two countries. Ultimately, the matter was discussed in Parliament and rejected.

During the Genoa conference in the spring of 1922, the matter was discussed again by the Soviet and Bulgarian delegates, with similar results. In the final analysis, there was little that Soviet Russia could offer to aid Bulgaria in her ordeal. Stamboliiski realized this full well. At no time was he prepared to antagonize the Western powers by undertaking a more favorable stand, despite persistent Soviet overtures.

The main thrust of Agrarian foreign policy was directed toward the Balkan regional setting. A distinction was drawn between relations with Greece and relations with the new Yugoslavia. The Agrarians were not prepared to accept the loss of western Thrace and said so repeatedly. On this issue, Stamboliiski took an extreme revisionist stand from which no Bulgarian government during the interwar period was to budge. Although futile, Bulgarian protests against Greek imperialism continued unabated.

Relations with Belgrade were a different matter altogether. Programmatically, the Agrarian Union favored the establishment of a southern Slav federation in which Bulgaria would be one unit, as would Serbia, Croatia, and Macedonia. Federation was to be achieved primarily through the cooperation of the various agrarian movements in the region. Stamboliiski's visions went even further. In a somewhat utopian vein, he believed that peasant internationalism could ultimately provide the basis for a broad federation of East European peasant states, whose nucleus would be the southern Slav federation. The political expression of this concept was the Green International, of which Stamboliiski was the chief architect. In 1921, Stamboliiski visited Prague, Warsaw, and Bucharest, where he hoped to muster official support for his grand scheme. In time, a permanent bureau of the Green International was set up in Prague. As conceived by Stamboliiski, peasant internationalism would constitute the foundation for a Green Entente of East European peasant states, which would be an autonomous political clustering immune to bolshevism and independent of Western political hegemony.

Imaginative as these ideas were, the fact that they had emanated from a defeated country constituted their fatal weakness. In a more immediate sense, the Agrarian international program depended on the good will of Yugoslavia for its realization. Stamboliiski's endeavor to reach a comprehensive understanding with Yugoslavia was never very fruitful. Belgrade remained suspicious throughout. In the fall of 1922, Stamboliiski met with Nikola Pasic. The talks between the two heads of state opened the way for the conclusion of a limited agreement between the countries which was signed on March 23, 1923. The Bulgarian side went a long way toward appeasing Belgrade. It promised to respect the new frontier and to restrain the paramilitary activities of IMRO bands. The Yugoslavs gave little in return, except a vague promise of support for Bulgaria's designs on Greece. The agreement was to be one small step on a long road leading to cooperation and harmony. However, the experiment collapsed from within. The agreement frightened Stamboliiski's political enemies at home and enraged IMRO. In consequence, the two combined their efforts, thus solidifying the anti-Agrarian conspiracy.

Stamboliiski's foreign-policy conceptions formed an important chapter in his political testament. The solutions he proposed contradicted the immediate prescriptions of realpolitik considerations. Although idealistic and somewhat visionary in its immediate context, however, Stamboliiski's foreign policy provided a unique and original answer to the uncertainties of Bulgaria's long-range position as a sovereign state. He took his stand independently of the interests and dictates of the Great Powers. The Communists appropriated some of his basic ideas in the years to come. Their total dependence on Moscow's will, however, always constituted the fatal flaw in their position. Belgrade became more receptive to Stamboliiski's ideas following his departure from the scene. This was manifested in the good will which Serb politicians showed the Bulgarian Agrarian émigrés after 1923. The latter, however, spoke for themselves and only one part of the Agrarian movement, not for a sovereign state. At best, the Agrarian exiles on Yugoslav soil could utter their hopes for an ultimate return to their homeland and reinstatement in positions of authority. This was not an advantageous bargaining position, by any means. Gradually, they became the object of interest of Great Serb chauvinism, which viewed them as a convenient instrument through which to harass the regime in Sofia. As far as the governments under the Yugoslav monarchy were concerned, their continuous flirtation with the Agrarians of the Pladne wing was nothing more than a debasement of Stamboliiski's great political vision. By not supporting Stamboliiski's foreign-policy approaches when support was still meaningful, the Yugoslavs followed a short-sighted policy which they later had reason to regret.[3]

After 1923, Stamboliiski's message was stamped with an official taboo within Bulgaria. Neither friend nor foe was allowed to speak out openly on the subject of a comprehensive "Yugoslav solution" as Bulgaria's means of escape from her international impasse. Stamboliiski's enemies wanted Macedonia to be annexed to Bulgaria rather than relegated to membership in a larger political formation of southern Slavs. His critics remained unconvinced of the feasibility of his foreign policies. They did not comprehend how a victorious Serbia could be expected to extend a friendly hand to defeated Bulgaria while undertaking to solidify Serb hegemony over the various nations within Yugoslavia. This skepticism was shared, after 1923, by many rank-and-file members of the Agrarian Union as well. Except for the Agrarian émigrés who helped form the Pladne group in the early thirties, the overwhelming majority of Agrarian leaders in the twenties deleted the more provocative clauses in Stamboliiski's foreign-policy program from their speeches. This was a political adjustment of practical significance. Without this modification, it is doubtful that any of the various Agrarian organizations would have received a sufficient degree of legitimacy to be allowed to operate on the Bulgarian political scene.

Thus, Stamboliiski's international outlook underwent a grad-

---

[3] As of the present time, no systematic study of Stamboliiski's foreign policy exists. In the main, his foreign-policy ideas are best reflected in his speeches before the Bulgarian *Subranie* as well as in those of his closest collaborators. His stands on the various international issues are summarized in the following sources: Macartney and Palmer, *Independent Eastern Europe*, pp. 174, 263; Wolff, *The Balkans in Our Time*, pp. 106–8; *Istoriia na Bulgariia*, 2nd ed., 3: 75ff. Todorov, *Balkan Firebrand*, gives what is probably the most favorable view of the foreign-policy undertakings of the Agrarian regime. On Stamboliiski's peasant internationalism, see George D. Jackson, Jr., *Comintern and Peasant in East Europe*. None of the above materials is truly satisfactory. The views presented here are the author's. They were arrived at deductively and were influenced by retrospection.

ual eclipse. Part of his ideas were revived in a much modified form by the Zveno group in 1934, by Boris in 1937, and by Dimitrov in 1947. All three cases involved no more than plagiarism of a serious and comprehensive outlook painstakingly worked out by the original founders of the Bulgarian Agrarian movement.

In the decade following Stamboliiski's assassination, Bulgaria reverted to a traditional foreign policy devoid of originality or innovation. The extension of the French defense system into the Balkans reaffirmed Bulgaria's isolation. While Yugoslavia and Rumania joined the Little Entente, Bulgaria continued to pursue an uncompromising traditionalist policy toward her neighbors. This was especially true of Bulgaria's policies vis-à-vis Greece. Although nominally a defeated country, following the Treaty of Lausanne of 1923, Turkey operated largely as a satisfied state and thereby precluded the possibility of harmonious cooperation with the Bulgarians. Throughout the twenties, Bulgaria's relations with Ankara remained cool but correct. The abortive Communist uprising of September, 1923, inspired by the Comintern and Moscow, overshadowed Bulgaria's relations with the Soviet Union, which remained mutually antagonistic. With the exception of the Communists, not one political group within the Bulgarian body politic advocated improvement of relations with Moscow, which was perceived as Bulgaria's staunchest enemy. While the latter was true, Bulgaria's anti-Soviet diplomatic posture proved too narrow of base to allow for an understanding with France or with her clients in Southeastern Europe.[4]

There was, however, one exception to Bulgaria's state of international isolation. In the twenties, Italy emerged as the organizer of the discontented countries in Europe. Although the Italians could not match the might of France and were, therefore, unable to erect a formal system of alliances, they could and did extend their support to the countries of the defeated camp,

[4] Khadzhinikolov, *Stopnaski otnosheniia i vruzki mezhdu Bulgariia i Suvetskiia suiuz do deveti septemvrii, 1917–1944;* although devoted to Soviet-Bulgarian economic relations, which were not significant during the interwar period, the monograph traces the rudiments of diplomatic relations as well. On Stamboliiski and Soviet diplomatic overtures toward Bulgaria, see *Istoriia na Bulgariia*, 2nd ed., 3: 76–77.

which included Bulgaria, Hungary, and Austria. In actual fact, Italy's support did not amount to very much. Italian diplomacy was imaginative and audacious, but Italy lacked the resources necessary for the establishment of an effective hegemony. In this sense, Italy substituted for Germany as long as the latter was weak and prostrate. In retrospect, it is obvious that the great energies expended by the Italians in Central and Southeastern Europe amounted to no more than a holding action. The change of guard came in the mid-thirties. One by one, Italy's clients were handed over for inclusion in Germany's new sphere of influence.

In Bulgaria, dependence on Italy was more than a diplomatic nuance. Italy was successful in penetrating Bulgaria's domestic political system by means of the Macedonians. The Italians had discovered the Macedonian terrorists long before 1923. Italian diplomacy had helped bring about the consolidation of the anti-Stamboliiski forces. The change of orientation which followed the successful coup of 1923 played directly into the hands of Rome. Italy was not satisfied with a mere rapprochement with the Bulgarian ruling regime. She went on to strengthen the hands of the most extremist factions within the Macedonian organizations in their internal struggles against the more moderate groups. While the official champion of an Italian orientation was General Vulkov, Bulgaria's war minister after 1923, Italy's favorite within the Macedonian movement was Ivan Mikhailov, the leader of the extreme Macedonian annexationists. In time, Mikhailov emerged supreme from the interfactional struggles against the more moderate elements of the Macedonian nationalists. On July 7, 1928, a Mikhailov gunman shot and killed General Protogerov, who had led the more moderate wing of the Macedonians. With Protogerov's removal, Mikhailov proceeded to consolidate his personal authority over the movement as a whole. He was backed by Bulgaria's prime minister, Andrei Liapchev, himself a Macedonian. Not all of the partners in the Democratic Alliance were of the same mind, however, on the Macedonian issue. Professor Tsankov, who had surrendered the premiership in January, 1926, inclined toward the Protogerov Macedonians, as did Atanas Burov, Bulgaria's foreign minister in the Liapchev government. Still, until the end of his tenure in power, Liapchev's view prevailed.[5]

The negativism of Liapchev's foreign policy was only slightly modified by a number of small concessions which Bulgaria was able to extract from the victors. In April, 1928, Bulgaria was hit by a catastrophic earthquake which brought wholesale destruction to large areas of the southeast. This provided the excuse for negotiating a foreign loan in the amount of five million pounds sterling with a group of British and French banking establishments, a loan which would be administered by the League of Nations. Although small in size, this stabilization loan helped prop up the Liapchev government, which was already sustaining the heavy burden of reparations imposed on Bulgaria in 1919. The outbreak of the Great Depression, however, made the payment of reparations unbearable. In January, 1930, the Liapchev government successfully negotiated a cutback in the over-all amount of reparations due, as well as an extension of the payment periods.

Bulgarian foreign policy did not undergo any significant revision after the People's Bloc came to power in 1931. Gripped by continual domestic upheavals during the premierships of Alexander Malinov and Nikola Mushanov, Bulgaria remained linked to Italy for lack of other meaningful alternatives. In March, 1932, Premier Mushanov visited Ankara for the purpose of improving relations with Turkey as a first step in breaking Bulgaria's Balkan isolation. While the tie with Rome remained intact, in the latter part of its tenure the government of the People's Bloc undertook several initiatives aimed at modifying Bulgaria's foreign-policy position. In September, 1933, Boris visited Alexander, the king of the Yugoslavs, in Belgrade. The Yugoslav monarch returned the visit in October of the same year. These were the early beginnings of a rapprochement with Yugoslavia which Boris was to pursue more energetically

[5] On the subjects of Bulgaria, IMRO, and Italy, see the following: Lukacs, *The Great Powers and Eastern Europe;* Seton-Watson, *Eastern Europe between the Wars, 1918–1941;* Logio, *Bulgaria: Past and Present.* Swire, *Bulgarian Conspiracy,* is best on Italian intrigue in the Macedonian question; Malinov's two volumes, *Pod znaka na ostrasteni i opasni politicheski borbi* and *Stranichki ot nashata nova politicheska istoriia: Spomeni,* are general but interesting, particularly in view of Malinov's position as the leader of the Democrats.

later in the thirties. Also in 1933, the Bulgarian government began to explore the possibility of establishing diplomatic relations with the Soviet Union. Bulgarian-Soviet trade relations were resumed, although the initiative was not brought to fruition before the May, 1934, coup. More significantly, in its last year the Mushanov government adopted energetic measures against the Macedonian terrorists. Here again, the undertaking was only a beginning. In November, 1933, the Bulgarian king met with the Rumanian monarch in an endeavor to improve relations between the two countries. After Hitler came to power, French diplomacy in the Balkans showed signs of intensified activity, but the effort to include Bulgaria within a widened Balkan system failed. When Rumania, Yugoslavia, Turkey, and Greece signed the Balkan Pact in February, 1934, Bulgaria stayed out.[6]

The coup of May, 1934, brought to power the Military League and the Zveno people. Zveno's foreign-policy conceptions had been formed long before the capture of power and were now expeditiously implemented. The new government sought improved relations with France, which were to be the direct by-product of an understanding with Yugoslavia. The Zveno people understood that Bulgaria could not effectively pursue a policy of revisionism along the entire spectrum of its political grievances. If relations with Yugoslavia could be normalized, Bulgaria could turn her attention to Greece. Since rapprochement with Yugoslavia depended on the attitude of the Bulgarian government toward the Macedonian extremists, one of the very first acts of the Georgiev government was to disband Mikhailov's organization. The latter fled the country; his followers were disarmed and some were imprisoned. This political feat was achieved by use of the regular army and with the cooperation of the more moderate Macedonians of the Protogerov wing, with whom Zveno had maintained a liaison since the late twenties. By late May, the new Zveno government had

6 Geshkoff's *Balkan Union* and Stavrianos' *Balkan Federation: A History of the Movement toward Balkan Unity in Modern Times* remain important contributions to the subject. Of the various political factions, the Bulgarian Social Democrats took the most active part in the movement for Balkan unity sponsored by a number of centrist and left-of-center political parties from neighboring countries.

negotiated a trade agreement with Yugoslavia. A number of cultural and educational accords had been concluded as well.

Bulgaria's relations with Rumania were likewise improved. In early November, 1934, the Rumanian foreign minister, Nicholas Titulescu, visited Sofia. To signalize the desire for better relations with France, Bulgaria's Francophile minister to Paris, K. Batolov, was named foreign minister in the Georgiev government. At the same time, Petko Stainov, a professor of public law who had found his way into Zveno by way of the Tsankov movement, was appointed Bulgaria's minister to France. Dimo Kazasov, the ideological founder of Zveno, became Bulgaria's minister to Belgrade. These two men were to re-emerge in the first Fatherland Front government set up after the entry of the Red Army into Bulgaria in September, 1944—the first as Bulgaria's foreign minister, the second as minister of propaganda.

In its "Manifesto to the Bulgarian People," issued by the new regime immediately after it assumed power, Zveno proclaimed its determination to restore relations with the Soviet Union. Talks were inaugurated between the Bulgarian and Soviet ministers to Ankara soon thereafter. On June 23, 1934, formal diplomatic relations were established by the signing of two Soviet-Bulgarian protocols. In September of the same year, diplomatic representatives were exchanged. Professor D. G. Mikhalchev, a well-known historian, became Bulgaria's minister to Moscow. He was to be reappointed to that post after September, 1944. Razkolnikov, the civil war Bolshevik hero, became the Soviet minister to Sofia. This was to be his last official post in the series of assignments which had marked his brilliant revolutionary career. Indeed, Sofia became a place of exile for him. During Stalin's Great Purge he chose not to return to his homeland and ended his life under tragic circumstances in France after having published an open indictment of the Stalin regime.[7]

Carrying out the above measures, meaningful as they were, all but exhausted the Georgiev government's foreign-policy

[7] On Razkolnikov in Sofia and his ultimate fate, see Oren, *Bulgarian Communism*, pp. 97, 125. The performance of the Georgiev cabinet in the foreign-policy sphere is summarized in *Istoriia na Bulgariia*, 2nd ed., 3: 288–91.

initiatives. The fact was that in the international domain Zveno had arrived much too late. The posture of France in Eastern Europe had grown weaker, even though the outward manifestations of this lower profile were not yet fully visible. For objective reasons, the Zveno government was not able to stop Bulgaria's drift toward Germany. In 1933, 36 percent of all Bulgarian exports went to Germany, while 38 percent of the country's imports consisted of German merchandise. A year later, the respective percentages were 43 and 41. In 1934, Italy accounted for only about 10 percent of Bulgaria's entire international trade. The number of Bulgarian youth who were going to Germany and Austria for their higher education was rapidly increasing. In the cultural and artistic spheres, Germany held a position of primacy. The industrial equipment which Bulgaria bought in her moderate endeavor to industrialize was almost entirely of German make. Nevertheless, the Zveno regime succeeded in temporarily stabilizing Bulgaria's international position and, to some degree, in lifting the country out of her stifling isolation. In this sense, the Georgiev government pursued an enlightened course, but this stood in striking contrast to its domestic policies, which were marked by the rise of autocracy.

Following the overthrow of the Zveno regime, Bulgarian foreign affairs passed entirely into the hands of Boris. In November, 1935, the premiership was handed over to G. Kioseivanov, a professional diplomat who carried out the king's will throughout his five-year tenure. The king was a wary man and, although his pro-German inclinations were undeniable, he avoided radical measures. The rapprochement with Yugoslavia, begun under Zveno, was continued, but the relationship had been emptied of its original significance by Yugoslavia's own reorientation toward Nazi Germany as signalized by Dr. M. Stoyadinovic's rise to power in Belgrade. To solidify its newly established influence in Yugoslavia, Berlin now became anxious to see an improvement in Bulgarian-Yugoslav relations. A pact of "eternal friendship" between Bulgaria and Yugoslavia was officially signed in January, 1937. The only real relevance of this treaty was that it guaranteed Bulgaria a free flow of German armaments via Yugoslavia. Bulgaria's rearmament program was started as early as 1936. The new military equipment was entirely of German manufacture. Germany's growing influence in Sofia was signified by the increasingly frequent visits of German officials to Bulgaria. Marshal Goering visited Sofia in mid-1935. A year later, in June of 1936, Dr. Schacht, Hitler's economics minister, visited Bulgaria. By 1939, the German share of Bulgaria's exports had climbed to 68 percent, while German goods accounted for 65 percent of Bulgaria's total imports.[8]

In an endeavor to counterbalance Bulgaria's alarming dependence on Germany, France and Britain undertook to satisfy some of Bulgaria's revisionist demands. Aided by their suggestions, in June, 1938, Bulgaria concluded the so-called Salonika Agreement with the countries of the Balkan Pact, which formally lifted the military restrictions imposed on Bulgaria by the Paris peace treaty. In view of the fact that Bulgaria was already rapidly rearming, this proved to be only a nominal concession. Bulgaria supported the sanctions against Italy voted by the League of Nations at the outbreak of the Abyssinian war. Officially, Bulgaria stayed out of the Spanish conflict and recognized the Franco regime only after the Western powers had done so. In the long run, however, Bulgaria's revisionism could fulfill itself only by means of harmonious relations with Germany, which was the only Great Power capable of delivering those goods in which Bulgaria was most interested.

In the second half of the thirties, the Bulgarian Communists took a number of initiatives, all of which, though invisible at the time, were significant in the long run. In one way or another, these Communist activities were linked to Bulgaria's foreign-policy stand.

As early as 1936, the Communists established a secret liaison with the leaders of Zveno. The coming together of these two seemingly incompatible political forces represented a phenomenon which can best be termed mutual recruitment. Having been both ousted from power and purged by Boris' henchmen, Zveno and the wing of the Military League with which it had cooperated found themselves in a political wilderness. Since

8 The unpublished dissertation of Pundeff, "Bulgaria's Place in Axis Policy, 1936–1944," remains the best monograph on Bulgaria's foreign-policy orientations in the last pre-Communist decade.

they had never sought nor received wide popular support, once again there was no direction in which Zveno could turn except that of political conspiracy. Under Georgiev's inspiration, the top-ranking Communist functionaries who had been dispatched to Bulgaria by Dimitrov were approached for the purpose of concluding a Zveno-Communist alliance. The Comintern was duly informed of these overtures and responded favorably. The responsible comrades within Bulgaria were instructed to maintain the link for whatever eventualities might yet arise. However, the suggestions proposed by Zveno, which explored the possibility of a political *Putsch* to be carried out with Communist assistance, were turned down by Moscow. Putschism would negate the popular front tactics and thus was considered inappropriate for the time being. Still, an informal friendship arose between functionaries of the Communist party and several influential personalities from Zveno and the Military League. This tentative collaboration became more fruitful in the latter part of the Second World War, when the Communists combined with a number of retired officers close to Zveno to carry out the coup of September, 1944. The political partnership between the two continued throughout the first stage of sovietization. The rapport which Zveno achieved with the Communists in the second half of the thirties did not, however, obligate Zveno to, or engage its followers in, a common front with the Communists. The Zveno leaders were much too shrewd to tie their hands in any way. They maintained their intimate contacts with spokesmen for the extreme right as well. Had the political winds blown the other way, Zveno might well have emerged in the democratic camp. As it was, circumstances toward the end of the Second World War favored the Soviet Union, and Zveno tailored its political behavior accordingly.[9]

As could be expected, the Bulgarian Communists became involved in the Spanish Civil War. Although officially Bulgaria remained neutral and the government did what it could to prevent the participation of Bulgarian citizens in the conflict, several hundred Bulgarian Communists and Communist sympathizers made their way into Spain via the clandestine channels

[9] Zveno-Communist links in the mid-thirties are discussed, analyzed, and documented in Oren, *Bulgarian Communism*, pp. 131–32.

set up by the Comintern in Paris. In Spain, they were joined by about one hundred Bulgarian Communist exiles who had come directly from the Soviet Union. Thus, after 1936, Spain became the meeting ground for a relatively large number of cadres from Bulgaria proper and from the Soviet emigration. In all, more than four hundred Bulgarians fought on the Republican side. Many of the Bulgarian émigrés acted as Soviet personnel and were not officially identified as Bulgarian volunteers throughout the war. When, in early 1938, Moscow began recalling its people from Spain, the Bulgarian émigrés returned to the Soviet Union, where some were purged, as were most of the other participants in the Spanish conflict. After the outbreak of the German-Soviet war in 1941, a number of Bulgarian "Spaniards" were dispatched to Bulgaria to take part in the underground Communist resistance. The Communists who had come directly from Bulgaria crossed into France after the collapse of the Republic and remained in French concentration camps until after the outbreak of the Second World War. Eventually, they were pardoned by the government in Sofia and allowed to return home, thanks to the intervention of Bulgaria's minister to the Vichy regime. A number of them participated in the Communist resistance during the Second World War. The "Spaniards" suffered a grim fate in the late forties, when any indication of cosmopolitanism, as Stalin had defined the term, acted to their detriment. A fighting record in Republican Spain gained value once more in the mid-fifties, when the surviving veterans were publicly acknowledged and awarded distinctions.[10]

In the latter part of the thirties, relations between the Bulgarian Communists and the Communists of Rumania came to the fore. The various national minorities had played a predominant role in the affairs of the Rumanian party during the interwar period. The Bulgarians were probably the most conspicuous of the lot. They were mainly natives of Dobruja who had come to communism via the road of their national grievances. In 1938, the Communist party in Bulgaria adapted its line to harmonize with the national aspirations of the Bulgarian people as a whole. The earlier ideas of Balkan federalism were

[10] *Ibid.*, pp. 133–38, covers the story of the participation of Bulgarian Communists in the Spanish Civil War.

dropped and the Communists came to insist that southern Dobruja rightfully belonged to the Bulgarian state. This placed the Bulgarian members of the Rumanian Communist party in direct conflict with their Rumanian comrades. The latter felt betrayed, particularly at a time when Rumania faced the grim prospect of being truncated by her revisionist neighbors. In the long run, the issue of southern Dobruja was decided not by the Communists but by the Great Powers, and by Germany in particular. The hatred which the issue aroused in the hearts of the Rumanian Communists did not diminish, however. The resentment persisted into the sovietization of the two countries and survives to this day.[11]

The last year of peace found Bulgaria's international position predetermined. In retrospect, it is obvious that Stamboliiski's experiments in the foreign-policy domain and the efforts of the short-lived Georgiev government to rearrange Bulgaria's foreign affiliations were little more than passing episodes. Although well conceived, the two endeavors suffered from insurmountable inner deficiencies which could not be easily overcome. Stamboliiski's originality was undeniable. Yet, for reasons of personal temperament and political ideology, he was never able to concentrate on select issues; instead, he sought to tackle everything at once. In this sense, his overwhelming confidence was also his undoing. He was incapable of striking temporary alliances with any of the domestic political factions in order to attain limited objectives. Rather, he committed himself and the Agrarian Union in a massive way to the entire spectrum of problems. His style of political action contained elements of naïveté. As a result, his enemies were able to unite in common action, despite their political heterogeneity.

The reasons for Zveno's failure are to be found in different quarters altogether. Essentially, Zveno and the Military League constituted a general staff without an army. Although politically astute, they commanded no popular support, nor did they

[11] *Ibid.*, pp. 138–43, traces relations between the Bulgarian and Rumanian Communist parties in general and the question of southern Dobruja in particular. Georgiev, *Dobrudzha v borbata za svoboda, 1913–1940*, is the most important Communist source on this intricate subject. Except for the unveiled bitterness they have expressed toward the historic role of Bulgarian communism, the Rumanians have yet to relate their part of the old conflict in any detail.

attempt to master the masses by means of political organization. They relied much too heavily on mass propaganda and generalized appeals to the people at large. Because of its self-perception as an elitist group, Zveno was incapable of setting up a political bureaucracy of its own. Finally, the coup of May, 1934, was carried out in an international context which was undergoing fundamental changes. By the time Zveno and the Military League had assumed power, the countries of Central and Southeastern Europe had already begun to drift toward Germany, which was probably unavoidable in the face of Western hesitancy.

The interwar experience proved once again the irrelevance of France and Britain to Bulgaria's modern political destiny. In terms of political culture, as well as considerations of realpolitik, the positions of the two Western democracies were too far removed from the immediacy of Bulgaria's international ordeals. Throughout the period, the geopolitical importance of Bulgaria was depreciated, if not altogether dismissed, by the statesmen of Paris and London. Bulgaria's objective requirement of at least one Great Power's support was thus served by neither. This small and embattled country stayed firmly entrenched within the magnetic field of Germany or Russia.

Within Bulgaria, those forces which alone could have provided the energy necessary to escape from Berlin's or Moscow's sphere of influence were too weak. As a class, the enlightened bourgeoisie was much too young and small to play a significant role. The urban middle class would have required another two generations, at least, to become a meaningful force. The urban and rural intelligentsia was economically destitute and therefore was highly susceptible to radical political moods. A sizable number went over to the Communists, among whom they sought support for their national and class grievances. The backing provided them by Stalinist Russia proved precarious. Moscow's political egoism always took precedence over the interests of Bulgarian revolutionism. The timetable for political action was regulated by Moscow and the Comintern without regard to the particular circumstances of Bulgaria's position.

As an institution, the dynasty remained crucially important

throughout the interwar period. The eclipse of the king's power under the Stamboliiski regime and the Georgiev government proved only temporary. In the realm of diplomacy, what little talent the country could muster drifted toward the court. Boris was better informed of world events than any of the many political groups. His intimacy with German politics, his family connections with Rome, and his frequent tours of the West made him best equipped to implement his own foreign-policy designs. Boris was not a dogmatic person. His natural wariness and endless patience gave him an advantage over his rivals. When the internal domestic quarrels had ended and the dust of battle had settled, all eyes turned to him for guidance. To the end of his life he retained the confidence of several political figures whose ideological positions were at great variance with his own. His tact, personal charm, and shrewdness helped immobilize many of his rivals at the most crucial junctures in the political development of Bulgaria. Under his leadership, Bulgarian diplomacy in the thirties followed a cautious course, never giving itself up to experimentation of any kind. Thus, the dynasty prevailed until the bitter end.

3: THE WAR YEARS: FROM PROFIT TO DEFEAT

Just as they imposed themselves on all other small states, the particular circumstances of the Second World War and developments in the larger world converged on Bulgaria and limited her range of choices. Crucial initiatives were not demonstrated, as they had been in the Balkan wars. Nor were the dilemmas of 1915 reproduced in 1940. The Bulgarians acquiesced to the forces of war, bending with the winds. As long as Germany's might lasted, Bulgaria reaped the fortunes of war.

In September, 1939, Bulgaria declared her neutrality. A few months later, Boris ordered new general elections, resulting in a Parliament that was more secure than the one produced by the 1938 elections. Only a handful of nominally oppositionist deputies found their way into the new house. The overwhelming majority consisted of hand-picked individuals who gave their support to the regime without resistance. They constituted the so-called co-opted majority. Political parties continued to be banned, as they had been since 1934. Governments were made and unmade by the personal decision of the king. Other than his careful nature, there were no institutional forces to balance his will. Following the sweeping purges that Boris instituted against the Military League in the 1930s, the army stayed compliant. Bulgaria remained effectively integrated within the German economic sphere. Until well into the middle of the war, the country enjoyed a moderate, but real, economic prosperity. Industrial capacity expanded continuously until 1942. Germany constituted a secure market for Bulgaria's agricultural produce. Even though she could not buy from Germany all that she wanted, and was forced to be satisfied with what the Germans were willing to sell, Bulgaria's GNP continued to rise for a time. The real income of the industrial working class experienced only moderate fluctuations. Eventually, the savings of the peasants were to be wiped out by rising inflation. For the time being, however, the countryside was satisfied as it had not been for years.[1]

On the eve of the war, Bulgaria entered into an extensive trade agreement with Soviet Russia. The agreement was politically motivated, and its economic significance remained limited. On the face of it, the government welcomed the Ribbentrop-Molotov Pact because it tended to neutralize the leftist opposition at home, just as the Munich Agreement had immobilized the democratic elements. At the same time, the secret clauses of the German-Soviet understanding, of which the Bulgarians were vaguely aware, left Boris uneasy. Since 1938, the Soviet government had demonstrated its designs on Bulgaria by making repeated approaches to Sofia. The division of Poland, the disposition of the Baltic States, and, above all, Hitler's neutrality during the agonizing battles in Finland increased the apprehensions of the Bulgarian Germanophiles. Repeatedly, throughout the winter and spring of 1940, Boris sought reassurances from his friends in Berlin that Bulgaria had not been promised to the Russians. In the summer and early fall of the same year,

---

[1] The following are but a few of the indicators of the state of the economy during the Second World War. All figures are derived from Natan, *Ikonomicheska istoriia na Bulgariia*. Published in 1957, this work cannot be suspected of endeavoring to show special favor to Bulgaria's economic progress during wartime capitalism, for it does the opposite. Industrial production rose by 18.2 percent between 1939 and 1941, and in 1943 was still 10.5 percent higher than it had been in the last prewar year (p. 506). The mining of coal almost doubled within a span of two years, from 2.2 million tons in 1939 to a little more than 4 million tons in 1943 (p. 527). The total production in the metal-working industries rose 12.7 percent between 1939 and 1942, while food and tobacco-processing industries increased their total production by 50.3 percent between 1939 and 1941, and in 1943 were still producing 12.7 percent more than they had in the last prewar year (p. 524). The index (1939=100) of real and adjusted average wages for the industrial workers was as follows: 95.5 in 1940; 93.7 in 1941; 80.3 in 1942; 85.9 in 1943; and 112.3 in 1944 (p. 545).

the Russian pressure on Bulgaria increased. The Bulgarians were asked to enter into an agreement of mutual assistance with the Soviet Union, being promised, in return, Moscow's support of Bulgaria's territorial designs on Greece and Turkey. During the November visit of Molotov to Berlin, the question of the future of Bulgaria was placed high on the Russians' agenda. Molotov's dogged insistence that Bulgaria rightfully belonged to the Soviet sphere of influence only added to Hitler's outrage at his unnatural partners. What little chance the Russians had of placing their foot on the Balkans had all but disappeared by then, primarily because of the disastrous Italian campaign in Greece. Hitler had resolved to come to the assistance of il Duce in order to extricate his embattled legions from the ill-fated venture into the Balkans. Bulgaria had to be held secure as a land bridge if the Germans were to reach the Aegean.

Developments during the winter of 1940/41 followed a pre-determined course. On the political side, detailed schedules were prepared for Bulgaria's entry into the Tripartite Pact. These were complemented by meticulously worked out military plans which secured the logistic side of the German crossing into Bulgaria on their way to the Greek frontier. For their services, and without being asked to participate in any military activities, the Bulgarians were promised Thrace. In February, the Boris regime cracked down on the opposition elements at home, arresting several hundred of them. Communist functionaries, as well as persons of Western and democratic leanings, were incarcerated together in a newly established detention camp erected for that purpose. On March 1, 1941, Bulgaria formally entered the Tripartite Pact while the German armies crossed into the country. The unexpected *Putsch* in Belgrade and Hitler's consequent decision to deal with the Yugoslavs as well added to the bag of spoils in which the Bulgarians were to share. The German lightning campaign followed in early April. Later in the spring, the Bulgarians received their reward in the form of Thrace and Macedonia. The much desired town of Salonika remained in German hands. The recently recovered territories were incorporated into the Bulgarian state, even though their formal disposition was left open till the end of the war. Bulgarian-Soviet relations remained intact after June, 1941, through early September, 1944. In December, 1941, Bulgaria declared war on the Western Allies.

The Bulgarian body politic did not undergo radical changes during the war. Throughout, the king maintained his primacy and ruled by means of the state bureaucracy, which was of his making. Relations with Nazi Germany continued to be amiable. Collaboration with the Germans on the military and secret police planes was complete. Although the Bulgarians adopted the German style of political action to a certain degree, Bulgaria did not become a thoroughly fascist state. The country resembled a traditional Balkan autocracy much more than a modern totalitarian state-in-the-making. Hitler was satisfied with Bulgaria's compliance in the political and economic spheres, and did not insist on ideological emulation. Only a few fringe groups were seriously affected by Nazi ideological appeals. The small size of the country, the relative poverty of its society, and the persistence of traditional political corruption provided the Bulgarian political system with a measure of built-in leniency and livability.

A fringe of the new intelligentsia did undertake to rewrite history, however, by removing Bulgaria's heritage from its Slavic origins. No other factor was nearly so powerful as the rising wave of national chauvinism fostered by the newly attained unification of the "Bulgarian tribe." The Bulgarians were now the largest people in the Balkans, and it was they who should remake the politics of the region. Such designs of newly discovered grandeur dwelt among parts of the urban middle class, however; the tastes of the peasants were more rudimentary. For the peasants, relative peace and moderate prosperity sufficed. Bulgaria's escape from the brunt of the war and the dismal fate of her neighbors loomed as the largest consideration of which the populace took account.

Oppositionist sentiments survived on the fringes. The traditional pro-Western democratic elements were split several ways. The majority came to constitute what was termed the tolerated opposition. A handful of them, led by Mushanov, sat in Parliament and uttered their reservations regarding the policies of the regime. Otherwise, the old leaders endeavored to maintain contact with their immediate followers as best they could. Their dilemma was that, despite their dislike of Nazi Germany, they were not averse to the fruits of victory made possible by German arms. Most of them preserved their individual freedom, which permitted them to pursue a certain amount of political lobbying.[2]

The only active opposition to the Germans came from a small segment of the Pladne Agrarians. Aided by the British and the Yugoslavs, Dr. Dimitrov set up a small underground network which was to execute sabotage activities against the German military establishment in Bulgaria. This meager organization did not survive long. It was uncovered in the spring of 1941, and its participants were tried and sentenced later that year. Dr. Dimitrov and a few of his close collaborators escaped and eventually established themselves in the Middle East, where, with British assistance, they organized radio broadcasts to Bulgaria. Within Bulgaria, Petkov undertook to collaborate with the Communists, who set themselves up as the one sizable underground movement.[3]

The circumstances which placed the Communists on top in 1944 were unrelated to their wartime record. In retrospect, it is clear that wartime Communist activities affected the future of their party much more than they influenced Bulgaria's wartime position. It is for this reason that Communist wartime fortunes must be briefly sketched.

Intraparty schisms and the purges of the cadres at home and in Soviet exile left their mark on the once-powerful organization. At the outbreak of the war, Communist party membership was a fraction of what it had been a few years earlier.[4] Unlike

[2] The fate of the tolerated opposition in all of its political ramifications is covered in Oren, *Bulgarian Communism*, chap. 8. Dimitrov, *Burzhoaznata opozitsiia v Bulgariia, 1939–1944,* and Petrova, *BZNS v kraia na burzhoaznoto gospodstvo v Bulgariia, 1939–1944,* are significant contributions on the same subject made public in Bulgaria in recent years. Dimitrov's work is the superior of the two, both in its scope and in its relative objectivity.

[3] The full range of Dr. Dimitrov's wartime activities is treated in Oren, *Bulgarian Communism*, pp. 162–65, 205, 223, 250n. Additional information is to be found in Sir. H. M. K. Hugessen, *Diplomat in Peace and War* (London, 1949), and Sweet-Escott, *Baker Street Irregular.*

[4] Party membership (including organized members of the Communist party and the Bulgarian Workers party) changed as follows: there were more than

most of their Western counterparts, the Bulgarian Communists were not shocked by the signing of the Ribbentrop-Molotov Pact. On the contrary, the rapprochement between the two dictatorships gave the Communists a degree of official acceptability to which they had long been unaccustomed. Momentarily, they became more trustworthy in the eyes of the regime than any one of the democratic groups. As long as the Berlin-Moscow harmony lasted, the Communists could and did speak out in favor of Bulgaria's revisionist designs without being hampered. The regime's desire to mend its relations with the Soviet Union reflected favorably on the position of the Communists. For all practical purposes, police repressions were suspended and, although the Communists were not allowed to organize openly, their presence on the political scene became much more visible. In the general elections held in the winter of 1939/40, they succeeded in electing ten deputies of known and acknowledged pro-Communist affiliation. Although modest in absolute terms, this achievement was more than respectable when compared with the electoral attainments of the democratic pro-Western elements, who, together, elected only as many deputies as did the Communists.[5]

Throughout the period, the Communist line closely followed the Balkan interests of Soviet diplomacy. The Russians supported the annexation of southern Dobruja by Bulgaria, as did the Western powers. The transfer of territory represented only one minor part in the truncation of Rumania. While benefiting from Moscow's attitude on the issue, the Boris regime failed to acknowledge the Soviets' assistance and did all it could to shift its official gratitude to the Germans. The Communists expressed resentment at such duplicity and voiced it in their illegal leaflets. Still, as long as the Russians hoped to affect Bulgaria's international orientation on the official diplomatic level, the Bulgarian Communists had to support the regime's foreign policy wholeheartedly. For his part, Boris was careful to appease the Russians—that is, as long as Hitler's determina-

---

30,000 in 1932–33; a low of 4,000 at the end of 1934; 7,252 in October, 1936; and 6,890 in mid-1940. See Oren, *Bulgarian Communism*, pp. 108–9.

[5] *Ibid.*, pp. 148–49.

tion to block Russia's designs on the Balkans was not clearly and firmly stated.

The situation changed in the fall of 1940, following Hitler's decision to intervene in Greece. At this point, Berlin gave the Bulgarians the green light which opened the way for Bulgaria's definitive refusal to comply with Soviet demands for a treaty of mutual assistance. Having failed in their Balkan game, the Russians undertook to pressure the Bulgarian regime from within. This signaled the parting of ways between the Communists and the Boris regime on the vital foreign-policy questions. The Soviet legation in Sofia passed on to the Bulgarian Communists the text of the proposed treaty, which was edited, then widely circulated all over the country. Only the most favorable clauses were included in the Communist version. In the massive underground Communist literature Russia was portrayed as Bulgaria's one and only benefactor. As it gathered momentum, the campaign assumed overt anti-German overtones. In the eyes of contemporary observers the anti-German stand taken by the Sofia Communists appeared to be a puzzling deviation. Only the few and best initiated grasped the full meaning of the campaign, which was its signification that Soviet-German relations had reached a point of crisis. For the Russians, this was a calculated risk which indicated their great anxiety over the fate of Bulgaria. In the end, Moscow's realism prevailed. By the end of the year, the Soviets realized full well that Bulgaria's commitment to the Axis was final and unalterable. They called off the Communist campaign and instructed their Bulgarian comrades to stay put. Molotov was prepared to go only a limited distance. The uneasy détente which the Ribbentrop-Molotov Pact had bought the Russians was not to be imperiled for the sake of Bulgaria. When the German armies crossed the Danube in early March, 1941, the Bulgarian Communists satisfied themselves with mild protestations. They made no move and undertook no meaningful action until June, 1941.[6]

From the spring of 1941 until the end of the war, the Bulgarian Communists faced a harsh dilemma. On the one hand, they endeavored to capitalize on Bulgaria's territorial gains; on the other hand, Germany's attack on the Soviet Union com-

[6] On the Soviet-proposed treaty and the Communists, see *ibid.*, pp. 153–65.

pelled the Communist party to take action in defense of the socialist motherland. While they were more than willing to follow the first requisite, they found themselves ill-equipped and, on the whole, disinclined to carry out the second. In the main, the inner conflict represented an insoluble clash between the instincts of nationalism and the sentiments of internationalism.

If Bulgaria and Macedonia had become a single country, why should the Bulgarian Communist party and the Communist organization in Macedonia not constitute a single party as well? The question was posed rhetorically. "One country, one party" became the new motto of the Sofia comrades. Subjectively, there was no other conceivable stand that the Bulgarian Communists could take. Much of the leadership of the Bulgarian party consisted of functionaries who were themselves of Macedonian origin. Many of them had become Communists precisely because of the frustrations fostered in their souls by the insurmountable Macedonian problem. This was not a game of duplicity, as Tito was to claim. The position was as natural and as logical for the Communists as it was for the Boris regime and for the people at large. From April, 1941, until the end of the war, the Bulgarian Communists attempted to integrate within their ranks all the Communists from the new territories, as well as all those willing to follow the Communist line.

Confrontation with the Communists of Belgrade was inescapable. It was inevitable, in the long run, that this jurisdictional dispute between the two parties would be shifted onto the Comintern and Moscow. Moscow's arbitration of the dispute retained a measure of ambivalence which was probably unavoidable. The case of the Sofia Communists was taken up by the Bulgarian Communists in Soviet exile. The merits of the dispute were never an issue for the Russians. Since Tito very soon proved to be much more capable of fighting the Germans, he became the nominal recipient of Moscow's support. The Soviet judgments were never clear-cut, however. Formally, the Bulgarians accepted Tito's predominance on the Macedonian issue. In actual fact, they endeavored as best they could to subvert his authority in Skoplje. Stalin trusted the Bulgarians more than he did the Yugoslavs, the wide discrepancy in their respective wartime records notwithstanding. When in 1944 Tito won the contest, the Bulgarians had to comply with the new reality but they did not accept the judgment as final.[7]

While the Macedonian problem mastered the Bulgarian Communists' diplomatic skills, the resistance effort required morale, arms, and extensive organizational work. These were not easily forthcoming. Following Germany's attack on the Soviet Union, the Politburo issued an appeal calling on the cadres to prepare for armed resistance. This appeal proved to be more a reflex action to the war requirements of the Soviet Union than an actual command. The disastrous experience of 1923, when the party took up arms after the opportunity had passed, was still fresh in the minds of the party's high command. The difference was that in 1941 the opportunity never arose.

After the spring of 1941 there were only a few German army units on Bulgarian soil. Resistance, therefore, had to be directed against the Bulgarian regime alone. Since Bulgaria was not at war with Russia, there was no conceivable way in which the Communists could help the Soviet war effort except by sabotaging, or at least hampering, the flow of Bulgarian agricultural exports to Nazi Germany. In other words, economic sabotage, even if it could be carried out successfully, had to be directed against Bulgaria's own economy. This being the sole means by which the Bulgarian Communists could prove their international solidarity, there was no way to mobilize the enthusiasm of even the most devoted followers of the cause. Still, the party went through the motions. A military commission was set up to plan and organize resistance. The majority view within the commission itself was that the party should not endanger its present and future by undertaking meaningful underground activities.

[7] On wartime Macedonia and the Bulgarian-Yugoslav Communist dispute as arbitrated by the Comintern, see *ibid.*, pp. 187–99. See also *Titovata banda, orudie na imperialistite: Dokumenti i materiali; KPJ i makedonskoto natsionalno prashanye; Istorijski arhiv KPJ*, vol. 7; Barker, *Macedonia: Its Place in Balkan Power Politics;* Clissold, *Whirlwind;* Mojsov, *Bulgarskata rabotnichka partija (komunisti) i makedonskoto natsionalno prashanye;* Dedijer, *Tito Speaks* and Djilas, *Conversations With Stalin.* A recently published two-volume memoir by Svetozar Vukmanovic-Tempo, a wartime Yugoslav Communist hero, is important regarding Tito's wartime relations with the Bulgarian Communist representatives in Skoplje. See the extensive review published in *Radio Free Europe Research,* February 11, 18, 25, 1971.

All that was left during this first stage of the war, therefore, was Communist rhetoric.

Dimitrov and his collaborators in Moscow viewed the situation differently. They organized a number of detachments from the Bulgarian Communist emigration in Russia and landed them on Bulgarian soil by means of Soviet submarines and aircraft. The undertaking proved a failure from the start. The great majority of the participants in the venture were captured by Bulgarian security forces immediately upon landing. Those who were not shot on arrival were rounded up, tried, and executed in the spring of 1942. Only a few survived to tell their story and describe the desperate nature of the entire affair.[8]

In the early months of 1942, the organizational superstructure of the party collapsed. For all practical purposes, the party's Central Committee ceased to exist. Aided by the Gestapo, the Bulgarian secret police penetrated and ultimately broke up the few intelligence networks the Russians had set up in Bulgaria. In desperation, the surviving party cadres turned to political assassination. A number of Bulgarian politicians were shot in revenge for their collaboration with the Germans or their anti-Communist activities. The overwhelming majority of the Communist intelligentsia remained in detention camps and awaited events. In the winter and spring of 1943, the Bulgarian Communist party reached its lowest ebb.[9]

Only after the summer of 1943 did the Bulgarian Communist organization show signs of revival. The German reversals on the eastern front had an inevitable impact on the Bulgarian scene. Aided by the Yugoslav partisans, as well as by the brutality of

[8] No other subject has produced so much attention or so many published materials in Communist Bulgaria since 1944 as the wartime resistance. This massive output is reflected only in small part in the bibliography. Vasilev's *Vuoruzhenata suprotiva* and Gornenski's *Vuoruzhenata borba . . . 1941–1944* are the two standard histories of the Communist resistance. *The Struggle of the Bulgarian People against Fascism* is a semiofficial English version of the Communist effort. Kostov's *Politicheskoto polozhenie i zadachite na partiiata,* published in early 1945 (but never reprinted), is the most important document on the state of the Communist party during the war. Kiril Vidinski, *Podvodnicharite: Spomeni* (Sofia, 1963), relates the details pertaining to the expedition of the Bulgarian émigrés sent from Russia in 1941. The Communist resistance as a whole is retraced in detail in Oren, *Bulgarian Communism,* pp. 166–220.

[9] *Ibid.,* pp. 180–87, 202–03.

71

the anti-Communist persecutions carried out by the Bulgarian security forces, a few partisan contingents came into being. They were never very numerous or effective. The bulk of their energies was consumed by tending to the needs of their own survival. They represented a mixture of the younger devoted followers of the party line and brigands of all kinds. They received no material aid from the Soviet Union except for Bulgarian-language radio broadcasts which emanated from Russia. In the summer of 1943, the Allied Mediterranean Command took notice of the slight Bulgarian underground. A British liaison mission was parachuted over Yugoslav territory for the purpose of establishing contact with the Bulgarian Communists. Several planeloads of arms were parachuted over Tito's free territory for distribution among the Bulgarian partisans. The Allied effort was small, and its impact on the fighting capability of the Bulgarian contingents remained slight. At about the same time, a number of Bulgarian Communist émigrés were dispatched from the Soviet Union to Tito's partisan headquarters. Their function was not to fight but to establish a political presence in Bulgaria's proximity.[10]

In the fall of 1943, the Bulgarian regime took notice of the changing fortunes of war and initiated a few tentative steps to improve relations with Soviet Russia. The detention camps were closed down, freeing those Communists who had been held by administrative decrees. Several of them rejoined the underground, thus reinforcing the ranks of the resistance. In the spring and early summer of 1944, the Bulgarian Communist resistance counted a few thousand participants. The armed effort did not amount to very much. It never attained much popular support. The war experience in Bulgaria confirmed that the influence and success of communism is correlated with national rather than class dissatisfaction. For those fanatically devoted to the Communist cause, this was a bitter lesson, but one which, nevertheless, had to be learned. The fact that the Bulgarians had performed better than their comrades in any one of the countries allied with Germany offered little consolation. What mattered most to the Bulgarian Communists was what

---

[10] On the Allied assistance and the émigrés sent from Moscow to Tito's headquarters, see *ibid.*, pp. 205–11.

they saw across their frontiers. The Yugoslav Communists, whom the Bulgarian party had patronized disdainfully throughout the interwar years, had become a formidable force, while their own might had shrunk. These were facts which postwar Communist historiography could not obliterate nor successfully rewrite.

Paralleling the resistance was the political dimension of Communist wartime activities. As early as 1942, at Moscow's instigation, Communist functionaries sought political collaboration with the leaders of the democratic camp. This was the origin of the Fatherland Front. Headed by Mushanov, the small Bulgarian Democratic party remained firm in its refusal to join the front. The leadership of the tiny but influential Social Democratic party split, with a few going over to the Fatherland Front and the veteran Pastukhov remaining aloof. The split among the Agrarians followed the lines of earlier schisms. The majority, headed by Gichev, refused to cooperate, while the Pladne group, led by Nikola Petkov, which had split off from the main body of the Agrarians in the early thirties, joined hands in the Fatherland Front. The leaders of Zveno went over to the Communists. The small Radical party remained unallied.

The Fatherland Front did not become a cohesive opposition group until the very eve of the coup of September, 1944. Throughout, it was a tentative alignment, of which the Communists constituted the core. Although the constituent parts of the front agreed with the program worked out by Dimitrov in Moscow, neither the Communists nor their partners remained fully committed to Fatherland Front discipline. In the summer of 1944, the Communists endeavored to come to terms with the government of Bagrianov. Petkov and the Social Democrats interacted with the political leaders of the opposition groups that had remained outside the front. For all practical purposes, the front remained an empty frame until August of 1944, when Russia's prospects in Bulgaria radically and suddenly improved. The organization acquired real significance only after it had assumed power.[11]

[11] The politics of the wartime Fatherland Front are described in *ibid.*, chap. VIII. See also Kazasov, *Burni godini;* Dramaliev, *Istoriia na Otechestveniia front;* Dimitrov, *Burzhoazanata opozitsiia v Bulgariia 1939–1944;* and Petrova, *BZNS v kraia na burzhoaznoto gospodstvo v Bulgariia, 1939–1944.*

Bulgaria's position at the end of the war was determined not by the shadowy existence of political parties at home but by international developments far removed from Bulgaria's reach. There is sufficient evidence to indicate that, after the German reversals in Stalingrad, Boris' anxiety over the ultimate disposition of his country increased. He was a man of intelligence and much political shrewdness. In the early summer of 1943, he initiated a few tentative approaches to the Western powers which were aimed at ascertaining their true inclination toward, and ultimate demands on, Bulgaria. Boris' capacity for determined action was never displayed, however, for he died suddenly in August, 1943, under clouded circumstances. Like all willful people, Boris had kept control of all decisive issues in his own hands. He was succeeded by a regency council whose authority was substantially less than his.

Although contacts with the Allies continued to be maintained and were, in fact, expanded in the winter of 1943/44, the approaches remained at a very low level throughout. Those in charge were too thoroughly committed to a pro-German orientation. This inhibited them in their foreign dealings and rendered them incapable of undertaking a decisive turnabout in Bulgaria's international commitments. Since Bulgaria was engulfed by Germany's military might in the Balkans, her room for maneuver was never very wide. She realized full well that Russia represented her greatest peril. The fact that Bulgaria had not become involved in war with the Soviet Union was judged an asset, and she endeavored desperately to preserve it. The regents remained essentially ignorant of the larger implications of developments in the international war. Their inability to generate any meaningful interest in Bulgaria among the Western Allies was their greatest failing. This alone made their wartime record pitiful.

To the very last, the regents clung to Bulgaria's acquisition of Macedonia and Thrace and hoped that the Red Army would stop its advance on the banks of the Danube after the Germans had evacuated the country. From the start, however, the game was largely out of their hands. While the political realities of the future were determined by military developments along the war fronts, the final verdict over Bulgaria emerged in the conference rooms of the Great Powers.

The main outlines of the inter-Allied diplomatic record are complete and need not be reviewed in detail here. To preserve Greece, Churchill was prepared to go a long way in accommodating Soviet demands. Stalin's designs on Bulgaria were quietly but forcefully presented and were accepted without resistance. The question of Bulgaria was only incidental in the extensive Anglo-Soviet diplomatic exchanges which commenced in the early spring of 1944 and which ultimately led to the "percentage-agreement." At best, Bulgaria commanded Churchill's complete disinterest; at worst, Churchill's attitude toward Bulgaria was colored by a strong feeling of repugnance. Bulgaria had won his lasting enmity as early as the First World War, when she joined the Central Powers and thus contributed to the failure of his favorite campaign, that in the Dardanelles. Moreover, Churchill's talks with the Soviet leaders underlined his inner conviction that Stalin would not be appeased unless Bulgaria were made a part of his postwar dominion. Thus, no serious attempt was made to bargain over Bulgaria.[12]

The impact of this outcome on the entire Balkan peninsula was no less than that on Bulgaria's own future. The fact that the lines of division between the wartime partners became set along the Bulgarian-Greek frontier rather than along the Danube brought about an irrevocable transformation in the geopolitical setting in the Balkans. The postwar positions of Greece, Yugoslavia, and Turkey were affected once Bulgaria

[12] U.S., Department of State, *Foreign Relations of the United States: Diplomatic Papers, 1944,* vol. 3 (Washington, D.C., 1965), pp. 300–554, and various entries in selected wartime volumes of the same series constitute the most comprehensive source material on the Allies and Bulgaria during the last stages of the Second World War. The two volumes of *Soviet Foreign Policy during the Patriotic War* are important for the Russian side of the story. Turkish-Bulgarian relations on the eve of the Red Army's crossing of the Danube receive a good account by Nikola Balabanov, Bulgaria's minister to Ankara, in his "A Year in Ankara," serialized in *Bulgarian Review* (Rio de Janeiro), 4–7 (1964–67). Churchill, *The Second World War,* vol. 6; Hull, *Memoirs,* 2: 1454; and D. F. Fleming, *The Cold War and Its Origins,* vol. 1 (Garden City, N.Y., 1961), are all important on the subject. Bozhinov, *Politicheskata kriza v Bulgariia prez 1943–1944,* is the standard Communist diplomatic history covering the last year of the German presence in Bulgaria.

succumbed to Soviet might. Blinded by hatred toward the Bulgarians for their occupation of Thrace, the Greek government-in-exile failed to see the long-range advantage of having Bulgaria neutralized, even if unpunished. It insisted on frontier rectifications, not recognizing the futility of such rearrangements once Bulgaria had become sovietized. The Yugoslav government-in-exile did much the same. The interest of the Turkish government in not having the Red Army entrenched along its European frontier harmonized closely with the interests of the wartime regime in Bulgaria. Yet, to the last, the Turks clung to the belief that the Russians would not cross the Danube. They did little or nothing to influence the Western powers to ensure that the Russians stayed at a distance. For the Turks, this proved to be a blunder in an otherwise brilliantly executed wartime diplomacy. Slight as it was, the prospect that Bulgaria would be set up as another Finland, as a country friendly to the Soviet Union but unoccupied by the Red Army, remained unexplored.

Judgments made in retrospect constitute all too easy a method of apportioning blame. The fact remains that the developments which converged on Bulgaria in the late summer of 1944 considerably limited the possibilities for a more favorable outcome. These developments can be enumerated briefly. First, there was the British government's agreement to recognize that Bulgaria rightfully belonged to the Soviet sphere of military activity. This acknowledgment was the logical conclusion to the decision made much earlier by the Western powers not to invade the Balkans. The result was that the British claim over Greece was to be effected only after the German armies had begun to withdraw from Greek territory. Furthermore, the collapse of Rumania on August 23, 1944, came suddenly and much sooner than expected. Overnight, as it were, the Red Army found itself on the banks of the Danube. The military position of the Germans in the Balkans thus became untenable. Yet, their withdrawal from Greece lingered on. In view of this, it was difficult to see how the Russians could continue their advance westward without securing their left flank. By early September, therefore, the crossing of the armies of the Third Ukrainian Front into

Bulgaria had become a military necessity which complemented and harmonized with Soviet political designs.

The Russians declared war on Bulgaria on September 5. The British and American ambassadors in Moscow expressed mild surprise, but did not protest the act. Thus reassured, the Red Army crossed into Bulgaria on September 8. This sealed the fate of the Muraviev government, which was made up of respectable democratic Bulgarian leaders who had assumed office on September 2. It also cleared the way for the coup d'état which Moscow's protégés carried out during the night of September 8/9. The fact that the Bulgarians had officially declared war on Nazi Germany a few hours before the coup had little effect. With their masterful maneuver, the Russians gained possession of the country as well as the juridical right to formal belligerence. The ill-started Cairo negotiations between Bulgarian representatives and representatives of the Western powers were brought to an abrupt halt. The Soviets' insistence that armistice negotiations be shifted to Moscow was duly honored. The road to tutelage was now wide open.[13]

It is difficult to see at what point in time and in what manner the Bulgarians could have changed the above-described sequence of events. Paradoxically, the ultimate national interest could have been served only by an act of irresponsibility. Had the Bulgarians perceived the future and become formally and actively engaged in military activities against the Germans in the Balkans right after the collapse of Rumania, they could conceivably have foreclosed the necessity, or the excuse, for the Red Army's crossing. Such perceptions were not easily forthcoming, however. Nor was a forceful and imaginative leadership readily at hand. Whether or not the late king could have lifted his country out of the abyss by emulating his colleague in Bucharest remains a moot question. The Zveno group, which had twice before taken power by the force of conspiracy, was largely committed to the Communists and thus was unavailable to carry out a maneuver aimed against Soviet interests. None would have found the Bulgarian army readily responsive, in view of its well-established pro-German officer corps. The fear

---

[13] On the Cairo negotiations, see the account in Moshanov. *Vunshnata politika na demokraticheskata partiia.*

of German military reprisals, which the Germans indeed contemplated, would have constituted a permanent deterrent in any case. The Bulgarian maze was intricate, and the escapes, if any existed, were few.

The *Putsch* of September 9, 1944, which brought the Fatherland Front to power, requires no detailed recounting. It was carried out and cast in Balkan fashion. The Bulgarian Ministry of War was captured with the aid of a few junior officers who unlocked the doors from within and allowed the revolutionaries-to-be to enter unopposed. The minister of war had been forewarned and, indeed, had been recruited. He was duly rewarded by being posted as commander-in-chief of the Bulgarian army. Having sensed the way the winds were blowing, the high command of the police in the capital, as well as critically placed bureaucrats, had come to terms with the Fatherland Front and remained aloof when not actively collaborating. The ministers of the Muraviev cabinet were rounded up without opposition. The services of the few Communist contingents which had been brought to the capital on the eve of the coup were not required. The capital and the provinces complied without resistance. The shot which was to signal the beginning of the most radical transformation in Bulgaria's modern history amounted to no more than a banal changeover, strikingly devoid of any ecstasy or sense of glory.[14]

Once established, the Red Army garrisons constituted the single overriding factor. Sovietization in Bulgaria did not require the active use of Soviet bayonets. The Soviet High Command intervened only occasionally to put right those things they disliked or feared. In the main, however, the sheer presence of the new overlords sufficed to maintain the new authority. Thus, a fixed and given element went into the making of the Communists' rule; the reordering of the Bulgarian setting, however, was the function of resources which sprang from within.

[14] The main events of the September coup are recounted in Oren, *Bulgarian Communism*, pp. 251–58. A good account of the short-lived Muraviev government is to be found in *Istoricheski pregled* (Sofia), no. 5 (1964): 3–33; the story of General Ivan Marinov, the war minister who switched sides at the moment of truth, is told by the General himself in his article published in *ibid.*, no. 3 (1968).

4: THE COMMUNISTS:
PUTSCH AND REVOLUTION

The Communist takeover of Bulgaria lasted about two years and coincided with the presence of the Red Army in the country. In retrospect, it is obvious that, once the Russians established their garrisons in the country, sovietization became inevitable. For the contemporaries, however, the outcome was not so clear-cut. As long as the peace treaty with Bulgaria was not concluded and the Western powers were present to some extent on the Bulgarian scene, nominal as this was, hope existed that Bulgaria could ultimately disengage herself from the Soviet grip.

From the outset, there was a great discrepancy between the formal and the actual state of political affairs. From a strictly legal viewpoint, Bulgaria was an enemy country, devoid of sovereignty, and ruled by the victorious Allies. Ultimate political prerogatives resided with the Allied Control Commission (ACC), which consisted of representatives of the Soviet Union, Great Britain, and the United States. In actual fact, however, the Western Allies had agreed that, while the war lasted, the Soviet representative on the ACC would be given primary responsibility for Bulgarian affairs. Although set in writing, the agreement was vaguely worded and open to varying interpretations. While Marshal Tolbukhin served as the chairman of the ACC, actual responsibility resided with his deputy, General S. S. Biriuzov. Until his recall in 1946, General Biriuzov was, for all practical purposes, the Soviet viceroy in Bulgaria, as well as the commander-in-chief of the Soviet armies in the region.

Together with his political advisers, he oversaw all political affairs and reported directly to Moscow. The Western representatives on the ACC were not kept informed and were convened only occasionally, for the purpose of ratifying decisions that had already been taken.[1]

The administration of the country was left in the hands of the Fatherland Front government. The state bureaucracy remained intact, even though the widespread purge which commenced immediately after the September coup served to replace many undesirable officials with Fatherland Front appointees. The formal governmental structure, however, represented only a small part of the actual distribution of authority. From the national level to the local, an entirely new bureaucracy was erected in the form of Fatherland Front committees. These were informal, but powerful, new organs vaguely patterned after the soviets of the early years of the Bolshevik Revolution. Their function was to supervise political and administrative decisions throughout the state bureaucracy. In effect, no measure of any significance could be taken without the approval of the appropriate Fatherland Front committee. Nominally, the committees were to be made up of representatives of the political parties that participated in the Fatherland Front government. In actual fact, the relative weight of the Communist functionaries and their appointees was overwhelming from the start. The continuous effort of the non-Communist ministers in the government to secure for their followers proportional representation in the committees was of no avail.[2]

[1] Biriuzov, *Sovetskii soldat na Balkankh;* these are Biriuzov's own recollections, which are invaluable in understanding the inner workings of the ACC as well as the particular relations between the Soviet High Command and the Fatherland Front government.

[2] Dragoicheva, *Politicheska, organizatsionna, i stopanska deinost na . . . Otechestvenofrontovskite komiteti . . .* , is the official report of a veteran female Communist functionary, delivered before the first large-scale gathering of the National Council of the Fatherland Front (held in the spring of 1945), of which she served as general secretary. The report is invaluable for the organizational and functional details given on the work and composition of the Fatherland Front committees. For a scholarly monograph on the place and role of the Fatherland Front within the framework of the old state establishment, see Sharlanov and Damianova, *Miastoto i roliata na Otechestveniia front v sistemata na narodnata demokratsiia.* On the legal and formal aspects of the new regime,

After September, 1944, the party map underwent radical transformation. Only those political parties represented in the Fatherland Front were given the right to organize formally. The party spectrum as it had existed in the past was drastically curtailed. From the center to the extreme right the old political formations were obliterated.[3] The governing coalition was set up on the basis of numerical parity among the Communists, the Agrarians, and Zveno, each of which held four portfolios. The Social Democrats received two ministries, while two more were handed over to nominally independent and unaffiliated individuals. The Communists took the Ministry of Interior, the Ministry of Justice, and the Ministry of Public Health. One Communist minister held no specific portfolio. The Agrarians were given one minister without portfolio (Nikola Petkov), as well as the Ministries of Transportation (Angel Derzhanski), Agriculture (Asen Pavlov), and Public Works (Boris Bumbarov). Zveno took the premiership, held by Kimon Georgiev, the Ministry of War, headed by Damian Velchev, the Ministry of Foreign Affairs (Professor Petko Stainov), and the Ministry of Education (Professor Stancho Cholakov). The Social Democrats were given the Ministry of Trade and Industry (Dimitur Neikov) and the newly established Ministry of Social Welfare (Grigor Cheshmedzhiev). Dimo Kazasov headed the Ministry of Propaganda, and Professor Petko Stoianov headed the Ministry of Finance, both as independents. The distribution within the cabinet bore no relation to the true or potential political strength of the participating parties. Nor did the persons within

---

see the following: Union of the Bulgarian Jurists, *Inquiry into the Legality of the Communist Rule in Bulgaria;* Stainov and Angelov, *Administrativno pravo na NRB;* Genovski *et al., Osnovi na durzhavata i pravoto na NRB;* Ianev, *Funktsiite na durzhavata v NRB;* and Charukchiev, *Kharakter i dvizheshti sili na narodnodemokraticheskata revoliutsiia v Bulgariia.*

[3] This was true, as expected, of all the right-wing and fascist-like factions, as well as of the Tsankov movement. Tsankov himself fled the country with the departing German troops, first to Germany and later to South America, where he spent his last days. Despite repeated requests by the Bulgarian government, his repatriation for the purpose of standing trial was never carried out. At first, both wings of the Democrats were banned. In the fall of 1945, however, the Democrats, under the aging Mushanov, were allowed to reorganize and to reissue their old party organ, *Zname.* Burov's *Narodniatsi* disappeared altogether, as did the Liberal Progressive party.

the government necessarily reflect their relative importance within their respective parties.

To the Communists, victory came suddenly and almost unexpectedly. There was an anomaly in their position: communism had been strong in Bulgaria, and the Bulgarian Communist party did not have to be reinvented, as it were. Nevertheless, the fact remained that the Communists were propelled to the top at a time when their morale and their fighting élan were somewhat blunted. The blame was not theirs. Their record throughout the war years has been surveyed and need not be repeated. Objective social and political conditions in Bulgaria prevented the Communists from harmonizing their party program, dictated by Moscow, with the national interest as perceived by the vast majority of Bulgarians. In almost all respects, the Bulgarian Communists in 1944 were substantially weaker than they had been in the early and mid-twenties. This was a striking deviation from the general direction of European communism. At the end of the war, radicalism was on the upsurge all over Europe, as were the parties of the radical left. While in Eastern Europe the contexts varied, in none of the countries was the position of communism similar to that in Bulgaria. The peoples of Yugoslavia, Greece, and Albania fought their civil wars while fighting the German and Italian occupiers. When liberation came, the Communist parties in these three countries were at the pinnacle of their prestige and influence. In the interwar years, the minute Rumanian Communist party was largely made up of the nationals of the many ethnic minorities. After the surrender in August, 1944, the party had to be almost made anew. The Communists in Czechoslovakia were substantially stronger at the end of the war than they had been in the interwar period. The Hungarian Communists were weak, as they always had been, the Bela Kun regime notwithstanding.

While in absolute terms the Bulgarian Communists were weaker than they had been before, their relative position on the domestic scene was favorable. This was so largely because they had been able to maintain a semblance of organized political life during the preceding decades, whereas their potential rivals had been all but decimated organizationally. The surviving Communist émigrés returned from Soviet exile and strengthened the ranks of the party, adding substantially to its political and administrative capabilities. The past schisms between "leftists" and "rightists" were now disregarded, and the large majority of Communists who had drifted away rejoined the party. The standing rules of admission were suspended; those who wished to enroll were admitted en masse, without being subjected to the standard candidacy period. Anxious to show its political muscle, the party took in tens of thousands of new members after little or no scrutiny. From a few thousand members at the time of the coup, Communist party membership increased to a quarter of a million a few months later. Finally, but not least in importance, the fact that the Ministries of Interior and Justice were headed by Communist functionaries gave the Bulgarian Communist party an enormous advantage. A new People's Militia was set up on the ruins of the old police force, and it became the most important political instrument in the conduct of domestic affairs. It was accountable only to the minister of interior, Anton Yugov, who reported directly to the party's Politburo. The reign of terror which ensued was directed against fascists as well as individuals judged to be undesirable.[4]

The Bulgarian Communist party was headed by a large Politburo into which young, new elements were co-opted. The Russians did not allow Dimitrov and Kolarov to return to their home country, for fear that their presence in Bulgaria might have undesirable repercussions abroad. At a time when the

[4] The literature on the state of the Communist party in the years immediately following the September coup is enormous. Ostoich, *BKP i izgrazhdaneto na narodnodemokraticheskata durzhava,* is probably the best monograph on the subject. Gindev, *Kum vuprosa za kharaktera na narodnodemokraticheskata revoliutsiia v Bulgariia,* is an orthodox-dogmatic interpretation of the nature of the Communist takeover. The best documentary source covering all political aspects of the takeover up until May, 1945, is *Ustanoviavane i ukrepvane na narodnodemokraticheskata vlast, Septemvrii 1944–Mai 1945: Sbornik dokumenti.* The problem of party membership and the social composition of party cadres is covered in Ivanov, *Chlenstvoto v partiiata i reguliraneto na neiniia sustav.* The establishment of proletarian dictatorship is interpreted in Popov, *Ustanoviavane, razvitie, i sistema na proletarskata diktatura u nas.* Finally, two monographs which discuss the state of the working class after 1944 are Isusov, *Rabotnicheskata klasa v Bulgariia, 1944–1947,* and Ivanov, *Sotsialisticheskata revoliutsiia i rabotnicheskata klasa v Bulgariia.*

Russians disclaimed any desire to see Bulgaria communized, it was deemed best not to have the former general secretary of the Comintern in Sofia. The return of the two veterans was delayed a full year. Kostov, who had survived the war years in the Pleven jail, became the new general secretary of the Bulgarian party.

Because of their size and appeal the Agrarians were the only political force which could meaningfully challenge the Communists. For a time, the old schisms persisted. Those who participated in the government of the Fatherland Front came from the ranks of the Pladne group, while the Gichev wing of the Agrarians became outcasts. Gichev and his close collaborators were tried and given jail sentences. Led by Petkov and the newly returned Dr. G. M. Dimitrov, who had spent the war years in Cairo, the Pladne Agrarians endeavored to absorb the various Agrarian factions of the past within the ranks of the newly re-established Agrarian Union. Despite constant interference from the outside and personal tensions within, the Agrarians became a formidable force.

The Social Democrats remained few in number, as they always had been. The old guard, led by Pastukhov, criticized their fellow Social Democrats for having joined the Fatherland Front, and stayed aloof. They were few in number and, for the time being, remained in political isolation. What influence the Social Democrats could muster centered on the enlightened middle-class intelligentsia, primarily of the teaching profession. The Social Democrats endeavored to re-establish their small trade union and their various cooperative enterprises, which, in the past, had constituted the base of their movement. In this undertaking they were impeded by the Communists from the start.

The Zveno group reorganized as a full-fledged political party. They disclaimed any connection with the Military League, which had disbanded. Numerically, Zveno was and remained a meager political creation. Its influence rested on the talents of its leaders and on their influence within the professional officer corps. The Bulgarian army was called upon to fight the Germans. The Russians realized that the professional officers, who were indispensable, would follow Velchev as minister of war rather than the Communists. As long as the war lasted, therefore, Zveno was given a period of grace. This did not relieve the uneasy relationship between Velchev and the newly appointed Communist military commissars. Nevertheless, in the absence of a sizable following in the country, Zveno stuck to the Communists.

For the time being, the Democrats were not allowed to re-organize. This was true of the wing led by Mushanov as well as of the Democrats who had split off from the historic party as early as 1923 and had participated in the various governments of the twenties. The tiny Radical party, led by the aging Kosturkov, refused to join the Fatherland Front because of its leader's belief in the ultimate victory of the Germans. For the present, it remained disbanded, though its chance for collaboration with the Communists was yet to come. Professor Tsankov fled the country with the retreating Germans. Some of his past followers were sheltered by Zveno; others were tried in the People's Courts. All of the remaining political parties withered away, never to be revived organizationally.

Developments during the first few months after the coup were crucially affected by two separate, yet related, processes. One was connected with the war against the Germans which Bulgaria was called upon to wage. The second was linked to the massive purges which culminated in the large-scale political trials held in the winter of 1944/45. Taken together, these events produced a political climate of continuous upheaval which helped the Communists produce a semblance of revolutionary un-settledness.

Germany's withdrawal from northern Greece followed a south-north axis across Yugoslavia. Since the Germans were unsure of forthcoming developments in Sofia, they endeavored to secure their right flank by capturing and disarming the command units of the Bulgarian occupation corps in Serbia, as well as elements of the Bulgarian Fifth Army in Yugoslav Macedonia. They were entirely successful in these military operations. In turn, having occupied Bulgaria, the Soviet High Command in the Balkans insisted that the Bulgarian army turn against its former ally by undertaking a campaign deep into Yugoslavia to cut off the German line of retreat. These Soviet instructions could not be immediately executed, however, because of administrative and political difficulties. The Bulgarian armies occupying Yugoslav territory found themselves in a state of disarray, for Tito's government was unwilling to have Bulgarian army units carry out military operations on its territory. Only in early October, following the personal intervention of Marshal Tolbukhin, were the Bulgarians allowed to regroup and undertake a campaign against the Germans on Yugoslav soil.

In the meantime, the Bulgarian army underwent a sporadic cleansing of its officer corps. This would have become a full-fledged purge had the Soviet High Command not intervened to stop it. Moscow was concerned to assure the maintenance of Bulgaria's fighting ability, even if this required the preservation of the old commanding cadres of the Bulgarian army. The compromise which was eventually worked out called for the dispatching of political commissars as deputy commanders at the army and divisional levels. They were organized within the framework of the newly established Institute for Deputy Commanders, which had been set up as part of the army's general staff and would be supervised directly by the Military Department of the Central Committee of the Bulgarian Communist party. A number of recently returned Communist émigrés who had had military experience in the Red Army were posted as deputy commanders in critical units of the Bulgarian army.

Throughout the campaign, friction between the Bulgarians and Yugoslav partisan units was unavoidable. The relative contribution of each to the liberation of Macedonia and part of southern Serbia has continued to be disputed by the military historians of both sides to this day. For the Bulgarians, the campaign constituted the first stage of what the Communists termed the War for the Fatherland. The second stage came after the Germans had been cleared from Yugoslav territory in the last weeks of 1944. At that stage, a number of Bulgarian army divisions, amounting to about 100,000 soldiers, marched alongside the advancing Red Army into Hungary and later into Austria.

The entire military venture remained politically unpopular among the Bulgarians. Despite wide-scale public indoctrination, the average Bulgarian could not comprehend why it was necessary to fight in order to return Macedonia to the Yugoslavs when three and a half years earlier they had gained Macedonia without fighting at all. The only meaningful rationalization which the new regime in Sofia could devise was the claim that by fighting the Germans Bulgaria would attain a status of belligerence which could eventually help the country secure better terms when the peace treaty was worked out. On the whole, the Bulgarian army fought well, largely because of the Prussian-like discipline with which it was infused. The support given the war effort by the non-Communist partners of the Fatherland Front regime was less than enthusiastic, especially during the second stage of the campaign. In all, about 500,000 Bulgarian soldiers participated in the war, of whom some 30,000 were killed. The material expense was substantial, particularly since it came on top of the great financial burden imposed on the Bulgarian taxpayers, who were obligated to pay the entire cost of maintaining the enormous Soviet occupation army. Coupled with two consecutive crop failures, agricultural Bulgaria emerged greatly impoverished. Despite these sacrifices, however, the Western powers refused to recognize Bulgaria as a belligerent country, thus denying the Fatherland Front regime its only conceivable dividend of political significance. In the annals of the Second World War the contribution of the Bulgarians has been all but disregarded, the detailed accounts emanating from Sofia notwithstanding. The requirements of the war permitted many professional officers to maintain ranks and military positions which they otherwise would certainly have lost. Only in the spring of 1946 was the army purged in earnest.[5]

While the psychological and material burdens produced by the war effort were great, the domestic upheaval caused by the

[5] The historiography produced by the Bulgarians on the subject of the war and, indirectly, on the purge and sovietization of the Bulgarian army is substantial. The following are the most important sources: *Otechestvenata voina na Bulgariia, 1944–1945*, constitutes the most detailed historical account of the war effort as well as of the restructuring of the army; Kirchev, *Otechestvenata voina, 1944–1945*, and Atanasov et al., *Kratka istoriia na Otechestvenata voina*, also are important monographs; Damianov, *Izbrani proizvedeniia, 1892–1958*, and Velchev, *Statii, rechi i zapovedi . . .* , are significant compilations of the speeches and public utterances of the two top-ranking men of the military hierarchy after 1944. Damianov headed the Military Department of the Communist Central Committee before becoming minister of defense.

purges at home and, more so, by the mass trials held by the so-called People's Courts was enormous. Several thousand people were executed or arbitrarily murdered by Communist partisans who began returning to their villages and towns in the early days of September. Inevitably, political motives mingled with personal vendetta. Even though the large majority of the victims probably deserved punishment, the arbitrary settling of accounts produced an atmosphere of terror and insecurity which affected the countryside more so than it did the towns. This was a time of revenge for the Bulgarian Communists, who for more than twenty years had suffered insult and terror of their own. It is possible that much of the upheaval was unavoidable, even had the new regime wanted to avoid it.[6]

While these were anarchic outbursts, the purge by trial was formally and efficiently organized from the start. The various decrees for the punishment of Bulgaria's war criminals were drafted by the Communist-controlled Ministry of Justice in the first weeks after the coup. In the late fall of 1944, numerous People's Courts were set up on the national and provincial levels. They were cast in the form of revolutionary tribunals staffed mainly by Communist functionaries and sympathizers. Ranging from the wartime regency council and members of the wartime cabinets, as well as deputies who had voted in favor of Bulgaria's declaration of war against Great Britain and the United States, down to local village mayors, tax collectors, and rural policemen, thousands of people were expeditiously tried, convicted, and sentenced.

Proportionally, the war trials claimed more lives in Bulgaria than in any other German wartime satellite. The desire to prove to the world Bulgaria's determination to cleanse herself of pro-German and cryptofascist elements was undoubtedly the regime's primary motive in holding the trials. Here again, the belief that Bulgaria's peace terms would be mitigated in proportion to the magnitude of the purge by trial played a domi-

---

[6] The number of people who perished at the hands of the Communist partisans after 1944 remains unknown. The man directly responsible was Minister of the Interior Yugov, who was in charge of the newly constituted People's Militia. The Communists eventually acknowledged the atrocities carried out during Yugov's tenure in statements made at the 1962 Party Congress, by which time Yugov had been purged.

nant role in influencing the actions of the new rulers. Such political considerations were successful in blunting, to some extent, the hatred and outrage of Bulgaria's main wartime victims in Greece and Yugoslavia. The effect which the trials had on the Western countries was more dubious. The fact that the ministers of the last two wartime cabinets—the governments of Bagrianov and Muraviev—also were tried and that Bagrianov himself was executed gave rise to some revulsion, particularly among those who knew of the two premiers' painful endeavors to disengage from Germany. With the exception of General Marinov, the minister of war of the Muraviev government who went over to the Fatherland Front on the eve of the coup, the members of the Muraviev government, who had declared war on Germany on September 8, were tried and sentenced. Among others, Gichev and Mushanov received jail sentences. This alone caused widespread resentment which could not be openly aired, for fear of what the People's Militia might do.

In the early days of 1945 there was little doubt that the Communists and their partners were using the mass trials to dispose of their enemies, real and potential. The immediate result was that opposition in the country stiffened. People at large, and the peasants in particular, began looking for a leader who would stand up to the Communists and utter their hearts' desires in public. In the long run, the impact of the trials was significant. A sizable segment of Bulgaria's tiny intelligentsia was exterminated. That most were people with rightist leanings and profascist sympathies did not alter the fact that many also were people of talent. On balance, the rapidity with which they were disposed of constituted a loss which a small peasant people could ill afford.

The above-described developments represented only one side of the Bulgarian coin. Throughout the period, the domestic scene remained closely linked to the international setting. In more ways than one, inter-Allied relations, as well as Bulgaria's relations with her neighbors, took precedence over the newly evolving patterns at home.[7] In October, 1944, the armistice with

[7] For a short time following the entry of the Red Army into Bulgaria, the Fatherland Front regime was still hopeful of being able to retain those territories which had been awarded to Bulgaria from Greece in April, 1941. For their part,

Bulgaria was signed in Moscow. The specific terms were not particularly harsh, nor were they of fundamental importance, since they formalized already existing conditions. The main significance of the armistice lay in the fact that the Russians presented themselves as Bulgaria's chief advocate. While the Bulgarian delegates remained docile throughout the negotiations, Molotov fought hard to extract all possible concessions on behalf of Russia's new protégés. The lesson was not lost on the British representatives, who, for their part, pressed the Greek demands for war indemnities and restitutions. It was at this time that Churchill worked out the informal "percentage agreement" with Stalin. Political influence over Bulgaria was to be divided between Soviet Russia and Great Britain on the basis of 75 and 25 percent, respectively. In December, the revolutionary eruptions in Athens and the forceful military intervention of the British were immediately reflected on the Bulgarian scene.

Although Russia was in physical possession of the country, the fact that Bulgaria was an enemy country under the nominal control of all three Allied governments, and that her formal status was yet to be worked out, made the Russians somewhat uneasy. Their immediate concern harmonized well with Tito's long-range plans. If Bulgaria were federated within Yugoslavia before the war ended, her final status would be transformed overnight, and she would be extricated from any possible designs that the Western powers might have. For a brief moment toward the end of 1944, the Russians appeared to have accepted

---

the Russians supported this ambition and in fact made a number of informal approaches to the Western Allies, sounding out their views on the question. The Greek government was outraged and so were the British. Before signing the armistice with Bulgaria, the British insisted that the Bulgarian army be withdrawn to the prewar frontier. After some hesitation, this was done. Bulgaria's relations with Greece remained strained for many years to come. Unlike the dispute with the Yugoslavs, the Communists and the anti-Communists in Bulgaria were firmly united on this issue, on the basis of an uncompromising anti-Greek position. On Bulgarian-Greek relations during the war and immediately following 1944, see the following sources: *Bulgarian Atrocities in Greek Macedonia and Thrace, 1941–1944;* Christopoulos, *Bulgaria's Record;* Gialistras, *Hellenism and Its Balkan Neighbours;* Xydis, *Greece and the Great Powers, 1944–1947;* and Woodhouse, *Apple of Discord: A Survey of Recent Greek Politics in Their International Setting.* The Bulgarian position is treated in Shterev, *Obshti borbi na bulgarskiia i grutskiia narod sreshtu khitlerofashistakata okupatsiia.*

this formula and, in fact, to have worked out a rapidly constructed federative scheme. The entire venture, which apparently was never thought through, failed in the face of protestations made by the government of Great Britain. Although the British were not averse to an eventual Balkan federation, Bulgaria was not to be allowed to escape punishment by taking shelter within a new political edifice.

The failure of this maneuver, which neither the Russians nor the Bulgarians regretted in the long run, did not discourage the Russians from seeking other ways and means of securing their play. Also in December, they began pressing for an immediate general election, which would confirm and formalize the Fatherland Front regime and thereby preserve and perpetuate the advantage the Communists enjoyed. In early January, General Biriuzov served Petkov with an ultimatum demanding the immediate removal of Dr. G. M. Dimitrov as general secretary of the Agrarian Union. Dimitrov had not joined the government; since his return from Cairo, he had concentrated his efforts on remolding the Agrarian Union into a viable political party, in order to render it the sole countervailing force against the Communists. His energy, his British connections, and, above all, his independent spirit made him suspect in Russian eyes. Petkov, on the other hand, was perceived by the Communists as the man best suited to lead the Agrarians into cooperation and eventual collaboration with them. At this early stage, the Agrarians decided to comply with the Soviet ultimatum. Dimitrov was indeed removed, and the Agrarian leadership was reorganized under Nikola Petkov.

The reshuffling of the Agrarian leadership proved to be a significant act, for it signaled the beginning of the end of the Fatherland Front coalition as it had existed since September, 1944. Led by Kostov, the Communists were confident that they could push through their electoral plans. From the outset, the Communists cultivated doubtful elements within the parties that were their nominal partners and, in the spring of 1945, attempted to install them at the top of their respective organizations. These maneuvers were not lost on the people at large. Gradually, a revulsion set in which gave rise to a formally organized anti-Communist opposition. Communist endeavors to maintain Petkov as the figurehead of a reorganized Agrarian leadership failed. While the victorious Allies were gathering at Potsdam, Petkov and his friends from the Social Democrats prepared a memorandum calling on the Allied governments to use their prerogatives to prevent the forthcoming elections which the Communists were certain to stampede. The petitioners resigned from the government and set themselves up as the leaders of the new united opposition. In the face of Western protestations, the Russians yielded and the elections were indeed postponed. The opposition was allowed to organize openly, and the Communists were forced to retrench.[8]

There were now two distinct, yet identically named, Agrarian and Social Democratic parties. Although the numerical distribution of power could not be precisely ascertained, because of constant Communist interference, the majority of the peasants gave their trust and support to Petkov, as did a large segment of the urban middle class. The minority followed the collaborationists, who, under Communist license, continued to operate within the Fatherland Front. Throughout the upheaval and the organizational reshuffling, Zveno and its ministers in the government remained true to the Communists. This served to give the government of the Fatherland Front, from which the democratic leaders had exited, a degree of badly needed legitimacy. To maintain the fiction of political pluralism, Kosturkov, the leader of the small Radical party, entered the Fatherland Front, as did a segment of his followers. It was a cynical move on both sides because Kosturkov, believing in the ultimate victory of the Germans, had refused to join the Fatherland Front before September, 1944. At the same time, the Democrats, led by Mushanov, established themselves as a separate opposition party.

[8] The full text of the memorandum is reproduced in U.S., Department of State, *Foreign Relations of the United States, Diplomatic Papers: The Conference in Berlin, 1945*, vol. 2 (Washington, D.C., 1960), pp. 724–25. The same volume contains important information on all aspects of the domestic upheavals as reported by Barnes, the U.S. ambassador to Sofia. The complete story, however, must be pieced together from the contemporary Bulgarian press, Communist as well as oppositionist. There are two brief but good accounts in English dealing with the anti-Communist opposition and with political conditions in general: Barker, *Truce in the Balkans*, and Betts, ed., *Central and South East Europe, 1945–1948*.

The new situation represented a turnabout in the traditional political positions of the past. For the first time in their history, the Communists found themselves a ruling party faced with an audacious and vocal opposition. Radically different from the past was the fact that this time the country was occupied by a foreign power determined to maintain its grip. Dimitrov and Kolarov were brought back from Moscow to reinforce the cadres at home and to boost their morale. The opposition in Bulgaria was a genuine force which did not require Western backing. Had the terms of the game been equal, the opposition would have prevailed over the Communists by the force of the ballot. But this could have been realized only if the Western powers had contained and in some way balanced off the Russian presence.

Bulgaria remained a very small component in the complex of interpower relationships which was about to degenerate into the cold war. Even though the United States was not a party to the Anglo-Soviet "percentage agreement," it could not alter the de facto military zones, which had been fixed at the end of the war. The American minister in Sofia, who represented his government on the Allied Control Commission, pleaded that his government stand fast and not allow the loss of the little that had been gained through the postponement of the scheduled elections. He was a man of character who knew the conditions in Bulgaria intimately. His perceptive dispatches were infused with an almost prophetic view of things to come. They were of no avail, however. A commission of inquiry, dispatched by President Truman to the Balkans, reported back the facts as they stood.[9] They did not change the underlying tendencies within the American government, which was striving to produce a modus vivendi with the Soviet Union. A few months after their postponement, the elections were held. The opposition leaders decided to boycott. Thus, the outcome was preset, and the Communists proceeded to convene a Parliament packed with their followers and their stooges. The opposition refused to carry out the joint recommendation of Secretary Byrnes and

[9] The report of the commission of inquiry is contained in Dennett and Johnson, eds., *Negotiating with the Russians*.

Molotov directing that two opposition leaders be included in the Fatherland Front government.[10] For their part, the Communists proceeded to complete the purge within the professional army through the early retirement of a few hundred officers. The purge brought about the complete emasculation of Zveno.[11]

Still, there was one more card to be played in the Bulgarian political game. As long as the peace treaty with Bulgaria had not been signed, the Russians and the Communists were obliged to tolerate the domestic opposition. A new election was scheduled. This time the opposition decided to take part in the voting. Despite police outrages, the elections of 1946 proved to Bulgarians at home and to those in the world who were still willing to listen that these peasant people continued to hope for political freedom against all odds. The opposition elected 101 deputies to the new Parliament. Even though they remained a minority, they set a record which was unrivaled within the Soviet domain. For a few months the voice of the opposition in Parliament was heard loudly and clearly. Although Soviet Russia could not be directly attacked, communism was. The fact that Bulgaria's future borders were being fixed at the Paris Peace Conference did not inhibit the Bulgarian opposition from attacking their oppressors at home. This left them open to charges of treason. It was to the credit of the Bulgarian opposition that, despite the cruel dilemma which faced it throughout, it continued to assault political tyranny. The moment the peace treaty was signed, the fate of the opposition was sealed. The record of Petkov's subsequent arrest and eventual trial is all too well known. His execution was followed by the removal and imprisonment of his collaborators and followers. In the years that followed, the jails and labor

---

[10] See Byrnes, *Speaking Frankly,* on Soviet-American negotiations on the matter.

[11] The man in charge of the army purge was none other than Kostov himself. The opening shot of the anti-army purge was fired in the spring of 1946 and was signaled by the arrest and trial of Pastukhov, the leader of the Social Democrats who had criticized Communist policies in the party organ. Pastukhov's remarkable speech, made at the end of his trial, is reproduced in *Svoboden narod,* June 23, 1946. Pastukhov was given a five-year sentence. He never emerged from jail, however, for he died (perhaps was murdered) in prison around 1949.

camps were the only forums where views other than those of the Communists could have a hearing.[12]

Those who collaborated with the Communists can be explained more easily than those who opposed them. Roughly speaking, the collaborationists divided into two groups: the great majority of them were opportunists; a small number were motivated by considerations that lay above their own personal interests. In a country as poor as Bulgaria, where very few private fortunes are to be found, even among the tiny middle class, the dependence on the state for pensions and other privileges has always been overwhelming. In this sense, collaboration provided a livelihood. In addition, there were frustrated politicians of the past who perceived and exploited the new opportunities in order to forge political careers. The collaborationists of higher motive were those few who considered Bulgaria's long-range national interest and saw that the preservation of her territorial integrity lay in the hands of Soviet Russia. They believed that the local Communists could be tamed and that Russia would not press for the communization of the country, in view of its overwhelmingly egalitarian peasant structure.

In large measure, the expectations of the opportunists were justified. Realizing their comparative weakness, and cognizant of the relative scarcity of trained and trustworthy cadres, the Communists agreed to shelter those individuals who had forfeited their class interests and their ideological convictions. Having been co-opted into the ruling regime, the collaborationists lent their names and former political records to the new government, which was eager to acquire legitimacy at home and abroad. Their presence within the government helped blunt the resentment of the great mass of oppositionists. For the convinced and resolute anti-Communists, the maneuver was too transparent to constitute a meaningful development. The Com-

---

[12] On the peace treaty with Bulgaria and the respective positions at the Paris Peace Conference, see entries in U.S., Department of State, *Foreign Relations of the United States, 1946,* vol. 4 (Washington, D.C., 1970). For Communist views of Bulgaria's international position, see Bozhinov, *Zashtitata na natsionalnata nezavisimost na Bulgariia, 1944–1947,* and Vasev and Khristov, *Bulgariia na mirnata konferentsiia, Parizh, 1946.* On Petkov's trial, see the following: Padev, *Dimitrov Wastes No Bullets; The Trial of Nikola D. Petkov, August 5–15, 1947: Record of the Judicial Proceedings,* and Vergnet and Bernard-Derosne, *L'affaire Petkov.*

munists, however, were after the masses, who were less political and therefore more easily manipulated.

In more objective terms, political collaboration with the Communists represented an infusion of political experience and technocratic skills into the new governing elite. This was a significant addition in a country with a meager intelligentsia. At the same time, with very few exceptions, the collaborationists did not attain top-ranking careers. Kimon Georgiev, the shrewd and capable Zveno leader, survived very close to the top of the political pyramid until the end of his life. He remained a member of the government in various cabinets and an outstanding member of the Fatherland Front National Committee. The fate of the Agrarian collaborationists was somewhat less fortunate. Obbov, the man who led the splinter Agrarians into the Communist camp, was pushed into political oblivion after his unenviable job had been carried out. Communist favors went to second-generation collaborationists, of whom Traikov was the most outstanding example. He became, in effect, an administrator of the agrarian section of the Communist party and retained a position of political prominence throughout. Having disbanded or incorporated all other political parties, the Communists retained a bogus Agrarian Union within the Fatherland Front regime, which continued to be headed by Traikov. Traikov's Macedonian origin may or may not have influenced the success of his dubious political career.[13]

After crushing the true Social Democratic party, the Communists proceeded to absorb the collaborationist wing. In the case of the Socialists, the Communists could afford a smaller degree of generosity. None of the Socialist collaborationists achieved a lasting career of any importance. The more compliant among them were given marginal positions in the trade-union movement or were awarded meaningless ambassadorial posts abroad. Dimo Kazasov, the shrewd minister of propaganda

13 For a Communist view of Communist-Agrarian collaboration, see Karadzhov, *Suiuzut na rabotnicheskata klasa i selianite.* On the bogus Agrarian Union, see Traikov, *Za narodna vlast.* On Zveno on the eve of its liquidation as an autonomous party group, see *Natsionalna konferentsiia na Narodniia suiuz Zveno.* Ultimately, all the collaborationist groups were amalgamated within the Fatherland Front, which was reorganized in 1948; on this, see *Vtoriiat kongres na Otechestveniiat front.*

in the first Fatherland Front government whose earlier political career had vacillated all the way from socialism to Zveno, stayed afloat during the early stages of sovietization and was retained as a court publicist in later years. Old Kosturkov, the leader of the Radicals, did not live long enough to benefit from the betrayal of his political principles. The Communists paid their debt to him by appointing his son mayor of Sofia. The great majority of Democrats were unwilling or unable to collaborate.

On a lower level, political collaboration with the Communists established a bridge over which a substantial number of professionals, technocrats, and managers walked safely into the era of communism. On balance, this was probably the greatest contribution made by the compromisers. The significance of this substantial infusion of technical skills into the Bulgarian social structure was considerable.[14]

In one crucial sense political collaboration with the Communists failed completely. Those who in 1944 and later hoped to tame the Communist party by exerting their influence from within soon saw the futility of their endeavor. Their guiding conviction was that not even Stalin would dare bolshevize Bulgaria's agrarian society without due regard for the egalitarian structure of the peasantry. Although they expected that Bulgaria would be forced to march a long stretch along the road of sovietization, they believed that their country would be spared full-fledged communism in the face of objective domestic and international conditions. It did not take long for their expectations to be shattered and washed away in the political climate of the cold war and in view of Soviet political maximalism. In one sense only could the collaborationists claim some credit for themselves. Under Soviet patronage Bulgaria's territorial integrity was indeed preserved. By joining hands with the Communists and responding to all Soviet designs, they facilitated—or so they believed—the preservation of the nation's

14 On the evolution of the new intelligentsia in Bulgaria, see Avramov, *Bulgarskata komunisticheska partiia i formirane na sotsialisticheskata inteligentsiia;* on the consolidation of the youth movements of the various political groups within the united Communist youth movement, see Dimitrov, *Izgrazhdane na edinen mladezhki suiuz v Bulgariia, 1944–1947.* Another monograph by the same author gives a good sketch of the entire period of sovietization: *Godini na prelom.*

boundaries in the face of Western antipathies and the revision-ism of their neighbors. This was scant consolation, if any, for the few collaborationists who had preserved their consciences.

The record of the Bulgarian anti-Communist opposition stands out in the annals of resistance to sovietization. The audacity, persistence, and élan of the opposition in Bulgaria are a source of amazement to the student of Balkan history. Objec-tive political conditions clearly did not favor the undertaking which fell to Petkov and his friends. On the face of it, the international constellation, the specific regional setting, con-crete military conditions, the historic Russophilism of the peo-ple at large, and the conventional national interest of the country all called for total compliance with the facts of life.

Unlike the Rumanians, the Hungarians, and the Serbs, the democratic elements in Bulgaria had few, if any, connections with the West. Bulgaria was not the object of good will; rather, she was perceived by most Western statesmen as an unruly and treacherous country with an unvarying record of doing the wrong thing at the wrong time. Her staunch nationalism, which had always bred irredentism, had forced even the most pro-nounced Bulgarian democratic leaders into a mold of uncompro-mising political introversion. The Bulgarians had no political lobbies in the Western countries. The only sizable contingent of Bulgarian nationals was to be found in the United States, and even there the great majority were of Macedonian origin and reflected all the ambivalence that this affiliation implied. Greece, the one safe bridgehead of the West in the Balkans, could be counted on to wish the worst for Bulgaria. This was true of both the Greek government and the overwhelming majority of Greeks; not even the Greek radical left could be safely relied upon to take a more generous view of Bulgaria's immediate destiny. In order to legitimize themselves in the eyes of their would-be followers, the Greek Communists, already tainted by their pro-Soviet orientations, could in no way show any amiability toward their northern neighbor, who had ac-tively participated in the truncation of their country.

In occupied Serbia, the Bulgarians did little to endear them-selves to the local populace. Furthermore, Tito's concept of Yugoslav federalism required that all of Macedonia be incorporated into the new political edifice erected on the ruins of the old Yugoslav kingdom. In September, 1944, Turkey found Red Army divisions securely deployed along the old Turkish-Bulgarian frontier. True, the Turks had done little or nothing to try to prevent the Red Army from crossing the Danube southward. By the late summer of 1944, Turkey was in a state of panic which persisted for a number of years. Bulgaria was viewed as no more than a Russian stooge ready and willing to help foster Russian designs in the Balkans. Even without her own ordeals, Rumania could not be depended on to provide Bulgaria with even a semblance of comfort.

While the above-enumerated configurations were of a peripheral nature, the physical presence of the Red Army within the country touched on the very core of Bulgaria's postwar situation. Wartime inter-Allied agreements stipulated that an Allied Control Commission be established to serve as guardian of Bulgarian affairs. Although the United States and Britain were represented on the ACC alongside the Soviet Union, it was the latter which by common agreement was empowered to carry the burden of day-to-day administrative and political responsibilities. The Anglo-American representation on the ACC was, from the first, small in size and strictly limited to the capital and its immediate vicinity. The real garrisoning of the country was in the hands of the Red Army, headed by General Biriuzov, who served as the authorized deputy of Marshal Tolbukhin. The presence of the Red Army was a formidable factor which could not be discounted by even the most optimistic among the democratic elements. For all practical purposes, it precluded any verbal criticism, overt or oblique, against the Soviet Union. Relations between the opposition leaders and the Western representatives on the ACC, and specifically the American representative Barnes, were intimate but sporadic at best. The latter could offer little comfort to the opposition spokesmen, who hoped for a turnabout in Western attitudes toward Bulgaria. General Biriuzov could and did intervene personally on behalf of his local Communist protégés. These interventions overshadowed whatever slight prospect Petkov and his followers had of gaining consideration for their views. Their material means were meager and their powers of patronage nonexistent. The Russians were feared but not hated by their followers. The Russophilism which had persisted for generations was beginning to wear out, but the thrust of its appeal had not disappeared.

These were disabling circumstances which, under normal conditions and in the absence of courageous leadership, should have stifled opposition from the start. Yet, the oppositionist sentiment in Bulgaria had been on the rise since the winter of 1944/45. It continued to increase until the summer of 1947, when it reached a pinnacle before being strangled by sheer physical force. Programmatically, the Agrarians and the Social Democrats, the two main columns of opposition strength, were not natural allies. The former were populists; the latter were doctrinaire determinists. Despite this divergence, coupled as it was with the differences in style of the respective leaders, the united opposition held firm. It established itself to the left of center, carefully dissociating itself from the rightist parties of the past, including the Democrats under Mushanov. The brutality with which the Communists pursued their consolidation of power helped bridge the old schisms, which were particularly endemic within the Agrarian Union. In the summer of 1945, following the postponement of the elections, Petkov undertook to restore unity between the followers of Pladne and those of Gichev, thus bringing to an end the bitter quarrel which had lasted since the early thirties. The discrepancies in ideology and temperament between Pastukhov and Lulchev, the two leaders of the Social Democrats, were also glossed over and repaired. The age-long rivalry between the urban parties and the Agrarians, which had helped ostracize Stamboliiski's followers for a full generation, was all but forgotten.

Actively or tacitly, Petkov received the unreserved support of the urban middle class, as well as that of the huge number of peasants for whom he had become an idol. The Bulgarian peasants were not reactionary, in the main. Ambitious and progressive-minded, they were apt to sacrifice much of their meager livelihood to provide their sons with an education they hoped would give the younger generation a better future. The overwhelming majority of Bulgarian peasants, although poor, were land proprietors. They were sufficiently astute to realize that their hunger for land could not be satisfied by robbing the nonexistent landed aristocracy. The Bulgarian peasants understood that appeals for land reform could travel but a short distance, for there was little to redistribute. Being a proprietary class, they were not easily led on by the promises of demagogues. While many of their sons had become Communists in past years, the great majority of old and young had given their allegiance to the sociopolitical solutions formulated by the Agrarian Union. Those who had remained on the land knew enough of the Russian kolkhoz to be gripped by a never-ending fear. The nightmares of Russian collectivization had not escaped the attention of the smallholders. They sensed the approaching peril, even though their leaders could not always reach them, for lack of means, all of which were in Communist hands.

Inexplicably, yet in a remarkable way, Petkov was propelled to the fore of an oppositionist wave which swept the country irresistibly. A strong communion evolved between the isolated peasants, harassed and intimidated by the newly arrived Communist village functionaries, and Petkov, who was himself besieged by the Communist apparatus and its mercenaries. In Parliament after 1946 and in the pages of the Agrarian daily organ, Petkov verbalized the fears and expectations of his following in a fashion that was well attuned to the political culture of the Bulgarian village. He possessed unreserved personal courage, which bordered on fatalism, as well as uncompromising fanaticism. The political murders that had claimed the lives of his father and brother provided him with an almost absolute immunity from fear. The style of his oppositionist utterings had little to do with the judicious political struggle. This infuriated his Communist rivals and exacerbated the political conflict between the rulers and their detractors. Petkov's convictions were so sharply formulated precisely because he had come from the political left and had proved himself a true believer in a lasting alliance with Russia. For most of his short-lived political career, he behaved as if he had been personally insulted by the treachery of his former Communist friends. The opposition in Bulgaria rode the high crest of political emotions. Until the very end the Communists were fully prepared to pay a high price to at least blunt the edge of Petkov's assaults, if not to recruit him to their cause.

The above are but sketchy outlines of the character of the Bulgarian opposition. The oppositionists saw themselves more as political missionaries than as political negotiators. At the very best, Petkov could have hoped that the process of sovietization in Bulgaria would not be culminated before the departure of the Red Army, following the conclusion of a peace treaty. He hoped that the Western Allies would prevent the complete foreclosure of Bulgaria's options under the specter of the Soviet presence. These expectations proved futile largely because the lines of delineation which had become set by the end of the war proved unalterable. The conduct of the cold war had become incompatible with political accommodations of any kind. Thus, the principal objective was not, and could not be, attained. Petkov, Pastukhov, Mushanov, Lulchev, and many others paid with their lives. Gichev spent thirteen years in prison, much of it in solitary confinement, before being freed on the eve of his death. The rank and file from the opposition camp paid dearly in the numerous ' concentration camps which dotted the country.

In one respect only did the Bulgarian opposition gain a significant objective. An entire generation of Bulgarian youth which had known little or nothing of democracy and which was to survive under totalitarianism was taught an object lesson in political pluralism during the brief period of the opposition's survival.

5: STALIN AND THE EDGE OF TERROR

The final liquidation of organized opposition marked the beginning of a new stage in the sovietization of Bulgaria. Opposition to the Communists persisted, but it became scattered and diffuse. Having conquered the summits of political power, the Communists undertook to subdue the villages, where bitterness against the new regime mingled with resentment. The process of strait-jacketing the Bulgarian countryside took many years and required the use of police terror and an administrative reshuffling of the old social order. Political institutions were recast to fit new needs. Sanctions were sharply raised against those who failed to comply readily with the ever-increasing number of decrees which emanated from party headquarters. Labor camps became a normal adjunct of Communist rule. The edge of terror was directed against the regime's real and potential enemies. The distinction between real and potential was as great as it was profound. The former required a direct assault, while the latter necessitated pre-emptive actions on a large scale.

The terror befell the Communist party itself. This was expected, if not inevitable. Hardly was the struggle against the opposition over when the Communists began to turn inward. Their monopoly of power meant that all vital political processes developed within one organ. Moreover, they soon realized that, while they reigned supreme in the land, true sovereignty was not in their hands. The cleavages within the Communist party would have taken place in any case, but they were accentuated by the massive intervention of Soviet will implemented by Stalin's secret agents, who had come to Bulgaria in the footsteps of the Red Army. Stalin became to the Communists what they had become to their domestic rivals. The purge of the purgers commenced after 1947, and the upheaval spiraled upward. Stalin's agents were not satisfied with persecuting suspects; Stalin had always had his own rationale for hunting down potential enemies as well. As a result, within a short span of time the Bulgarian Communist party was all but decapitated.

Terror from within and from without converged in the late forties with yet another development which shook the country to its foundations. Ever since the conquest of the country by the Red Army, the Bulgarian Communists had been haunted by fear of the Yugoslavs and their new chieftain, whose ambitions threatened the very essence of national communism in Bulgaria. Tito's designs on the Bulgarian part of Macedonia had become manifest even before the takeover. When communism had safely installed itself on both sides of the boundary, Tito began to press his claims uninhibitedly. The Bulgarian Communists could not effectively resist the Yugoslav assault overtly. Until the peace treaty with Bulgaria was ratified, they conveniently took cover behind Western opposition to any territorial reshuffling in the Balkans. For more than three years the ordeal of the Sofia Communists was compounded by the fact that they could not publicly express their resentment of the Yugoslavs, which was very real from the start. The problem was further aggravated by the fact that many of the leading Bulgarian Communists were of Macedonian origin; the challenge to Bulgarian Macedonia constituted a painful threat to their own identities. Were they to be the ones to negotiate away the land of their birth and origin? As long as circumstances compelled them to make concessions to Belgrade, they could not easily disengage themselves from the cruel dilemma. Then, suddenly, the problem was resolved, almost overnight. The general consternation caused by Tito's break with the Cominform was matched in Sofia by a profound sense of relief. After 1948 the Bulgarian Communists were happy to freeze Bulgaria's western borders and to insulate themselves as best they could from Tito's reach. In this sense, Stalinism had its blessings.

Having salvaged their part of Macedonia, the Bulgarian Communists proceeded to remake Bulgaria into a homogeneous nation-state; there was to be no more risk-taking. Those Macedonians within Bulgaria whose allegiances were suspect were resettled away from the disputed frontiers, deep in the hinterland. The 50,000 Bulgarian Jews were allowed to leave the country in a mass exodus. A large segment of the Turkish people, who had lived in Bulgaria for centuries, was ruthlessly expelled across the frontier and into Turkey. Together, these crucial developments remade the country.

The two upheavals, the change in party leadership and the eruption of the quarrel with the Tito Communists, occurred almost concurrently. Within the relatively brief period of two years, the three highest-ranking party leaders departed, never to return. The hand of fate and of the executioner intervened to remove Kostov, Dimitrov, and Kolarov from the political scene. Their disappearance touched only the apex of the pyramid, however. Almost overnight, the party high command was turned over to the second echelon of Communist party functionaries. Yet, the entire party hierarchy was shaken, the tremors of the massive purge being felt all through the invisible body of the hidden iceberg. Not since the Great Purge of the Bulgarian Communist emigration in the Soviet Union had the Bulgarian Communist party undergone as profound a shakeup as it did in the late forties and early fifties. As in the past, the anti-Kostovite purges helped sever yet another link with the party's heritage. Gradually, but unmistakably, the revolutionism of the past was buried, being replaced by the inevitable process of bureaucratization.

To be sure, the Bulgarian drama of the late forties was fully shared by most, if not all, other newly communized East European countries. While the underlying motives for the purges were much the same, as was the impact of the devastating blows, in one fundamental sense the situation in Bulgaria differed from that in the other bloc countries. Because of their particular history, and primarily because of the Communist uprising of 1923, the Bulgarian Communist functionaries as a group could not easily be divided into the two well-known categories of Moscovites and homebred cadres.

The old guard, which had triumphed over the so-called left sectarians and survived Stalin's Great Purge, returned to Bulgaria after the 1944 coup, following a continuous absence of almost twenty years. Some of them had visited Bulgaria clandestinely during those two decades and were, therefore, fairly familiar with the conditions that prevailed in the country. Dimitrov and Kolarov exemplified the former, while Damianov, who in 1944 became the head of the Military Department of the Communist Central Committee, typified the latter. Taken together, the veterans of the old guard constituted a sizable contingent within the Politburo that was formally elected early in 1945. Kostov represented yet another category within the party high command. Although he had spent most of the interwar period inside Bulgaria, in and out of jail, he had served in Moscow as a functionary of the Cadres Department of the Comintern during three separate periods in the decade preceding the outbreak of the Second World War.

Even the youngest members of the postwar Politburo, who had come to political maturity after 1923 and had gradually developed into full-time functionaries of the party apparatus at home, had received their professional Communist training in the various Comintern schools within the Soviet Union in the thirties. Thus, there was hardly anyone within the first postwar Politburo, or within any other important adjunct of the high command, who had not been exposed to the realities of Soviet political life.

This meshing of the professional careers of the party's leaders made the Bulgarian Communists more homogeneous than their East European counterparts. A distinction could be drawn between those who had been in Bulgaria during the Second World War and their comrades in Soviet exile. Still, such differences were mitigated by the relatively unheroic performance of the Communist underground in Bulgaria. Only after the passage of time had successfully blurred wartime realities and had permitted the evolution of a wartime heroic mythos of sorts could the very young, headed by Zhivkov, claim for themselves the uppermost positions of power.

On the day following the 1944 coup the supreme leadership of the party in Bulgaria passed into Kostov's hands. From the

Pleven jail, where he had been incarcerated since 1942, he moved directly into party headquarters as the general secretary of the Central Committee. Dimitrov, still in Moscow, was elected president of the Central Committee. In terms of seniority and his commanding personality, Kostov was the inevitable choice for the top position. He epitomized the intellectual professional revolutionary within the party. Within the Politburo he was a towering figure. His political personality had been forged in the jails of Bulgaria's czarist regime, in clandestine organizational work, and in the halls of the Comintern in Moscow. Having been dispatched to Bulgaria in the mid-thirties by Dimitrov in Moscow, Kostov had spearheaded the purge of the left sectarians inside Bulgaria. He had been the leading spirit behind the party's popular front effort in the mid-thirties, the Communist reorientation vis-à-vis the Dobruja problem in the late thirties, and the initial efforts of the Communist underground right after the outbreak of the German-Soviet war. When all of Macedonia was awarded to Bulgaria in April, 1941, Kostov did what he could to integrate the Macedonian Communist organizations into the framework of the Bulgarian Communist party. His early clashes with Tito won him the lasting hatred of the Yugoslav Communists, who could neither forgive nor forget his persistence in favoring Bulgaria's primacy in all Communist Macedonian affairs. Although of Macedonian origin himself, in these matters Kostov spoke for the Bulgarian party as a whole.

Kostov's loyalty to bolshevism and Stalinism was never in question. His cardinal sin was that his unreserved devotion to Stalinist Russia sprang from an inner conviction regarding the rightness of the Stalinist position rather than from fear or inertia. Furthermore, it is possible that Kostov, unlike the bureaucratic stereotypes of the Stalinist mold, perceived institutionalized communism not as an end in itself but as a means to attain a richer material and, ultimately, spiritual life. Bulgaria's economic backwardness preoccupied him from the first. He appears to have been convinced that the modernization of Russia under Stalin had to be duplicated in the Bulgarian context with as few modifications as possible. It is doubtful that he could have conceived of the modernization of Bulgaria by any means other than the closest possible emulation of the Stalinist formula. In any case, his personal preoccupation with economic matters was fully demonstrated in the very early stages of sovietization. In view of the safety of his position within his party, he chose to devote much, if not most, of his time to problems of industry, electrification, and mining. In so doing, he neglected the personal cultivation of the party bureaucracy, which expanded by leaps and bounds after 1944.

In the final analysis, however, Kostov's ultimate political fate probably was not connected with any practical blunders he might have committed. When Stalin struck at the Communist parties within his domain in 1948, his primary motive was to emasculate them in order to bring them into an even greater servitude than that into which they had already fallen. As in the case of his Great Purge of the thirties, the blows were aimed not at deviationists as such but at prominent figures, who were to be put down as object lessons, for those picked to survive, on the apportionment of ultimate sanctions. By choosing Kostov as his chief victim, Stalin intended to reveal the depth of the abyss to everyone under him on the Bulgarian Communist scene. If Kostov could become a traitor overnight, there was no immunity for anyone.

From the end of 1948, when the charges against Kostov were first concocted, until the mid-fifties, when he was given a post-mortem exoneration, Kostovism served as the whip with which the Bulgarian Communist party was persecuted until it was bled white. Kostovism was not Titoism; nor was it Bulgarian nationalism, in the sense in which that could be perceived as a threat to Soviet hegemony. No meaningful common denominator ever united the tens of thousands who were victimized as Kostovites. The political analysts who endeavored to isolate particularistic features in Kostovism as a specific political line of action were inevitably frustrated.

In the bleak inquisition that was thrust on Eastern Europe, the public trial of Kostov was a singular exception in that the accused remained unbroken to the end. When the initial accusations against Kostov were made, he chose to go to the Soviet Union and attempt to answer the charges leveled against him by the Bulgarian Politburo. To the bitter end Kostov remained convinced that Stalin was mistaken about his own interest. Kostov's defense in the courtroom was less a self-defense than an attempt to show the Soviet Union that it was damaging itself by purging him. The fact that he was a fearless man made his stand even more pathetic intellectually. From beginning to end, the affair rivaled the best that historians could possibly unearth from the annals of medieval clerical purges.[1]

The case of Dimitrov, the one outstanding international figure produced by Bulgarian communism, was no less intriguing. For tactical considerations, Stalin blocked Dimitrov's return to Bulgaria for one year. When at last Dimitrov did return, toward the end of 1945, the hero of Leipzig was all but a broken man. Fame and substance correlated inversely in Dimitrov's political career. His abilities and revolutionary élan were expended during his long years as an underground Comintern functionary, while his years as general secretary of the Comintern were all but devoid of real meaning. After 1935, the year of his election to the highest position in the so-called general staff of the international proletariat, Dimitrov was no more than a convenience, a mere label concealing Stalin's counterrevolutionary designs. Back in Bulgaria, Dimitrov undertook to organize the new Communist regime. In Sofia no less than in Moscow, however, he continued to be besieged by Stalin's paid agents, who constituted his invisible, immediate entourage.[2]

There is little doubt that Dimitrov, unlike the overwhelming

[1] On Kostov's earlier career, the particular circumstances of his imprisonment during the war, and the ultimate pardon granted him by the court, see Oren, *Bulgarian Communism*, esp. pp. 183–84. Kostov, *Izbrani statii, dokladi, rechi*, contains many of Kostov's public utterances after 1944; they are indicative of his permanent preoccupation with matters concerning Bulgaria's economic development. On the accusations made against Kostov, see Kolarov, *Antisuvetskata i antipartiina deinost na Tr. Kostov*, as well as *The Trial of Traicho Kostov and His Group*. Some interesting observations on the behavior of Kostov during the trial are made in Leites and Bernaut, *Ritual of Liquidation*.

[2] Blagoeva, *Georgi Dimitrov: Biografichen ocherk*, remains Dimitrov's standard biography. Written by the daughter of the founder of "narrow" Socialism in Bulgaria, this work, which has undergone several editions, is altogether unsatisfactory. The multivolume selected works of Dimitrov, *Suchinenia*, are valuable on the man and his work. Western accounts of Dimitrov and his earlier career are numerous. On his career in the context of Bulgarian politics up to 1944, see various sections of Rothschild, *The Communist Party of Bulgaria*, and Oren, *Bulgarian Communism*.

majority of Bulgarian Communists, nourished a certain personal admiration for Tito, probably less because of Tito's particular political ways than because of what Dimitrov would have liked to become had circumstances been different. Dimitrov's deeds and thoughts during the last year of his life remain conjectural to this day. Yugoslav Communist chroniclers have never tired of reassuring those willing to listen that Dimitrov favored a Yugoslav-Bulgarian federative plan, by means of which he hoped to construct a countervailing posture vis-à-vis Moscow's maximalism. These contentions probably contain a grain of truth. If so, Dimitrov, himself of Macedonian origin, was more willing to forego Bulgaria's obsession with Macedonia than was the great bulk of his party. His death at the height of the crisis with Belgrade, and his early position as a godlike figure in the Bulgarian Communist pantheon, helped throw a blanket of fog over his true motives and last impulses. Largely because of the state of mediocrity into which Bulgarian communism sank in the decades following Dimitrov's death, Bulgarian Communist historians have continued to cling to Dimitrov's image as the one safe link to a more glorious past.[3]

Kolarov was the third leg of the tripod which collapsed in the late forties. Unlike Dimitrov and Kostov, who were self-made men, Kolarov was a professional intellectual-turned-revolutionary. A trained lawyer, he had been exposed to the wider world of socialism during his stay in Geneva well before the outbreak of the First World War. He had emerged as Blagoev's chief lieutenant and crowned successor, the number one Bulgarian Communist in the twenties. As with Dimitrov, Kolarov's career within the Comintern during the long years of exile had gone far beyond the narrow confines of the Bulgarian Communist emigration in the Soviet Union. Unlike Dimitrov, however, Kolarov did not become a world-known figure. The unprece-

---

[3] There is no hard evidence on Dimitrov's true intentions vis-à-vis the Yugoslav-Bulgarian plans for federation. Dimitrov's apparent admiration for Tito may not have been one-sided. In the second half of the thirties, when the émigré leadership of the Yugoslav Communist party perished in the Great Purge, Dimitrov appears to have helped Tito restore the little that remained of the shattered organization of Yugoslav Communists. For these and other interesting, if unconfirmed, speculations, see Djilas, *Conversations with Stalin,* and Dedijer, *Tito Speaks.*

dented success which the Reichstag affair brought his younger corevolutionary haunted Kolarov to the end of his days. Within the Comintern, Kolarov's formal specialty was agriculture and the peasantry. Having sided with the Stalin forces as early as 1923, however, Kolarov's particular vocation was purging any deviationists in the European (and Mongolian) Communist parties. In the mid-thirties, Kolarov emerged as chief executive of the purge of the Bulgarian left opposition in exile. His rich experience in such matters was once again put to good use in the late forties, when Kostov and the Kostovites became the objects of Stalin's wrath. Following Dimitrov's death, Kolarov succeeded to the Bulgarian premiership, which he held until his own death in 1950.[4]

Kostov's execution and the death of his elder colleagues ended the semblance of collective leadership which had lasted since the coup of September, 1944. In the years that followed, the rule of Communist Bulgaria passed into the hands of Chervenkov, yet another member of the younger generation of Stalinist functionaries. As long as Chervenkov's supreme reign lasted, it provided Bulgaria with its own special period of a *Yezhovshchina* and *Zhdanovshchina* combined. A man of some brilliance and unlimited ruthlessness, Chervenkov was a product of the Stalinist educational system which he himself helped perfect. Having lived in exile in the Soviet Union since the mid-twenties, Chervenkov graduated from a Soviet secret police academy and continued on to the various Comintern party schools. In the latter part of the thirties, following the cleansing of the Comintern intelligentsia, Chervenkov was given charge of the entire educational and propaganda system of the Comintern. Following his return to Bulgaria in 1944, a few days after the September coup, Chervenkov's special assignment was to manage the Department of Agitation and Propaganda and to serve as one

[4] Kolarov's *Spomeni* (Sofia, 1968) is an interesting autobiography of the man, even though the period covered pertains to his youth and his formative years as a Marxist. Borov, ed., *Vasil Kolarov: Bio-bibliografiia*, provides a good sketch of Kolarov's life and his writings. *Izbrani proizvedeniia* is a three-volume edition of Kolarov's selected writings. Unlike that of Dimitrov, in recent years the name of Kolarov has witnessed a slight but noticeable eclipse. This is largely the result of a hidden dislike nourished against Kolarov by a great many older Communist functionaries.

of the secretaries of the Central Committee. After Kolarov's death, he exercised the dual function of premier and general secretary of the party.[5]

The period of Chervenkov's unchallenged supremacy over Bulgaria was relatively brief. At the same time, the alterations forced on Bulgarian society were extreme. In the early stage of sovietization, the Communist party grew indiscriminately in terms of rank-and-file membership. The floodgates were raised, and, for all practical purposes, anyone willing to join was admitted without much scrutiny. At the time of the Fifth Party Congress, held in December, 1948, total party membership approached the half-million mark. Twice the membership of early 1945, and more than twenty times the size of the party immediately following the coup of September, 1944, this spectacular increment was made possible by the incorporation within the party's ranks of a large number of peasants, which in turn reflected the essentially peasant nature of the Bulgarian population. At the end of 1948, about half of the total party membership was of peasant stock, while workers accounted for only slightly more than a quarter of the total membership.

The Bulgarian experience, as well as that of most other East European countries, departed sharply from the earlier Soviet experience. Whereas the Bolsheviks in Russia had insisted on strict qualitative selection in terms of both the size and the social composition of their party's membership (at least during the first three decades following the October Revolution), the Bulgarian Party could hardly qualify as the vanguard of the socialist revolution in view of its relative enormity. Even though the general elections of 1945 and 1946 were rigged, the numerical size of the Communist party was deemed important in gaining electoral victories and carrying out an intensive social mobilization and politicization of the people at large.

In actual fact, the crisis within the Communist party had become acute even before the Fifth Party Congress convened

[5] On Chervenkov's career in Bulgaria and in the Soviet Union, see various parts of Oren, *Bulgarian Communism*. A sample of Chervenkov's collected writings appears in the bibliography of the present volume. Chervenkov, *Bio-bibliografiia, 1900–1950*, provides a good sketch of his life and a bibliography of his writings.

in December, 1948. Chervenkov's rise to power was marked by a drastic curtailment of the size of the party, and this was effected by wide-scale purge. By 1950, close to 100,000 members had been expelled from the party. The streamlining had yet another goal, which was to increase the proportion of workers as compared to peasants. The massive purge achieved its purpose, even though the proportion of peasants remained larger than that of the working proletariat. This "achievement" notwithstanding, the Bulgarian Communist party was, and remained, a party with a disproportionately large peasant element.[6]

The purge affected the summits of the party hierarchy as well. Anton Yugov, the minister of the interior who had brutally managed the breakup of the opposition after September, 1944, was demoted and pushed aside. Dobri Terpeshev, the folkish, yet energetic, commander-in-chief of the Communist wartime resistance who after 1944 had become chief economic planner under Kostov, was publicly criticized and dropped. Tsola Dragoicheva, the top-ranking female functionary who had served as general secretary of the National Council of the Fatherland Front, was another victim of the Chervenkov purge. Other party leaders were tried, convicted, and imprisoned. Among these were Petko Kunin and Professor Ivan Stefanov, outstanding economic and financial planners. There were many more, some of whom perished in the Bulgarian jails. The newly reorganized army was not spared; the old political leadership of the armed forces was all but obliterated. General Slavcho Trunski, the one genuinely popular partisan leader, disappeared from the scene, as did many more Communist functionaries who had been elevated to the rank of general officer after 1944.[7]

As the purge of the party ran its wild course, wide-scale terror affected the society at large. Under Chervenkov, Bulgaria took a giant step toward becoming a totalitarian state. Owing to the use of indiscriminate terror, Bulgarian society underwent a process of atomization, accompanied by alienation, which all but

---

[6] A sense of the extent of the purge is conveyed in *Treta konferentsiia na BKP*, which reproduces the minutes of the Third Party Conference, held in 1950.

[7] Those who did not perish in Bulgaria's jails were eventually rehabilitated and restored to their party or army posts.

113

tore apart the traditional social fabric. Collectivization of the land was launched in earnest. The semivoluntary campaigns of the mid-forties were replaced by the systematic destruction of private landholdings and of the village structure as a whole. In the early fifties, Bulgaria stood at the vanguard of the agricultural collectivization movement in Eastern Europe.

The statistical indicators of the collectivization campaign told but a tiny part of the gigantic human drama which unfolded in the Bulgarian countryside. The fact that Bulgaria had traditionally been one of the most egalitarian agricultural societies in Europe, with a large degree of voluntary consumer and marketing cooperation, made collectivization all the more unpopular. The regime tried to direct the resentment of the peasantry against a landed aristocracy or a class of large landholders, but it failed simply because such classes were nonexistent. Nor was the Leninist tactic of driving a wedge between the poor and middle-level peasants successful. Furthermore, the Bulgarian peasantry had been highly politicized for many years; it possessed a political consciousness of its own which had been forged by the Agrarian Union. The peasants were poor but not desperate. Under Petkov, the Agrarian Union had carried out a vigorous campaign which had revitalized the political and social self-perceptions of the peasantry. The bogus Agrarian Union under Traikov commanded neither the respect nor the obedience of the village population. Traikov's organization was useful largely as a corruptive institution because of the bribes it was able to distribute via the patronage left in its hands. In the main, however, the Chervenkov regime could not neutralize the peasants as the Bolsheviks had done to their peasantry in the twenties. The Bulgarian peasants had to be oppressed, persecuted, physically molested, and ultimately subdued into obedience.

The beginning of massive collectivization constituted one major element of the socioeconomic revolution launched in earnest by the Chervenkov regime. Industrialization was the counterpart of the social reordering. As far as the regime was concerned, the latter took precedence over the former. Here again, the Soviet formula was applied meticulously and without due regard for the immense discrepancies in the size of the countries, the particularities of the land, and the levels of economic development. Collectivization was to achieve two main objectives. The first was to substitute administrative constraints for the peasant market economy. Among other things, this change would secure for the regime comprehensive control over the countryside. The second objective was to ensure a substantial outflow of surplus labor from the agricultural sector and, at the same time, to install a mechanism by means of which the regime could extract the "surplus" savings generated within this sector and commit them to the industrialization effort.

The guiding principles of this formulation were not new. They had been worked out in Soviet Russia in the mid-twenties and were the end result of the intense intraparty debates between Bukharin, speaking for the central-rightist majority, and Preobrazhenski, speaking for the Trotskyite left. When the intra-Bolshevik struggles for the succession were over, Stalin chose and implemented the leftist program of Preobrazhenski-Trotsky. Thus, in the early fifties, the Bulgarians were merely imitating Stalin, who had copied the ideas of his rivals.

In essence, the general line adopted by Chervenkov provided that the Bulgarian countryside become, in effect, Bulgaria's internal colony, which was to be squeezed and exploited on behalf of urbanization and industrialization. In the absence of any sizable capital importation, agriculture was to be harnessed to the effort to generate a so-called internal capital accumulation, without which it would be impossible to construct factories at a rapid rate. Agriculture was to be starved; in the overall allocation of the state budget, it was to contribute much more than it was to receive. As always, the burden was placed on the peasants' backs. Whatever the human muscle could extract from the land was to be consumed in the cities, while the peasants' level of consumption was to be frozen close to the subsistence line.

The scheme offered one important benefit to the village population, however; it promised employment in industry for the sons and daughters who could not earn their livelihood working the land. Overpopulation in the countryside had been one of the gravest problems in the country for many decades. Industrial expansion in the interwar period and during the initial stages of the Second World War had advanced at too slow a rate to effect a sizable diminution of hidden unemployment, or underemployment, among the peasantry. In the early fifties the rudimentary preconditions were created for a relatively rapid siphoning off of the rural population into the cities.

In the Bulgarian context, the problem of modernization could be tackled in three different ways. The solution provided by the Agrarians stipulated that Bulgaria remain essentially agricultural. They contended that, in an international division of labor, Bulgaria's advantage lay in intensifying and modernizing those branches of agriculture for which the country was best suited in terms of its topography, climate, and existing skills. The growth of tobacco, Bulgaria's chief hard-currency earner, the specialized cultivation of fruits and vegetables, and their processing for export, were conceived as the means to attain greater welfare and riches. If the Agrarians could have had their way, the bulk of the country's capital investment would have been directed into the countryside.

The same fundamental problems were answered differently by the more enlightened bourgeois parties. In economic terms, their approach was more akin to that chosen by the Communists than to the policies promulgated by Stamboliiski as spokesman for the more extreme Agrarian-populist viewpoint. Like the Communists, the middle-class parties realized that, in the long run, urbanization was inevitable and that its attainment would be made possible by exploiting the villages on behalf of industry. Capital loans from abroad were to supplement the process of capital formation at home. In the opinion of the bourgeois economists, the market mechanism had to be regulated so as to bring about the overpricing of industrial goods relative to agricultural produce. At the same time, none of them, not even the most ambitious, envisaged a rate of urbanization and industrialization as rapid as that proposed in later years by the Communist regime. The People's Bloc regime of the early thirties, an alliance between the Gichev Agrarians and the Mushanov Democrats, had endeavored to make the Agrarian and bourgeois economic policies compatible by modifying both in order to reach a workable compromise. Much more so than Stamboliiski in earlier years, Gichev was receptive to the idea of regulated economic coexistence, which would satisfy the basic needs of both the peasants and the industrialists and tradesmen. Similarly, the old Democratic party was willing to make concessions to the agricultural interests, in part because of the degree of support it found in the countryside. Under the Boris dictatorship of the mid-thirties and early forties, the requirements of industry took precedence over those of the peasants.

The Communist approach, which began to be implemented in the early fifties, was the antithesis of Stamboliiski's populism. It differed from the economic concepts of the bourgeois past because the Communists were immensely more ambitious in their plans for industrialization and because they relied on administrative-police constraints rather than on a free market interplay. Furthermore, the Communists placed overwhelming emphasis on capital investment in basic industries, as opposed to processing and light industries, which had been favored in earlier years. Finally, the Communists were prepared to starve all services except those directly related to the development of heavy industry. Their bias was vividly reflected in the standard of living of the population at large, which dropped radically. Obsessed by their pursuit of material modernity, the Communists could contemplate without much hesitation sacrifices of which no traditional politician would have dared to dream.

To implement their economic program the Communists relied on arbitrary administrative and police measures complemented by numerous governmental decrees and new laws. Summary penalties for real or assumed disobedience and alleged sabotage, which included tardiness or absenteeism from work, were distributed in a massive manner. The victims became part of the vastly expanded labor–concentration camp system, which developed into an important economic sector based on slave labor. Systematized terror thus became economically profitable, even though the regime's primary objective was probably less economic in nature than psychological. The threat of arbitrary punishment caused widespread demoralization, which immobilized any meaningful passive or active opposition. Severe restrictions regarding registration, travel, size of domicile, and staying at one's job were strictly applied to the entire population.[8]

Large numbers of Russian citizens began to participate openly in all spheres of Bulgaria's economic life. They were exempted from the stringent restrictions and were paid salaries many times higher than those received by the Bulgarians. The Russians took an active part in managing the various Soviet-Bulgarian economic enterprises.[9] This massive Russian intervention in the day-to-day management of Bulgaria contrasted sharply with the state of international isolation in which Chervenkov endeavored to place the country. On February 20, 1950, the United States broke diplomatic relations with Bulgaria. This event occurred within three weeks of Chervenkov's assumption of the premiership. A break in diplomatic relations became inevitable following the implication of Donald R. Heath, the American ambassador to Sofia, in the Kostov trial.

The self-imposed siege under which Chervenkov chose to carry out his policies signified the degree of fear and insecurity which prevailed within the regime. There were deeper motives, however, which pushed the Bulgarians into self-inflicted isolation. The state of utter helplessness of the Bulgarian Communists vis-à-vis Tito's federative designs from 1944 until the Yugoslav break with the Cominform had had a profound effect on the once-proud Bulgarian revolutionaries. The Yugoslav encroachments into Bulgarian Macedonia touched the very essence of Bulgaria's national sovereignty. Even worse in Bulgarian eyes was the seriousness with which some of the Bulgarian Macedonians in the Pirin District had reacted to the concept of a united, autonomous Macedonian republic within Yugoslavia. The exchange of teachers, politicians, and functionaries across the borders of the two countries had brought to the fore the grave perils facing Sofia. Even though the Bulgarians were the last to acknowledge that their Macedonian

[8] See Baldwin, ed., *A New Slavery*, and Carlton, ed., *Forced Labor in the People's Democracies*, on the scope of the concentration- and labor-camp system established in the fifties.

[9] On the magnitude of Soviet economic intervention, see Spulber, *The Economics of Communist Eastern Europe*, and Wolff, *The Balkans in Our Time*. Popisakov, *Ikonomicheski otnosheniia mezhdu NRB i SSSR*, is the most systematic monograph on Soviet-Bulgarian economic relations from 1944 through the mid-sixties.

population was a national minority, maintaining as always that the Macedonians were an integral part of the Bulgarian nation, after the break with Tito they were compelled to take a second look at the entire issue of national groups residing in Bulgaria.[10]

The revolutionary frenzy which the Communists had imposed on the country as a whole was exploited in resolving once and for all the problem of multinationalism, the purpose being to make the Bulgarian nation as homogeneous as possible. During the Chervenkov years the regime turned its attention to the texture of Bulgaria's national society and opened separate fronts involving the Macedonians, the Bulgarian Turks, and the Bulgarian Jews.

The Bulgarian-Yugoslav frontier was sealed immediately upon the outbreak of Tito's quarrel with Moscow. Overnight, the two-way traffic across the boundary was halted. The Bulgarians sought to provoke border incidents in order to heat up the frontiers and effectively insulate the immediate hinterland. The Yugoslavs responded in kind. Vladimir Poptomov, the old IMRO man and a long-time Communist who had spent twenty years in exile in the Soviet Union, was appointed Bulgaria's

[10] The Bulgarians have not added substantially to our fund of knowledge on the dispute with Yugoslavia. Once the break had been made, Sofia responded with insinuation and a stream of ill-documented accusations. The famous Bled Agreement, which was to have opened a new chapter in Bulgarian-Yugoslav relations by instituting a federation, became a passing episode. If Moscow had shown a qualified interest in seeing Bulgaria linked to Yugoslavia at the end of 1944, interest in that federation had all but disappeared by the end of 1947. By that time, international conditions had changed radically, and Bulgaria had become firmly secured. Dimitrov's ambivalent stand has already been noted. The affair as a whole has by now become well documented. The following are a few of the more significant sources on the subject. Royal Institute of International Affairs, *The Soviet-Yugoslav Dispute: Text of the Published Correspondence,* supplies the basic materials. Djilas, *Conversations with Stalin,* and Dedijer, *Tito Speaks,* give vivid and valuable evidence on Yugoslav-Bulgarian relations as well as on relations between Belgrade and Moscow. Vlahov, *Govori i statii, 1945–1947,* and *Svobodna Makedoniia i federalna Yugoslaviia,* are important for the views of the Macedonians who sided with Belgrade. Ulam, *Titoism and the Cominform,* and Armstrong, *Tito and Goliath,* supply most of the relevant narrative on the Moscow-Belgrade break, its antecedents, and its aftermath. On the Bulgarian side, the following are the more significant sources: Ormandzhiev, *Federatsiia na balkanskite narodi; Krizata v Yugoslavskata komunisticheska partiia;* and *Titovata banda, orudie na imperialistite: Dokumenti i matariali, 1948–1951.* Finally, the book by Mitrev, *Pirinska Makedonija vo borba za natsionalno osvoboduvanje,* represents an interesting polemic.

foreign minister on August 6, 1949. His appointment signaled the beginning of a savage campaign against Titoism and all that Belgrade represented in the eyes of Stalinist orthodoxy. Those Macedonians within Bulgaria who had foolishly let themselves be carried away by Tito's federalist appeals were quickly rounded up and incarcerated. The Sofia regime did not hesitate to undertake a large-scale resettlement of doubtful elements in the Pirin District away from the frontier regions and into the Bulgarian interior. An end was put to the publication of literature printed in the Macedonian dialect, which the Yugoslavs had helped foster since Tito's rise to power. From the local functionary to the university academician, the intellectual resources of the Bulgarians were employed to prove to the world and themselves that the Macedonian people were identical to, and inseparable from, the Bulgarian people, and that any idea of separateness was no more than a Yugoslav imperialist treachery.

As far as the Bulgarian masses were concerned, there is little doubt that the anti-Tito campaign involving the Macedonian question was widely popular. On this sore point neither the reactionary right nor the elements of the dissolved democratic groups could disagree with the otherwise hated Communist masters. Thanks largely to the Bulgarian obsession with Macedonia, the potential appeal of Titoism as a political doctrine was stifled from the beginning. There was no other path for Bulgarian chauvinism to march along except the road to Moscow.

The problem of the Turkish population in Bulgaria was of an altogether different nature. The ambivalence which existed in the case of the Macedonians in Bulgaria concerning their precise ethnic and national affiliation did not exist with regard to the Turks. The latter were a homogeneous group, more or less compactly settled in the northeastern part of the country, and distinguished from the majority in terms of nationality and religion. During the interwar period the Turks in Bulgaria numbered about 700,000. They were the residue from centuries of Turkish occupation. About 100,000 more Turks were added in 1940, when southern Dobruja reverted to Bulgaria. Bulgaria's record of minority treatment, unlike that of her neighbors, was relatively good for most of the interwar period. In 1925 the Bulgarian and Turkish governments signed a convention regulating the voluntary migration of the nationals of both countries across the frontier. On the basis of this agreement, some 100,000 Turks had left Bulgaria for Turkey by the outbreak of the Second World War. The number of Turks leaving Bulgaria annually varied from year to year. Emigration was at its lowest in the early thirties under the regime of the People's Bloc and at its highest at the outbreak of the Second World War, which indicated a clear correlation between the number of Turks desiring to leave and the relative degree of political freedom existing in the country.

The Turks in Bulgaria were virtually all peasants. They were poor and politically docile. From the September, 1944, coup until 1950, the Communist regime discouraged emigration, which indeed dwindled to a trickle. The Bulgarian Communists were determined to emulate the Soviet pattern applied to the various Muslim populations in the Soviet Union. Those willing to leave were termed reactionaries. Mosques and Turkish schools were nationalized, as was the entire educational system. Likewise, collectivization of the land was applied to the Turkish settlements as well.

These policies were sharply reversed in 1950 owing to purely economic motives and the aim of achieving greater national homogeneity. The Bulgarian government was keenly interested in nationalizing the Turkish lands, particularly those in southern Dobruja, where large-scale experiments in reclamation and collectivization were being carried out. In August, 1950, 7,000 Turks were permitted to leave. This was a tenfold increase compared to the number who left in January of the same year. At the same time, the Bulgarian government notified Ankara that a quarter of a million Turks had expressed the desire to immigrate to Turkey. The Bulgarians accused the Turkish authorities of issuing only a limited number of entry visas and insisted that Turkey agree to accept forthwith all 250,000 Turks. Understandably, the Turkish government refused to comply with this outrageous demand. Insisting on the right to set its own immigration policies and to refuse entry visas to undesirable elements, the Turks closed their frontier with Bulgaria in September. For their part, the Bulgarians proceeded to forcibly drive across the border large numbers of Turks whose lands in Dobruja had already been confiscated. To the thousands of destitute Turkish peasants boxed into the no-man's-land along the frontier, the Sofia government added a few thousand gypsies, of whom it wished to rid itself in the bargain.

In response to these outrageous acts of the Bulgarian authorities, the Ankara government threatened to bring the whole issue before the United Nations. The implication in this threat was that the problems of the Muslim population in the Soviet Union would be discussed as well. The Bulgarians had no choice but to modify their stand. Still, in the period 1950–51, an estimated 150,000 Turks were, in one way or another, pushed out of Bulgaria. Southern Dobruja was all but cleared of its Turkish population. Bulgarian relations with Turkey remained near the boiling point for several years.

Having resigned itself to retaining a relatively large Turkish population in the country, the Communist regime eventually undertook to provide the Turks with a degree of cultural autonomy. There were 656,000 Turks in Bulgaria according to the official census of 1956, and an estimated total of 746,755 in 1965. Only in the sixties did relations with Turkey begin to improve markedly, as a direct consequence of the Soviet-Turkish rapprochement. In 1968 the two governments reached a new agreement on the regulation of emigration quotas.[11]

The Jews of Bulgaria were much fewer in number than the Turks, and their ultimate fate was more cheerful. There were about 45,000 Jews in Bulgaria on the eve of the Second World War, half of whom resided in Sofia. Being few in number, they never constituted an acute problem for Bulgaria. While in most other East European countries the urban preponderance of the Jewish population constituted a threat to the rising native middle class, in Bulgaria the conflict of interests did not arise.

[11] Wolff, *The Balkans in Our Time,* and Brown, *Bulgaria under Communist Rule,* provide the basic facts on the Bulgarian Turkish minority as well as on Sofia's relations with Ankara. The most important monograph which looks at the problem from Turkey's point of view is Kostanick, *Turkish Resettlement of Bulgarian Turks, 1950–1953.* On the state of the Muslims in Communist Bulgaria, there are two Bulgarian sources—namely, *The Turkish Minority in the People's Republic of Bulgaria,* and Mizov, *Islamut v Bulgariia.*

Although moderately influential in the economic life of the country, the Bulgarian Jews played no political role of any significance. They were an unassimilated and largely introverted national group. Historically, the Jews had been barred entry into the state bureaucracy and the professional army. They were left in peace, however, to develop their own ethnic cultural life.

Lacking meaningful identification with the national and nationalistic aspirations of the Bulgarian majority, the Jews of Bulgaria identified more closely with the ideals of modern Jewish nationalism, of which political Zionism became the dominant expression. Prior to the First World War, as well as during the interwar years, active affiliation by Jews with any one of the various political parties in the country was generally the exception. The only party which succeeded in making substantial inroads into the Jewish community was the Communist party. The proportional representation of Jews within the Communist-led wartime resistance movement far exceeded their proportional representation within the general population. This situation was a natural reaction to the rise of authoritarianism, with its cryptofascist admixtures. Politically, the overwhelming majority of the Jewish population operated only within the framework of the Jewish community. Jewish political energies were largely exhausted by infighting—first, between Zionists and anti-Zionists, and, in later years, with the emergence of the Zionists as the preponderant majority, among the various Zionist factions.

The Bulgarian Jews escaped the Nazi holocaust with their lives. In 1940, the regime began legislating anti-Jewish laws, which gradually became more and more severe. The Jews were dispossessed, their freedom of action and occupation was restricted, and their male population was incarcerated in special labor camps. Intent on proving its allegiance and reliability to its German protectors, the wartime regime was fully prepared to surrender the Jews to the Germans. Yet, at a crucial point in 1943, plans to expatriate a large number of Bulgarian Jews to the German-occupied eastern territories were temporarily shelved. The postponement was responsible for the survival of the Bulgarian Jews, for the expatriation scheme was never resumed. This turn of events, unique among developments within the German domain, was the result of a massive outcry on behalf of the Jews delivered by the antigovernment opposition and, even more significant, an outburst against the government's antisemitic designs from the government's own parliamentary majority. By this time, the realization that Germany was losing the war had become widespread. Influential elements within the left, the center, and even the reactionary right, had come to realize the futility and the possible adverse future consequences of Bulgaria's allowing the Jews to be exterminated. This interplay of political forces constituted striking proof of the existence within the Bulgarian body politic of political pluralism, which had survived even at the height of the crypto-Nazi regime.

The coup of September, 1944, was an act of deliverance for the Jews. All the discriminatory legal restrictions were abolished. Although the new Fatherland Front regime did not hasten to restore to the Jewish community its confiscated property, in due time reparations were made. In the elections after 1944, as in the years preceding the Second World War, the overwhelming majority of Jews voted for the government in power. A special Jewish section was set up within the Bulgarian Communist party whose primary function was to muster Jewish support for the regime while fighting the now re-established Zionist political parties.

In Bulgaria, unlike most other East European countries, Jewish influence within the Communist party was moderate, if not meager. While a few Jewish Communist intellectuals did play a role, particularly in the educational and propaganda fields, the popular sentiments of the Jewish community were directed at political Zionism more so than in previous years. In ever-increasing numbers the Jews expressed a desire to leave for Palestine. At first, official consent to emigration was not readily forthcoming. As in Soviet Russia, Zionism was identified as little less than treason, even though the various Jewish nationalist organizations were allowed to operate. Until 1947 only a small number of Jews emigrated from Bulgaria.

The change in the official line followed the abrupt shift in Soviet policy toward support of the Jewish cause in Palestine, which was expressed by the Russian delegates to the General

Assembly of the United Nations. Beginning in 1948, Jewish emigration from Bulgaria rose steadily. In 1949, the floodgates were all but lifted. Within a few years, the vast majority of Bulgarian Jews departed for what by then had become the State of Israel.

The mass exodus took place after the Soviet government lost its initial enthusiasm and, in fact, reverted to its antagonistic posture vis-à-vis the Jewish problem as a whole. Thus, while the initial outflow of Jewish emigrants harmonized with Soviet policy on the Middle Eastern question, the departure of the great majority was in marked dissonance with the over-all Soviet orientation. This aberration in Bulgarian Communist behavior cannot simply be attributed to altruism or good will. The good fortune of the Bulgarian Jews resulted from the convergence of their own interests with the determination of the Chervenkov regime to rid the country of as many minority members as possible in pursuit of national homogeneity.[12]

[12] The three volumes published in Hebrew by Kishales, *Korot yehudei bulgariya*, are an important contribution to the entire spectrum of the Jews in Bulgaria. Meyer *et al.*, *The Jews in the Soviet Satellites*, is a brief but substantial account of the state of Bulgarian Jews during the Second World War and after. The most comprehensive history of the particular circumstances which befell Bulgarian Jews during the Second World War is the yet unpublished dissertation by Chary, "Bulgaria and the Jews: 'The Final Solution,' 1940 to 1944." For an analysis of the same subject, see Nissan Oren, "The Bulgarian Exception: A Reassessment of the Salvation of the Jewish Community," *Yad Vashem Studies* (Jerusalem), 7 (1968): 83–106. The two volumes by Grinberg, *Khitleristkiiat natisk za unishtozhavane na evreite ot Bulgariia* and *Dokumenti*, are important factually as well as in terms of the author's particular viewpoint. The monograph by Arditi, *Yehudei bulgariya beshnot hamishtar hanatsi*, is a comprehensive account with a particular viewpoint. Finally, the book by Piti, *Te, spasitelite*, is of interest largely because of the author's personal view on the role of Bulgaria's rulers vis-à-vis the Jewish issue.

6: PROGRESS AND REACTION IN A HOUSE OF QUARANTINE

Alone among the East European states under Soviet dominion, Bulgaria sailed through the post-Stalin era in a cloud of political obscurity. The permanent strains under which the regime operated did not produce any noticeable eruptions. Gradually, power passed into the hands of a younger generation of Communist functionaries. Only a few of the old Communists whose reputations had been acquired during the Comintern era survived. The successors were men of no distinction. The country succumbed to political exhaustion, which helped the new faceless managers govern. Although Bulgaria continued to stagnate politically, the country and the people underwent a steady transformation at a rapid rate. The conservative, if not reactionary, nature of the political culture fostered from above concealed from the outside world the great physical progress achieved in the span of two decades.

Stalin's death brought a slight but noticeable decline in the state of terror. Without removing the underpinnings of the political regime, Bulgaria launched a "new course" of her own which was of no great consequence for the people at large. At the same time, Chervenkov's hegemony within the party began to be dismantled. The shortage of time, rather than Chervenkov's consent, was the true reason why his victims were able to make a political comeback. The latter were neither "liberals" nor Communist "nationalists." Their temporary downfall had been the result of Chervenkov's grasp for supreme personal power rather than of major substantive political disagreements.

The reshuffling of personnel within the party high command altered but did not shatter the inner balance of the ruling caste. Chervenkov lost his supremacy, but he continued to share the powers of government for another decade.

The new equilibrium which evolved was made possible by the introduction of a number of political "dark horses" into the centers of party control. These were mainly younger people whose political careers had been made after 1944. For much of the fifties their main function was to act as keepers of the balance between the Chervenkov forces and the forces of the newly restored old guard, headed by Yugov. This triumvirate composed of three loose cliques broke up only in the early sixties, when the "center" successfully disposed of Chervenkov and Yugov. As long as it lasted, this temporary alliance of three distinguishable elements provided the party with a useful tripod on which the government could balance itself in times of crisis. An unmanaged, yet real, division of labor of sorts was established among the components. Following Khrushchev's secret speech at the Twentieth Party Congress, Yugov castigated Chervenkov as the epitome of Bulgaria's "cult of personality." Nevertheless, after the Hungarian revolution, Chervenkov was once again called upon to apply his special abilities in restoring order to some Bulgarian Communist intellectuals who had gone too far in their libertarian utterings. In no small measure, the Bulgarian Communists were able to withstand the upheavals of the mid-fifties precisely because of the factional coalition established after 1953.

Between the death of Stalin and the Sixth Party Congress (February, 1954) the party underwent no structural changes. The signing of the Balkan Pact by Yugoslavia, Greece, and Turkey (February 28, 1953) had the effect of further isolating Bulgaria from her Balkan neighbors. Although the end of 1953 witnessed a certain relaxation in the relations between Bulgaria and Greece, Bulgaria's relations with Yugoslavia remained tense and hostile.[1] One of the chief immediate causes of the constant friction was the growing number of Bulgarians fleeing to Yugo-

---

[1] On December 5, 1953, the Bulgarian and Greek governments signed a limited trade agreement; a few weeks later (December 30), representatives of the two states signed a frontier settlement in Salonika.

slavia. According to the Yugoslavs, from 1948 to the middle of 1953 some 7,000 Bulgarians fled across the frontier in search of refuge in Yugoslav territory.[2]

In September, 1953, Chervenkov announced the launching of the "new course." The few changes that were introduced were limited to economic matters. Consumers were promised several concessions. On October 3, collective farmers were granted a remission of overdue income taxes to the end of 1952. Irrigation and drainage charges were lowered, and debts owed to the Machine-Tractor Stations were canceled. More significantly, a special government decree reduced the compulsory delivery quotas. These concessions were made possible thanks to the good harvests of 1952 and 1953. In his speech of September 9, 1953, Chervenkov emphasized the need for more consumer goods. He stated that, in the future, Bulgaria would not have to develop all branches of heavy industry but would concentrate instead on those industries for which the most favorable conditions existed within the country. Earlier, the government had decreed price cuts averaging 10 percent on foodstuffs and 20 percent on industrial goods. These were the most important features of the "new course."[3]

Though the "new course" brought no immediate political changes, Bulgaria did not remain totally unaffected by the emergence of the new post-Stalin regime in the Soviet Union. There were no new purges throughout 1953. Kostovism was still discussed in editorials of the party press, but the issue was toned down. By the end of the year, Chervenkov began to speak of "greater collectivity in party leadership." At about the same time, formal communications from the Politburo began to conclude with the names of the signers arranged in alphabetical order rather than in the order of their political importance. These small variations were indicative of the new political climate which was beginning to emerge.

The Sixth Party Congress was held from February 28 to March 5, 1954. The main report on the state of the party dur-

[2] *New York Times,* July 9, 1953.

[3] The economic features of the "new course" were incorporated into the Second Five-Year Plan (1953–57), which was announced in May, 1953, but was not published in full until the beginning of 1954.

ing the past six years was presented by Chervenkov. He declared that, even though the elimination of Kostov had represented a great triumph, the enemies of the party were still active. At the same time, he warned against automatically identifying as enemies of the party all those who in the past might have been associated with Kostov and his collaborators. He went on to urge that those who previously might have been hostile to the regime of the Fatherland Front now be given the right to re-educate themselves. The report concluded with an appeal on behalf of greater collective work within the leadership.

The crucial change introduced by the Sixth Party Congress was the abolition of the post of general secretary of the party, a position held by Chervenkov since Dimitrov's death. In its stead, the Congress elected a Secretariat of three, with Todor Zhivkov serving as first secretary. The other two members were Dimitur Ganev and Boris Taskov. Chervenkov retained the premiership and his membership in the Politburo. Of the eleven Politburo members elected by the Fifth Congress, only five were re-elected by the Sixth Congress. These were Chervenkov, Yugov, Georgi Damianov, Georgi Chankov, and Raiko Damianov. Dimitrov and Kolarov were dead, Kostov had been executed, and Dobri Terpeshev had been dropped from the Politburo as early as 1950. Dr. Mincho Neichev, the minister of justice in the first Fatherland Front government, and Titko Chernokolev, both of whom had been candidate members of the 1948 Politburo, were absent from the new body. While Neichev was retained as a member of the Central Committee, the failure to re-elect him to the Politburo (of which he had become a full member in 1949) was considered a setback for Chervenkov. Chernokolev, the former minister of agriculture who had headed the agricultural drive during the most difficult years of collectivization, was dropped altogether. He had been dismissed as early as June 23, 1951, after being accused of failing to fulfill the collectivization plans with the necessary speed.

Among the members of the Politburo elected by the Sixth Party Congress were some who in 1948 had not even been members of the Central Committee. This was true of Generals Petur Panchevski and Ivan Mikhailov, whose elevation to top party leadership resulted from their military, rather than their political, qualifications. Also new to the Politburo (although he was a Central Committee member in 1948) was Encho Staikov, chief of the Education and Propaganda Department of the Central Committee.

The Sixth Party Congress elected a new and enlarged Central Committee. The Central Committee elected by the Fifth Congress had numbered forty-seven full members and twenty-eight candidates (or alternate members); the respective numbers in the new Central Committee were sixty-five and thirty-two. The increase in the size of the Central Committee was due in part to the rehabilitation of several Communists who had been purged following Kostov's downfall. Generals Boian Bulgaranov and Ivan Kinov were re-elected to full membership. As yet, however, these comebacks did not signify the rehabilitation of former Kostovites, for none of those involved had ever been directly accused of Kostovism.

The most striking change adopted by the Sixth Congress was the election of Todor Zhivkov as first secretary and the resulting curtailment of Chervenkov's personal domain. Why Chervenkov, the old *apparatchik,* chose the premiership instead of the party secretariat remains a moot point. It is plausible that the choice never lay with the Bulgarians. For the time being, however, Chervenkov's demotion within the ruling hierarchy was only nominal. His predominance over everyone else continued unhampered for at least two more years.[4]

Zhivkov's sudden elevation surprised the Bulgarians as much as it did the outside world. Zhivkov was a "dark horse" par excellence. At the time of his election he was in his early forties, the youngest first secretary in the Soviet bloc. A man of little formal education, he joined the Communist party in the 1930s while earning his livelihood as a printer's apprentice. He became a full-time functionary of the Sofia District party organization during the war, when he served as a liaison between the Sofia center and the "Chavdar" partisan brigade operating in the vicinity of the capital. The wartime link with the "Chavdar" people proved significant in later years. It gave the first secretary a certain reputation as a fighter which he augmented by ele-

---

[4] The full minutes of the Sixth Party Congress were eventually published in volume form as *Shesti kongres na BKP.*

vating many "Chavdar" partisans. Notable among the latter was the brigade's military commander, Dzhurov, who was to become Bulgaria's minister of defense. Immediately after the coup of September, 1944, Zhivkov was appointed commandant of the uniformed militia, a position which secured him a seat in the Central Committee as a candidate-member. He was elected to full membership in 1948 by the Fifth Party Congress. Zhivkov's career as a party functionary was built within the party apparatus of Sofia. In 1949 he was concurrently first secretary of the Sofia City party organization, president of the Sofia City organization of the Fatherland Front, and president of the Sofia City People's Council. In the following year, he joined the party secretariat, becoming a candidate-member of the Politburo. He attained full membership in the Politburo in 1951.

It soon became clear that the Bulgarians, who had always been responsive to developments in the Soviet Union, would not introduce fundamental changes while the question of the post-Stalin leadership in Moscow remained in doubt. As long as the Malenkov-Khrushchev combination lasted, Chervenkov was determined to continue as before. There were moderate changes in political style. Stress was placed on persuasion and the use of incentives rather than on coercion. Attempts were made to restore a degree of respectability to the bogus Agrarian Union, which, in the course of time, had become almost entirely submerged. In 1954 and early 1955, a number of former Agrarian leaders were freed from prison. They were put to use as speakers at peasant gatherings. Asen Pavlov, the Agrarian minister of agriculture during the first Fatherland Front government and a close collaborator of Petkov, was one of the more prominent figures within a large group of people who found themselves compelled by force of circumstance to enter the ranks of those who for many years had persecuted them.

A change in nuance and a series of minimal concessions were all that the regime was prepared to undertake. For a full year after the Sixth Party Congress the Bulgarians held firm. They remained subservient to Moscow and settled down to await developments. These came in quick succession. Among them, the downfall of Malenkov and the dramatic reconciliation between Khrushchev and Tito were the most significant signposts along the road that would culminate in the Twentieth Party Congress in Moscow and the famous secret speech.

The fateful gathering in Moscow found the Bulgarians out of step. First Secretary Zhivkov was not even included in the Bulgarian delegation, which was headed by Chervenkov, who also served as Bulgaria's official rapporteur.[5] The delegation to Moscow included Anton Yugov, then a deputy premier, Raiko Damianov, Dimitur Ganev, and Todor Zvezdov. The unexpected turn of events in Moscow was immediately reflected on the Bulgarian scene. Shortly after the delegation's return from Moscow, several steps were taken which pointed in the direction of the important changes that were soon to follow. At the beginning of March, the official party organ reprinted a *Pravda* article whose central theme was an attack against the cult of personality. This was followed by a number of editorials dealing with the same subject. At the same time, the regime announced its decision to call the National Assembly into an extraordinary session to be held in April. The importance of this decision was emphasized when the government made it known that an invitation to the opening of the extraordinary session had been extended to a Yugoslav parliamentary delegation. The climax came on April 8, 1956, when the Bulgarian party organ revealed that an extraordinary plenum of the Central Committee had been held in Sofia from April 2 to April 6. The plenum had reportedly been addressed by the party's first secretary, Todor Zhivkov, who had spoken on the significance of the Twentieth Party Congress. The same issue carried a long editorial which, after attacking Chervenkov, stated that, were it not for his personality cult, Bulgaria's achievements would have been much greater.[6]

Immediately after the plenum, top party leaders began visiting local party organizations throughout the country in an attempt to explain the new developments. It was at these meetings that the public was first informed of the substance of the plenum's decisions. On April 14, the party organ reported the contents of a speech delivered by Zhivkov at a meeting of party activists held in Sofia on April 11. Among other things, Zhivkov

[5] *Rabotnichesko delo,* February 17, 1956.
[6] *Ibid.,* April 8, 1956.

was reported to have stated that "a harmful consequence of the cult of the individual is a violation of legality. As a result, innocent comrades have been wrongly accused and condemned." Zhivkov went on to claim that the charges of criminal links with Yugoslavia raised against Kostov and those tried after him had been fabricated. These accusations were now rescinded, and all those detained in connection with the trials were freed. Zhivkov promised that in the future the Central Committee would be guided by the principle of strict observance of the concept of party collectivity. Significantly, Zhivkov did not speak of "rehabilitation," but stated simply that those involved in the Kostovite trials had been freed. Only later was the public informed of the creation of a special commission to investigate the issues involved in the trials. Since the conclusions of the commission would not be presented to the Central Committee until September, 1956, Zhivkov's April announcement indicated that the party had reached its decision to free the Kostovites before receiving the commission's report.

The extraordinary session of the National Assembly opened on April 16, 1956. The Yugoslav parliamentary delegation, headed by Mosa Pijade, attended the opening session. The Yugoslavs had not come in vain; they would witness Chervenkov's downfall. Chervenkov's resignation from the premiership was announced the day after the session opened. He was succeeded by Yugov, who, having survived his purge in the early fifties, now emerged victorious. Chervenkov was down but not out, however; he retained his position in the Politburo and was appointed deputy premier.

The April plenum, which came to be viewed by the Bulgarians as the equivalent of the Twentieth Party Congress in Moscow, represented no more than a minimal readjustment to the new spirits emanating from the Soviet capital. The link between this partial turnabout and the Yugoslavs was indirect, as was the connection between Belgrade and the rehabilitation of the Kostovites. It was clear from the outset that, in their recantation, the eyes of the Bulgarians were turned toward Moscow rather than toward Belgrade. For their part, the Yugoslavs welcomed the reconciliation with the Soviet Union, and insisted on visible evidence that the state of siege in which

Belgrade had been placed since 1948 had been lifted. Thus, the Bulgarians were compelled by their Russian overlords to pay a share of the price which the Soviet Union had promised Tito as part of a general undertaking to settle the Moscow-Belgrade dispute. Similarly, Yugoslavia's insistence that the Sofia leaders rehabilitate Kostov was aimed at punishing his executioners rather than at restoring the good name of Kostov. The latter had always been perceived by Tito as Yugoslavia's archenemy. Intricate as these relations had become, it was clear that Belgrade had chosen to use one of its dead enemies in order to disestablish its Sofia enemies who were still alive.

Following the April plenum, the Bulgarian press intensified its attacks against the cult of personality. Such utterances remained largely meaningless, however, for the political atmosphere in the country changed only slightly after Yugov's assumption of the premiership. The lack of democratization was best characterized by Vladimir Topencharov, the editor-in-chief of *Otechestven front* (the organ of the Fatherland Front), on May 5, 1956, when he called for a frank discussion of all questions and declared that fear of independent thinking had crushed intellectual initiative. Topencharov stated that dogmatism was being offered in the place of clearly formulated principles, theories in the place of honest analysis, and slogans in the place of serious consideration of important problems. The Yugov regime, however, was not ready to tolerate observations of this kind. Topencharov was admonished and was immediately forced to write an article of self-criticism. Even after his retraction he was dismissed.[7]

Just as the April plenum had been timed to coincide with the visit of the Yugoslav parliamentary delegation to Bulgaria, so the next step taken by the Bulgarian leaders came as a Bulgarian Communist party and government delegation was about to visit Yugoslavia. At the beginning of September, 1956, the Yugoslav news agency announced that a Bulgarian delegation, headed by First Secretary Todor Zhivkov, was due to arrive in Yugoslavia

[7] Topencharov was related to Kostov. His liberalized views were late in coming, however. In the forties, he had played an important role as one of the staunchest Communist intellectuals in the struggle against the Bulgarian opposition; on this, see Topencharov, *Istoriiata shte mine pokrai tiakh.*

on September 22. On September 19, Khrushchev arrived in Belgrade for a short visit. On the same day, the Bulgarian party organ published the text of two decisions made by the Bulgarian Central Committee at a plenum held a few days earlier.[8] It was stated that the plenum had convened to consider two problems: achievements in the area of combatting the cult of personality, and the report of a special commission appointed by the Central Committee in April, 1956, to investigate the Kostov trials. In the future, the decision stated, in order to guarantee the further strengthening of socialist legality, the work of the minister of the interior, the procurate, and the courts would be improved. The procurate's supervision of police work was to be tightened.

The second decision of the Central Committee dealt directly with the Kostov trials. Among other things, this decision stated that the Central Committee "approves the conclusions reached in the report of the commission empowered to review the Kostov trial and all the trials connected with the latter. Taking into account the fact that the above were convicted without any basis, the party restores to party membership all those who were convicted in connection with the so-called Kostov affair and considers proper that all those convicted in the above trials be also legally rehabilitated." This decision was intended to supplement the decisions made at the April plenum and thus to put an end to the whole Kostovite problem. Having been freed in April, those party members who had been convicted as Kostovites were now legally rehabilitated and restored to party membership.

Following this declaration, the Bulgarian delegation, headed by Zhivkov, proceeded with its visit to Yugoslavia. On their arrival in Belgrade, the Bulgarians were met by Pijade. Tito, who in the meantime had accompanied Khrushchev back to the Soviet Union, returned to Yugoslavia on September 27. Only on October 7, the eve of the delegation's return to Sofia and ten days after Tito's return from Moscow, did Tito receive the Bulgarians for a short audience. On the following day, the Yugoslav official organ published an article expressing the hope that, after the meetings between the Bulgarian and Yugoslav

[8] The full text of the two decisions appeared in *Rabotnichesko delo*, September 19, 1956.

Central Committee members, relations between the two countries would be improved. According to the semiofficial Yugoslav news agency, however, no meeting of minds between the Bulgarians and the Yugoslavs had been achieved. The Yugoslavs had decided to place the Bulgarians "on probation."

The process of deterrorization in Bulgaria, triggered by the Twentieth Party Congress and registered by the April, 1956, plenum, inevitably and unmistakably spilled over beyond the strict confines of the world of Bulgarian realpolitik. The Sofia bureaucrats were soon caught in the domestic crossfire of the Bulgarian Communist intelligentsia. The changeover in Moscow and the vacillations within the Bulgarian Politburo could not help but affect Bulgaria's literary world, which in turn contributed to the political ferment.

In the decade after 1944, the Communist regime fostered a new type of literature cast in the mold of socialist realism. This was perceived as an auxiliary instrument which was to help transform Bulgaria into a socialist country. The novel became the main vehicle of the new literary output, which was closely patterned after the stereotyped Stalinist literature in Russia. The immense volume of the new literature contrasted sharply with its literary value. Mediocrity characterized the creations of the new writers, who enjoyed generous state subsidies. There were a few exceptions which protruded through the blanket of boredom. Dimitur Dimov's *Tobacco,* published in 1951, was an outstanding example of the better type of novel produced during the period. Condemned at first by official censorship, *Tobacco* was eventually hailed as one of the finest Bulgarian novels. In the early fifties, while the terror was at its height, Chervenkov himself had come to realize that the quality of the new literature would have to be upgraded, even if this required slight concessions. A number of outstanding novelists of the interwar period were reinstated in the regime's good graces and were encouraged to write. Many of the literary classics from the period of Bulgaria's national revival and from the decades that followed her liberation from the Turks began to reappear in large, new editions. This controlled censorship underwent radical changes after 1955, and even more so after 1956.

Springing from within the Communist milieu, a new wave of

critical literature began to gather momentum in the mid-fifties. The Bulgarian writers did not go so far as their Polish and Hungarian colleagues did in the prerevolutionary ferment of 1955–56. Still, the Bulgarian dissidents undertook a sustained attack against some of the more stringent restrictions which they believed were leading the country into a state of moral bankruptcy. The more audacious among them began to accuse the official leadership of hypocrisy and dishonesty. They protested governmental interference and insisted on the legitimacy of forms of literary expression other than the socialist-realist type. Their protests and iconoclastic views were aired in literary "clubs," in private meetings, and occasionally in the press itself. Following the April plenum, at which Chervenkov had been demoted, the "rebels" demanded an extraordinary party congress to carry the program of the Twentieth Soviet Party Congress further than the regime had shown itself willing to go. This unprecedented demand indicated that the vanguard of the new liberal literati was prepared to invade political spheres and assault the very heartland of the official preserve.[9]

The leading figures in the Bulgarian writers' "rebellion" were Emil Manov, Todor Genov, Liuben Stanev, Stoian Daskalov, and Liudmil Stoianov. With the exception of Stanev, all were party members. The main forum for the expression of their views was the periodical *Plamuk,* launched by the Writer's Union at the outset of 1957. The protest spread, however, into more conservative literary organs, including the official *Literaturen front.*

The unorthodox and revisionist literature produced during the period of literary ferment had as its landmarks a number of creative pieces which aroused endless controversy. Emil Manov, in *An Unauthentic Case,* ably described the conflict between a higher party organization and a lower party unit over a decision connected with the expulsion of a member. Communist opportunism was vividly portrayed in a novel by Stanev called *The Laskov Family.* The lust for power by a once high-minded Communist who has risen high on the party ladder was the central theme of Todor Genov's play entitled *Fear.* The

[9] On the demand for an extraordinary party congress, see *East Europe,* March, 1958, p. 15.

exploitation of the poor by the rich in contemporary Communist society was the main subject of T. Nesnakomov's *Benefactors*. A short story by Kiril Toromanski, "Anna, the Comrade of the District," published in mid-1957, depicted a devoted Communist worker forced out of her job by a petty tyrant who ruled over the district party organization. These were but a few of the more outstanding literary deviations. Manov, an editor of *Plamuk*, emerged as one of the most outspoken rebels. His main contention was that the artist should be free in his choice of methods and in choosing among the prevalent ideological positions, provided that he remain basically "democratic." [10]

The literary turmoil was still gaining momentum when the Polish and Hungarian upheavals took place at the end of 1956. Fully aware of the significant role played by the intelligentsias of these two countries before and during the eruptions, Sofia's Communist officialdom became frightened. The Politburo closed ranks and resolved to fight a battle of retrenchment. In February, 1957, Chervenkov was called upon to head the Ministry of Education. He was reinforced by Todor Pavlov, the leading Bulgarian Marxist theoretician who, as head of the Academy of Sciences, had fostered the revival of a Bulgarian type of Zhdanovism. The official counterattack against the literary dissidents coincided with a new grand-scale purge. The labor camps, which had become somewhat depleted after 1955, began to be filled once again with an immense number of Communist as well as non-Communist doubtfuls who soon became known as the "Hungarian prisoners."

The purge spread to the uppermost echelons of the party hierarchy. In July, 1957, First Deputy Premier Georgi Chankov was dropped from his high-ranking official position and disgraced. He was the most prominent figure in the so-called counterparty group, which also included Dobri Terpeshev and Yonko Panov.[11] The harsh charges leveled against the three men remained vague. They were accused of having ganged together

10 On the writers' "rebellion" and their ultimate supression, see the following: "Bulgarian Writer's Revolt," *East Europe, ibid.*, pp. 15–23; "Texts and Documents," *ibid.*, September, 1957, pp. 47–48; and "Texts and Documents," *ibid.*, May, 1958, pp. 50–56. Brown, *Bulgaria under Communist Rule*, chap. 11, provides the best survey and analysis of the entire cultural scene under communism.
11 *Rabotnichesko delo*, July 17, 1957.

to subvert party discipline in order to impose their own leadership. Chankov was somewhat of a star, having made a good record for himself during the underground years and the period after 1944. He had been a leading functionary of the Communist youth organization and as such had been sent to Moscow in the mid-thirties for further training. After the outbreak of the Second World War he found himself in a concentration camp, but succeeded in escaping sometime around 1943 and joined the underground. Immediately after September, 1944, Chankov joined the Politburo and became one of the three party secretaries (together with Kostov and Chervenkov) in charge of the Cadres Department. He successfully sailed through the purges of the late forties, gathering ever-increasing power. Chankov may well have resented Zhivkov's rise to the top. Since his motives and his particular stand on the political issues of the day were never made clear, it is quite plausible that Chankov attempted to supplant Zhivkov by jumping to the head of the long waiting line. Whether or not he "conspired" with his two fellow victims remains unclear.

Terpeshev, on the other hand, was a genuine old revolutionary. He enjoyed authentic popularity within the party and without, even though his folkish manners and countryside style had more than once brought him ridicule. His demotion in the aftermath of the Kostov trial has already been related. Terpeshev succeeded in making a partial comeback, first as Bulgaria's ambassador to Bucharest and later as commandant of the civil defense organization set up in the early fifties. At the time of his downfall, however, he was not a member of the Politburo.

Panov was a different type altogether. In the mid-thirties, he had sided with the left sectarian opposition and had been one of the leading spokesmen against Dimitrov and Kolarov's old guard. As late as December, 1948, at the Fifth Party Congress, Panov had gathered enough courage to stand up and defend the positive revolutionary qualities of the left sectarians. By that time, he had rejoined the victorious majority. Having established a good resistance record during the war, he had earned the post of commander of all the border-guard units after 1944.

With the purge of these three men, one more fragment of the historic party was chipped off. Chankov's ambitions and the colorful and somewhat original personalities of the other two were probably too much for the ruling coalition, which in mid-1957 set itself the goal of restoring the threatened Communist bureaucracy to its former position by means of new terror.

Throughout the remainder of 1957 and much of 1958, the Communist regime came to realize that, while political unity could be restored by the use of administrative constraints, "unity of the mind" among Communist intellectuals and artists was not so easily attainable. Having been ousted, the so-called antiparty group, headed by Chankov, remained silent as far as the public at large was concerned. The many thousands of newly arrested who repopulated the labor camps and the various places of detention became nonpersons. Only years later would their dreadful fate be pieced together by word of mouth voiced in private following their gradual release. At the same time, it became obvious that the literary ferment had all but flooded the inner bastions of the regime's own cultural domain. Between February, 1956, and February, 1957, the period of Chervenkov's political eclipse, a large proportion of the well-established men of letters found themselves manning the barricades of literary opposition. Many had become intoxicated by the sudden release of emotional energies made possible by an uncertain censorship.

The quick repairs made by Chervenkov after February, 1957, in the somewhat flexible ideological lines of the party gradually brought about a new stifling atmosphere. Still, the "rebellious" literati were not ready to surrender unconditionally. Their answer to the mounting threats and intimidations was a "silence strike," not unlike that of the Hungarian writers under Kádár. This tactic of passive resistance infuriated the regime's reactionaries. On October 17, 1956, an article in *Literaturen front* charged the irreconcilable writers with using silence as a form of argument. "It is not a question of writers being passive and aloof out of private reasons, but of exploiting 'silence' as a means of opposing Party views on literature. These writers are not really silent at all; on the contrary, they are very talkative and 'heroic,' when they speak from their own rostrums, over a glass of wine in homes, in the two clubs and certain editorial offices." The same article accused the dissidents of having assumed the posture of martyrs. It went on to remind the writers that "everybody is free to write and say what he pleases. . . . However, every free union of people, including the Party, is free to expel members who use the Party label to preach anti-Party views. . . . The borderline between what is pro-Party and what is anti-Party will be determined by the Party program, by the tactical Party resolutions and Party statutes. . . . This is how things will be in our Party, gentlemen—adherence of bourgeois 'freedom of criticism.'" In the October 24 issue of the same periodical, Emil Manov wrote in defense of his ideas that the message he had wanted to convey was simply that "sometimes man is more important than the institution" and that "our theory—that man is the goal for which our society struggles—must not be separated from our practice, even in special cases." The latter exchanges were typical of the vein in which the debate was carried out in the latter part of 1957.

At the beginning of 1958, Vladimir Topencharov, the man who had spearheaded the oppositionists' outcry after the April, 1956, plenum, lost the office of president of the Bulgarian Union of Journalists. In February, the editorial board of the official party philosophical monthly, *Filosofska misul*, was criticized for its revisionist views. A wholesale purge of the writers' elite took place in April, 1958, at a meeting of the Union of Writers. Eight members of the union's board, including Manov and the old-time Communist writer Orlin Vasilev, were dropped from their official positions, while five of the six members of the union's secretariat failed to be re-elected. In May, the regime scored its greatest victory by extracting a mild and dignified apology from Emil Manov. Following the Seventh Party Congress in June, 1958, Chervenkov left the Ministry of Education and Culture. He had successfully restored order among the unruly intellectuals. Although the situation on the literary front would never revert to what it had been in pre-1954 days, the refreshing uproar which many a novelist, playwright, and short-story writer had created had come to an end.

There is little doubt that the early curtailment of the Bulgarian intellectuals' "revolt" owed as much to the turn of events in Hungary and Poland as to the onslaught of the party bureaucracy. The revolutionary upheavals in Hungary and Poland and their ultimate suppression precluded a successful outcome for the cause for which the "rebellious" Bulgarian intellectuals had become spokesmen. Although grown on native soil, the ferment in Bulgaria had been nourished and encouraged by the widespread critique which developed in Hungary and Poland. The moment the strength of counterrevolution was brought to bear upon the freedom-seeking elements in both countries, the fate of the Bulgarian experiment was sealed. The march of the Red Army into Budapest had frightened the party leadership and had made possible Chervenkov's partial return to power.

Although not lacking in courage, the Bulgarian writers had never challenged the legitimacy of Communist authority. At no time was there even a hint of anti-Sovietism in their utterings. They were preoccupied with general problems that touched on elementary humanism in the conduct of politics and they criticized the political behavior of the bureaucracy. In a deeper sense, they endeavored to verbalize the exhaustion of a people who had labored for more than a decade under conditions of extreme strain and trepidation. Although they never expressed it in so many words, the best and the most sensitive of the intellectuals were silently crying for a slowdown in the rate of change which the rulers had mercilessly imposed upon the populace. In many ways, this was the real challenge which they presented to the ruling political elite. This challenge ran counter to the firmly established traditions of Bulgarian communism, which, in addition to its dogmatism and unbending orthodoxy, had persistently counterposed itself to Bulgaria's material backwardness and the poverty of her people. Because of her dependence on, and servility to, Russia and the Bolsheviks, Bulgaria's urge to catch up with the advanced nations had been blurred in the eyes of the outside world. It is doubtful whether so many thousands of Bulgarians—and by no means the worst among them—would have placed their trust in the tenets of communism before and after 1944 had the tacit promise of modernization and greater wealth not been made by the Communist party.

The Seventh Party Congress, held in June, 1958, proved an uneventful affair. It approved the Third Five-Year Plan, which was moderate compared to the economic experiences of the past.

Hardly had the new plan been announced, however, when, in October of the same year, the press launched a widespread harangue calling for the fulfillment of the Five-Year Plan "in three to four years." At the end of 1958 the Central Committee approved a radical upward revision of the planned economic targets. The new goals were made public in the so-called Zhivkov Theses published via the press in January, 1959. The total volume of industrial production, according to Zhivkov, was to increase twofold by 1962, and from three- to fourfold by 1965, over the volume in 1957. In agriculture, the theses provided that the value of production in 1959 be twice as large as it had been in 1958, and three times as large in 1960. This was the beginning of the Bulgarian "great leap forward," a term which the Bulgarians adopted freely from the Chinese experiment.[12]

The new targets were as fantastic as was the energy required in order for the people to reach them. The nation was pushed into an unparalleled frenzy of activity. The press, the mass media, and, above all, the officials of the Agitation and Propaganda Department set out to stimulate mass enthusiasm for the cause. The uproar resembled that which was produced by Stalin in Russia in the early thirties. The campaign demanded social mobilization of a magnitude and depth unprecedented in the experience of Communist Bulgaria. This was the antithesis of what the liberal writers had sought only a short time earlier. Instead of being relaxed, the social fabric was further tightened until it threatened to tear.[13]

The Bulgarian "great leap forward" stood in sharp dissonance with developments in the other countries within the Soviet bloc. For a time, it appeared as if the Chinese revolution had spilled over into the Balkans. Unlike Albania, whose attachment to Peking was motivated largely by considerations of realpolitik rather than by economic motives, Bulgaria was copying the very technique of Mao's impatient reach for modernization. In October, 1958, Chervenkov led a parliamentary delegation to

[12] Zhivkov, *Za uskoriavane razvitieto na narodnoto stopanstvo* . . . and *Po niakoi osnovni vuprosi na nashata partina i obshtestvena rabota.*

[13] The best analysis of the "great leap forward" in Bulgaria, its targets, its execution, and its ultimate fate, is contained in Brown, *Bulgaria under Communist Rule,* chap. 5; the author is greatly indebted to this work for much of the economic discussion which follows.

Communist China. This identified him and his fellow conservatives with the new frenzy. The man in the street, who had little or no knowledge of the processes of decision-making within the Politburo, began to speak of "the China faction" in the Bulgarian Communist leadership. Indeed, at first, Chinese slogans and modes of action were often borrowed and used by the mass media. Only when the Sino-Soviet dispute erupted openly did Chervenkov make a consistent effort to dissociate Bulgaria's endeavors from those of Peking.

The motives behind the "great leap forward" consisted of a melange of political and economic considerations. Of the two, the former were secondary. For many a Bulgarian functionary, particularly those bred and raised in Stalinist schools, the pragmatic, erratic nature of Khrushchev's style of work could not be easily assimilated. This was particularly true of Chervenkov, though not of him alone. A certain quiet admiration for Mao's manner of political conduct had become moderately evident in many of the East European Communist parties. In this sense, the Bulgarians were not an exception, although their temperamental affinity with the seriousness, solidity, and revolutionary dignity of the Chinese was more pronounced. Within the leadership, Chervenkov was probably the most conspicuous, but by no means the sole, exponent of an instinctive, if not a natural, inclination toward the Chinese revolution. A feeling of mutual antipathy between Khrushchev and Chervenkov was accepted by all as a given fact. Since the former's rise to power had contributed to, if not caused, the latter's relative eclipse, it was natural that Chervenkov be in the forefront of those who adopted the new orientations.

Still, it is doubtful whether preferences in style alone would have sufficed to make the Bulgarians emulate Peking. There were, from the outset, compelling economic reasons which led the Bulgarian leadership to turn to the Chinese example. Foremost among them was the embarrassing rate of unemployment which had become epidemic in the Bulgarian economy. In the second half of the fifties, the unemployed numbered about 350,000. They were a painful symptom of the great scarcity of capital which had always haunted Bulgaria. The collectivization and mechanization of agriculture had created a large surplus of labor within the rural population, but industrial growth had not been sufficient to provide enough jobs for their absorption into the urban sector. For several years the Bulgarians had tried a number of unorthodox methods aimed at utilizing at least part of the surplus. These had ranged from the massive employment of civilians in a variety of jobs within the military sector, to the import of raw cotton from Russia for processing in the Bulgarian textile industry and eventual re-export to the Soviet Union, to the dispatch of thousands of young Bulgarians to the Soviet Union for employment in various projects there. The unorthodox undertakings had somewhat mitigated the acute problem, but they had not resolved it.

It was in this context that the Chinese example appealed to the Bulgarian planners, and even more so to the Communist leaders of the old radical band. The Chinese experiment appeared to offer an easy way of converting surplus labor into a capital resource to be applied in yet one more push of the rickety, half-primitive, half-modern economic machine. In addition, there were structural deficiencies in the economy which the "great leap forward" was meant to remedy in haste. During the first decades of Communist rule the Russians had shied away from applying the principles of an international division of labor to the countries within their domain. The Bulgarians, along with the other East European countries, proceeded to reproduce the Soviet model by developing all branches of industry parallel to those in the remaining socialist countries. With Khrushchev's rise to power, however, and particularly after 1956, the Bulgarian economy was called upon to specialize more and more, within the framework of the Comecon. Bulgaria was allotted an ambitious quota of fruit and vegetables for export to the Soviet bloc in semiprocessed and processed form. The "great leap forward" provided for a restructuring of the agricultural economy away from production of wheat and other grains and toward greater specialization in those edible commodities in which the Comecon market was interested. Thus, capital investment in the agricultural sector was increased radically.

The production norms set up in January, 1959, were, of course, not attainable. It is altogether doubtful whether they were ever taken seriously by Zhivkov and his comrades. Whatever else may be said of the campaign, the "great leap forward" did help reduce very substantially the rate of unemployment. The targets of production, however, were never even remotely reached. While the campaign was still in full swing, the Bulgarians quietly but skillfully changed their semantics in an effort to accommodate their rhetoric to reality. While the original Zhivkov Theses had called for more than a doubling of the volume of production, later in the campaign, references began to be made to doubling the rates of growth in the various sectors. The substitution of rate of growth for volume made all the difference. Even those who possessed only the most elementary understanding of economic matters did not fail to notice the shrewd switch. Yet, the semantic deception was carried out openly, and no attempt was made to explain to the Bulgarian public and to those in the outside world who were interested the crucial modification of the "great leap forward."

Having decided to swap horses in midstream, at the end of 1960 the regime proceeded to claim credit for itself by announcing that the Third Five-Year Plan had indeed been fulfilled, and two years ahead of schedule. The truth was that the actual progress made was not very different from the progress prescribed for the first three years of the Five-Year Plan as originally published. After terming the entire experiment an unqualified success, the Politburo hastened to shelve the undertaking and reverted to the more traditional forms of economic planning. By that time, the Sino-Soviet dispute had come into the open, and the slogans of the Chinese revolution had become altogether inappropriate. Despite some initial hesitation, the Bulgarian leadership as a group, including Chervenkov, faithfully joined Moscow in the barrage of insults and harangues aimed at the Chinese.

The "great leap forward" was the last major undertaking carried out by the factional triumvirate made up of Chervenkov, Zhivkov, and Yugov. The anticlimax came at the end of 1960, at which point the frenzied undertaking was wound up. In the absence of any tangible results from the massive effort into which the entire country had been mercilessly thrown, a feeling

146

of disappointment, helplessness, and widespread bitterness was inevitable.

For their part, the Russians came to realize that the erratic behavior of their Bulgarian protégés had gone too far. The swing between the liberal reaction of 1956–57 and the super-orthodoxy of 1959–60 was much too sharp in Moscow's eyes. While experimentalist by temperament, Khrushchev was less inclined to underwrite tactical vacillations in a vassal country than in his own house. He therefore proceeded to give his unhesitating support to that faction to which he felt personally most akin. Indeed, after two long years of stepped-up revolutionary change, the Bulgarians reverted to the most traditional activities—political infighting and the pursuit of personal power. In the period of a single year, between November, 1961, and November, 1962, the party triumvirate was dismantled. Backed by Moscow, Zhivkov successfully disposed first of Chervenkov and later of Yugov and his followers. For a man as lacking in distinction as Zhivkov was, this was a remarkable political performance. In a sense, his greatest asset was precisely his mediocrity. The Russians were perfectly satisfied to see their most secure Balkan fortress in the hand of an average man who was fully dependent on their will.

The initial blow fell on the "reformists." The strains produced by the "great leap forward" had, from the outset, taxed the unity of the party leadership. Early in 1959, Boris Taskov, the minister of trade, was dismissed from his government post. In April of the same year, he was dropped from the Politburo and the Central Committee. His downfall was the most conspicuous purge since the assault against the "antiparty group" in July, 1957. Taskov was accused of having deviated from the party line and of having cast doubt on the party's ability to carry out the "great leap forward." The pressure on the "reformists" continued to be maintained after the "great leap forward" had come to an end. In the early spring of 1961, Nikola Kufardzhiev, a secretary of the Central Council of Trade Unions, was publicly disgraced and purged. Somewhat belatedly, his name was linked with those of Terpeshev and Panov. A number of district party secretaries were expelled as well. The accusations made against all of them were that they had adopted foreign revisionist solutions and had tried to force them on the Bulgarian party. In May, 1961, Todor Prakhov, chairman of the Central Council of Trade Unions, and a number of lesser-known secretaries were dismissed from their posts. Although Prakhov's specific personal affiliations remained obscure, it was obvious that the trade-union organization had become a shelter, if not a fortress, for the more moderate elements of the opposition within the party leadership who had begun to criticize the extreme nature of the leadership's political behavior.

The dogmatists came next. The Twenty-Second Party Congress in Moscow, which constituted a sharp turning point in the Sino-Soviet dispute and marked the final expulsion of Albania from the Soviet bloc, became the main forum for Zhivkov's assault on the superorthodox faction within the party's top leadership. At the Central Committee plenum held at the end of November, 1961, a full month after the Twenty-Second Party Congress in Moscow had ended, Chervenkov's fate was finally sealed. He was dismissed from the Politburo and the Central Committee, as well as from his post as deputy premier. The accusations against him were lengthy. He was charged with consistent disobedience and vicious methods of work, which he had persistently manifested before and after the April, 1956, plenum. He had overstepped Leninist legality and had disregarded the elementary interests of the Bulgarian peasants and their rightful political spokesman, the bogus Agrarian Union. Portraying Dimitrov as Bulgaria's Lenin and Chervenkov as Bulgaria's Stalin, Zhivkov drew a contrasting picture between the two men, much as Khrushchev had done earlier. Chervenkov did not recant his mistakes and indulge in self-criticism. His remaining authority within the party apparatus was made fully evident by the large-scale purge of lesser provincial functionaries carried out in the following months.

The same plenum which had purged Chervenkov had also elevated to full membership in the Politburo Stanko Todorov and Mitko Grigorov, two of Zhivkov's staunchest supporters. In May, 1962, Khrushchev visited Bulgaria as head of a large party and government delegation. The aim of the visit was to support Zhivkov against his domestic opponents. Khrushchev undertook an extensive tour of the country, delivering his famous pep talks, which overflowed with compliments to the Bulgarian first secretary. The Soviet leader pressed for greater harmony between Bulgaria and Yugoslavia, a subject high on his agenda, particularly in view of the great effort being made by Moscow to reach a new rapprochement with Belgrade. Finally, Khrushchev went out of his way to praise the Bulgarian Agrarian Union, then numbering 120,000 members, and Georgi Traikov, the architect of peasant support for the Communist regime. In 1964, following the death of Dimitur Ganev, Traikov was made titular head of state by being appointed chairman of the Presidium of the National Assembly.

The Eighth Party Congress, originally scheduled for August, 1962, was finally convened in November of that year. It proved an amazing gathering, not so much because of Zhivkov's assumption of supreme power, but because of the way in which the disposal of the last residue of opposition was effected. In the months that preceded the congress, several indicators marked Yugov as the next political victim. As early as March, 1962, Georgi Tsankov, Yugov's personal protégé, had lost his post as minister of the interior. His promotion to the position of a deputy premier did not conceal the significance of his removal from one of the most powerful ministries, which he had headed since 1951.

At the end of October, only a few days before the opening of the congress, the party held a special plenum at which it was presumably announced that Zhivkov would assume the premiership in addition to retaining his position as first secretary, which he had held since 1954. The plenum was then interrupted by Zhivkov's departure for Moscow to confer personally with Khrushchev. Zhivkov returned to Sofia on November 3 and reconvened the plenary session. When the congress opened on November 5, Zhivkov announced the ouster of Yugov as premier. Yugov and Tsankov were dropped from the Central Committee, and Chervenkov was expelled from the party's ranks. Yugov's many sins, real and presumed, were recounted in detail by the first secretary and by a number of Politburo members before a stunned congress. He was publicly ridiculed for his cowardice during the wartime Communist resistance, and for

his cruelty as Bulgaria's first Communist minister of the interior
(1944–48).[14]

These revelations supplied valuable information to the contemporary historian of Bulgarian politics. For the Bulgarian
public, however, Yugov's cruelty and that of his lieutenants in
the Ministry of the Interior and in the People's Militia required
no documentation or verification. Yugov's downfall came as no
great surprise. The only remarkable feature of his purge was
that it occurred only a few hours before the Eighth Party Congress convened. This, together with Zhivkov's hurried trip to
Moscow, indicated the first secretary's ineptness and the devastating degree of his dependence on Bulgaria's real masters. It
was obvious that Yugov and his colleagues had fought bitterly
to the end to gain support within the Central Committee. In
fact, the quarrel had spilled over into the provinces, particularly
into the regional party organization of Plovdiv, where Yugov
had erected a powerful personal following which dated back to
his days as a Communist organizer of tobacco workers in the
latter part of the thirties.

Having won his dubious victory, Zhivkov proceeded to make
a clean slate for himself. The technique of bunching together
all those who were purged, irrespective of their individual
political inclinations, was once again resorted to. Yugov was
accused of having consorted with Chervenkov, as well as with
the people of the "antiparty group," which had been purged
as early as 1957. "Reformists" and dogmatists were all placed
under the same roof. The various security organs of the state,
where Yugov's personal influence had predominated for many
years, were cleansed and brought under the tighter control of
the new Politburo. The purge of the purgers was a device of
great convenience which the Bulgarians could copy from the
rich Soviet experience.

The remaking of Bulgaria by the Communists modified but
did not completely change some of the age-old characteristics
of that Balkan country. Because of the smallness of the country,
its political heights had always been overcrowded with people

[14] *Rabotnichesko delo,* November 6, 1962, reproduces Zhivkov's report before
the congress. Details of the purge of Yugov were pieced together from information
made public at the congress itself.

of ambition who engaged in relentless strife in an attempt to exert influence on the country's development. If smallness was the cause of political overcrowdedness, the latter was the cause of a degree of overt intimacy in the country's political processes. Personal intimacy and familiarity have always mingled with personal rivalries nourished by long memories of having worked together. These maladies had been epidemic in the political parties of the interwar period, and the Communists were no exception.

Regionalism, always a significant factor in the Bulgarian political context, constituted another important element in the character of Bulgaria's body politic. A degree of regional particularism persisted despite the supercentralism fostered by the Communist regime. This factor protruded once again in the mid-sixties in a bizarre, abortive conspiracy which intrigued the world and confirmed the resilience of the deeply rooted political mores. In April, 1965, the regime announced the uncovering of a conspiracy directed against it. Collusion between a number of middle-rank Communist functionaries and several general officers of the army's political administration had produced a plot aimed against Zhivkov's hegemony. Somewhat embarrassed by the sudden resurrection of the history-long phenomenon of putschism, the regime revealed neither the true motives of the conspirators nor the details of the plot. In true Balkan fashion, the affair ended with the suicide of the chief conspirator and the trial and conviction of his collaborators. From the meager evidence supplied by official sources, it is clear that the threat to the regime was never imminent. Prompted by the palace revolution which had overthrown Khrushchev in the Soviet Union, the Bulgarian would-be-putschists had made a similar attempt against their first secretary.

From beginning to end, the conspiracy seemed to be an intraparty affair. The implication of a number of army men in the plot was of interest largely because of the apparent connection between the April plot and the perennial nature of military intervention in Bulgarian politics throughout the country's modern history. Whether the conspirators, had they been successful, would have launched Bulgaria on a course of liberalization or on a course of superorthodoxy (in the pattern set by the

Chinese) continues to be a moot point. As it was, the affair remained no more than a single incident in the otherwise dull and eventless decade that followed the double purge of the early sixties.

In November, 1966, the Communist party held its Ninth Congress. The gathering followed a predetermined course and produced no surprises. Zhivkov, retaining his dual function as first secretary and premier, revealed himself to be a man of caution and a functionary of growing experience, with which his long tenure could not fail to provide him. In order to placate the veteran Communists who had remained unrepresented since the purge of Chervenkov and Yugov, two elderly Communist leaders were added to the newly elected Politburo. These were Todor Pavlov, Bulgaria's renowned Marxist theoretician of a clear Stalinist bent, and Tsola Dragoicheva, the veteran female Communist who had headed the National Council of the Fatherland Front after 1944, but who had sunk into relative political obscurity following the purge of the Kostovites. On the other hand, Mitko Grigorov, the young and aspiring party intellectual whom Zhivkov had brought into the inner circle after the 1962 purges, was dropped from the Politburo without explanation. His undoing was probably the result of too great a degree of personal ambition. Otherwise, the Ninth Party Congress did little that could be classified as remarkable or memorable.

In September, 1962, the party publicized the draft directives of a Twenty-Year Plan of Economic Development that had been closely patterned after the Twenty-Year Plan of the Communist party of the Soviet Union. Although ambitious in its over-all scope, the new plan envisaged no overly pretentious achievements such as had been projected during the "great leap forward." Industrial priorities remained high on the agenda, with special emphasis being placed on the construction and expansion of heavy industry. The Bulgarian economy was committed to the development of a number of gigantic industrial complexes, the most conspicuous of which was the Kremikovski combine for the production of pig iron and steel. In agriculture, wheat and tobacco, the two traditional hard-currency earners, were to be denied priority in favor of the intensive and specialized agricultural production of fruits and vegetables. A moderate but steady increment in the general population's standard of living was stipulated. As before, services would receive relatively moderate attention, even though much effort would be devoted to the further development of the tourist industry, which was to become a major hard-currency earner. Essentially, the Twenty-Year Plan was a prescription for the future. Its implementation depended on a large number of circumstances, not all of which were under the control of the planners.

7: NATIONALISM, CONSTITUTIONALISM, AND THE RULE OF THE PARTY

In November, 1968, the Historical Institute of the Bulgarian Academy of Sciences published *The Macedonian Problem: Historical-Political Aspects,* which set forth in detail the Bulgarian position on the Macedonian question.[1] For the first time, the Bulgarian party leadership undertook to deal comprehensively with some of the earlier inconsistencies in the party's attitude toward Macedonia by declaring the party's interwar position, which, on occasion, had advocated Macedonian self-determination, a mistake.

The document began by castigating Yugoslavia for distorting history in order to prove the existence of a Macedonian nationality. Yugoslavia was accused of attempting to denationalize the Bulgarians of Macedonia by denying them and their prominent figures and heroes their Bulgarian nationality, and by asserting the historical existence of a Macedonian Slav state separate from Bulgaria. The document then turned to historical evidence to

[1] The document was first published in booklet form by the Bulgarian Academy of Sciences in November, 1968. The material was used as the basis for a series of Radio Sofia broadcasts for Bulgarians abroad. The booklet was not made available to the general public, but was distributed as background material to party activists. On February 4, 1969, however, it was published in *Pirinsko delo,* the semiweekly newspaper of the Pirin District (the Bulgarian part of Macedonia). On February 10, Radio Zagreb announced that the Commission for Foreign Affairs of the Macedonian (Skoplje) Parliament had denounced the illegal distribution of the pamphlet within Yugoslavia. An English-language version of the booklet appeared in *Radio Free Europe Research* (Munich), February 17, 1969.

prove that Macedonia was solely a geographical area, not an ethnic or national entity. Historical sources were cited which referred to the Bulgarian nature and leadership of the uprisings that had occurred in Macedonia, as well as in the rest of Bulgaria, after the country had fallen under Byzantine rule. Likewise, the document claimed that the development of a Bulgarian nation and of the Bulgarian national liberation struggle in the eighteenth and nineteenth centuries, under Turkish rule, occurred in Macedonia, as well as in the rest of Bulgaria, and that several of the leaders of the Bulgarian national awakening were Macedonians. Macedonian personalities who had struggled on behalf of the Bulgarian nation and against the Hellenization of the Macedonian population, and who had ultimately proudly proclaimed themselves Bulgarians were cited. Much was made of the participation of Macedonians in the Bulgarian uprisings against the Turks.

Following the Russo-Turkish war and Bulgaria's deliverance from Turkish rule, the Peace Treaty of San Stefano included Macedonia within the frontiers of Bulgaria. According to the Bulgarian Academy of Sciences, Britain, Germany, and Austro-Hungary, fearful of a large Bulgaria, which might become dominated by Russia, rejected the treaty and imposed instead the Berlin Treaty, which excluded Macedonia and other areas from the Bulgarian state. By breaking up the nation, the document continued, the Berlin Treaty had caused the Macedonian problem and many of the conflicts in the Balkans.

Under the centuries-long Turkish rule, the people of Macedonia and Odrin Thrace suffered national oppression and economic discrimination, which ultimately led to an organized liberation effort. The leaders of the Macedonian-Odrin revolutionary movement possessed a Bulgarian national consciousness and were influenced in no small measure by Dimitur Blagoev and the Bulgarian Social Democratic party. Despite the existence of a Bulgarian national consciousness and the predominance of Bulgarians among the population of Macedonia, the organization sought autonomy for Macedonia and Odrin rather than union with Bulgaria, in order to avoid the intervention of the imperialist countries and conflict among the Balkan states.

Having achieved autonomy, Macedonia could more easily become part of Bulgaria.

According to official Turkish statistics, around 1900 approximately 52 percent of the people in Macedonia were Bulgarians. The figures made no reference to a Macedonian ethnic group. Other statistics confirmed as well that around the same time more than half the population was Bulgarian. The Bulgarian Academy of Sciences reminded its readers that Dimitur Blagoev and Georgi Dimitrov were of Macedonian origin but considered themselves Bulgarians.

After the Second Balkan War, most of Macedonia was seized by Serbia and Greece. During the First World War, the people of Macedonia welcomed the Bulgarian army as a liberator. After the war, the Vardar and Odrin Aegean areas of Macedonia became part of Yugoslavia and Greece, respectively, while the population was subjected to assimilation campaigns by both governments. Only when it had become obvious that the Bulgarians were unassimilable did Yugoslavia begin to claim the existence of a separate Macedonian nationality which was neither Bulgarian nor Serb.

Following the Second World War, Aegean and Vardar Macedonia remained parts of Greece and Yugoslavia, respectively, Vardar as a Macedonian republic within Yugoslavia. Belgrade denied the Bulgarian character of the people and their language, despite the fact that the dialects of Macedonia are part of the Bulgarian language.

The early Bulgarian Communist party position, which advocated self-determination for Macedonia, was now labeled "incorrect" and "non-Leninist" by the Bulgarian Academy of Sciences, since the majority of the population of Macedonia was Bulgarian. The current Bulgarian Communist party and regime recognized the Socialist Republic of Macedonia as part of Yugoslavia, but opposed Yugoslavia's distortions of history and her attempts to denationalize the Macedonian Bulgarians and turn them against Bulgaria and Bulgarian culture. These endeavors were seen as violations of Marxist-Leninist principles on the nationality question and as injuries to Bulgarian-Yugoslav relations.

The document was less significant for its content than for the timing of its publication and its official nature. The historiographic exposé and the principles outlined were not new. They had been repeated on numerous occasions during the years of Communist rule. This time, however, the Bulgarian Communist regime, using the Bulgarian Academy of Sciences as its mouthpiece, made a definitive and determined effort to set down and delineate the dichotomy between the political nature of the question involved and the nationality principle. While the requirements of international politics could not be overlooked at any given stage, the Bulgarians could not compromise on the essence of the national problem, which stipulated that Macedonia was a part of Bulgaria's heartland and indivisible from the metropole. The uproar which the document produced in official and scholarly circles in Belgrade and Skoplje was tremendous.

In the years following publication of the document, discussion continued to center on the age-old historical and theoretical aspects of the issue. Once again, in 1971 controversy arose with the appearance of an article in the Bulgarian press which reasserted the Bulgarian nationality of the Macedonians. The article brought a sharp response from the Yugoslav press, which accused Bulgaria of irredentism. With increased frequency, Bulgaria began broadcasting material on the subject of Macedonia through Radio Sofia's Rodina program for Bulgarians living abroad. These programs continued to discuss the Bulgarian nationality of the Macedonians, insisted that Bulgarian culture be made more readily available to the people of Yugoslav Macedonia, and repeatedly recalled Bulgaria's assistance to the Yugoslav partisans after September 9, 1944. For its part, the Yugoslav press denounced not only Bulgaria's territorial designs but also her "greater Bulgarian chauvinistic indoctrination" of Pirin Macedonia and the jamming of Radio Skoplje's broadcasts to the Pirin District.

Despite the polemics, economic ties between Bulgaria and Yugoslavia tightened with the conclusion of a goods-exchange protocol in November, 1971, and, soon thereafter, a tourism protocol as well. The remarkable feature of the latter was that it was signed in both Bulgarian and Macedonian. Prior to this, Bulgaria had refused to sign documents presented by Yugoslavia in Macedonian, so as to avoid implying recognition of the existence of a Macedonian nationality. Other indicators of a desire to improve relations were remarks voiced around the same time by Bulgarian leaders and the press concerning further technical cooperation between the two countries and the development of good-neighbor relations. On December 21, 1971, the Radio Rodina broadcasts were ended. Since these broadcasts had been a source of controversy with Yugoslavia, their discontinuance represented a further step in improving relations with Yugoslavia. The shift in relations was probably connected with Brezhnev's visit to Yugoslavia and his stopover in Bulgaria in September, 1971. Bulgaria's efforts to improve relations with Yugoslavia and her other Balkan neighbors were undoubtedly part of the Soviet Union's policy of détente in Europe. In pursuit of this policy, Moscow began seeking closer ties with Greece and Turkey, thus loosening the NATO alliance, while attempting to maintain and strengthen its ties among the Eastern bloc countries. Although the Soviet Union desires improved relations with Yugoslavia, it is not in her interest to put a complete end to the Macedonian issue, which might become exploitable once again in a post-Tito Yugoslavia torn by nationalist discord.

In 1971, the Bulgarian Communist regime turned its attention to yet another basic issue which had lingered on unresolved for a very long time. A new constitution, the first in a generation, was drafted, debated, and finally adopted. From 1879 until 1946, Bulgaria was governed by the Turnovo Constitution. During this time, the Constitution had been revised twice, suspended twice, and violated on numerous occasions. According to the Turnovo Constitution, Bulgaria would be set up as a constitutional monarchy with a parliamentary government based on the principle of separation of powers. Executive powers belonged to the king, but could be exercised only through the ministers, whose appointment had to be approved by Parliament. Legislative power was shared by the king and Parliament, which consisted of the Ordinary National Assembly and the Grand National Assembly. The former was elected by universal suffrage; the latter was convened only in extraordinary circumstances. Judicial power belonged to the courts, but the power to interpret laws rested with Parliament. The Turnovo Constitution also included provisions guaranteeing civil liberties.

Upon seizing power in September, 1944, the Fatherland Front government declared its adherence to the Turnovo Constitution. In fact, power was exercised by the Ministries of the Interior and of Justice, the political commissars of the army, and the National Committee of the Fatherland Front.[2]

Soon after consolidating power, the Communists held a plebescite (September 8, 1946), which declared Bulgaria a republic. On October 27, 1946, elections were held for a Grand National Assembly which was to prepare a new constitution. This was the last election in which the "tolerated opposition," headed by Nikola Petkov, was allowed to participate. The first draft of the new Constitution, known as the Dimitrov Constitution, which appeared in May, 1947, preserved many of the liberal principles of the Turnovo Constitution. By the time the final draft was presented in November, the opposition in the Assembly had been silenced, Petkov had been executed, and the new Constitution had been transformed into what was almost a copy of the Soviet "Stalin" Constitution of 1936. In December, 1947, the Dimitrov Constitution was approved by the Grand National Assembly and it remained in force until 1971.[3]

The Dimitrov Constitution proclaimed Bulgaria a "people's republic" governed by a "people's democracy." It rejected the principle of separation of powers, recognizing instead the principle of the "unity of the State power," which eliminated checks and balances and gave the Communists effective control over all state bodies. Formally, power was vested in the people, and the minimum voting age was lowered from twenty-one to eighteen. The Constitution stipulated state control of economic planning

---

[2] The literature on the Turnovo Constitution is enormous. Black, *The Establishment of Constitutional Government in Bulgaria*, remains the best English-language source on the subject. The most substantial history of the Turnovo Constitution published in Bulgaria is Vladikin, *Istoriia na Turnovskata konstitutsiia*.

[3] *Konstitutsiia na NRB*. This document has been interpreted and reinterpreted by numerous legal writers. Several such works have already been cited. Genovski *et al.*, *Osnovi na durzhavata i pravoto na NRB*, is as good as any of the works that have come out of Communist Bulgaria. Sharp, *New Constitutions in the Soviet Sphere*, remains a useful source on the general subject of constitutionalism in Stalinist East Europe. Various articles in Dellin, ed., *Bulgaria*, provide factual as well as interpretative material on the so-called Dimitrov Constitution of 1947.

and state ownership of the means of production. Responsibility for social welfare was placed exclusively on the state.

Provisions concerning the National Assembly (*Subranie*), the only legislative body, imitated the Soviet pattern. Among its other functions, the Assembly was to elect the Presidium and appoint the government, both of which were to be, in theory, responsible to it. In practice, the Assembly became a rubber stamp for governmental acts and decisions. The Presidium of the Assembly fulfilled both executive and legislative functions. It promulgated and interpreted laws, and could legislate by decree. The president of the Presidium became the titular head of state.

Executive authority was vested in the government, or in the president of the Council of Ministers, the deputy premiers, ministers, and the chairmen of the various commissions. The government was to be responsible to the Assembly and, when the latter was not in session, to the Presidium, which was to remain in permanent session.

The highest judicial authority was to be the Supreme Court, elected by the National Assembly for a five-year term. Judges and lay assessors were in fact chosen on the basis of political cooperation and could be dismissed at any time. The chief prosecutor also was to be appointed by the National Assembly for a term of five years. His chief function was to prosecute all those guilty of crimes affecting "the state, national, and economic interests of the People's Republic." Always a trustworthy Communist, the chief prosecutor appointed prosecutors to the lower courts and, together with the minister of justice, controlled the judicial system on behalf of the Communist party.

The Constitution divided the country, for administrative purposes, into districts and communes. These were to be administered by the executives of the local People's Councils. In 1949, provincial People's Councils were added to the already existing communal and district councils. In 1951, the local administrative system was changed (without any amendment to the Constitution), and the Soviet system of People's Councils of the Deputies of the Working People was instituted. These councils existed on the provincial, district, urban, suburban, and village levels. In 1959, the system of local government was reorganized, and a territorial system of administration was introduced. By bringing all political, economic, and cultural matters under the supervision of each district authority, greater efficiency, as well as decentralization, was achieved.

The Constitution included a wide range of guarantees in the areas of civil liberties and social welfare. While civil liberties were limited by accompanying qualifications and were never observed, the principles of social welfare were implemented to a significant degree.

The Dimitrov Constitution contained no reference to the Communist party, whose Central Committee and Politburo were the real supreme authorities. While formally the National Assembly was the "supreme organ of the State power" and "the only legislative organ," its members received the prior approval of the Communist party, and its legislative role was limited to approving the legislation of the Presidium, the government, and the party. The Presidium, the center of legislative, executive, and judicial functions, also served as a vehicle for party rule. Its president and the majority of its members were also members of the Central Committee of the Communist party. In theory, supreme power rested with the legislature. In fact, power rested with the executive, the Council of Ministers, and legislation was usually enacted by governmental decree, although the Constitution did not give the government this power. The ultimate authority, of course, was and is the Communist party, which, as stated above, was not even mentioned in the Dimitrov Constitution. Furthermore, Communist theory recognizes the supremacy of "the will of the ruling class" as expressed by the Communist party. Thus, any legislative act of the government or of the Central Committee of the party supersedes constitutional provisions.

Communist constitutions are intended to be statements of ideology and legal expressions of the situation at the time and stage at which they are adopted, rather than inviolable principles of law. Hence, new laws can be enacted and old ones counteracted without amending the Constitution. In the early sixties, Bulgaria announced its intention to revise its Constitution in order to bring it up to date with socialist achievement.

The revision was delayed until 1971, when, on March 30, the

original draft of what was to become the new Bulgarian Constitution was made public. Following this, the draft was submitted to the Tenth Party Congress (April, 1971), the National Assembly, and a May 16 referendum for approval. Of the 99.70 percent of the eligible voters who did vote, 99.66 percent voted in favor, and the Constitution was proclaimed law on May 18. Very few of the proposals for change made during the nationwide discussion of the first draft which preceded the referendum were taken into account, and only slight modifications appeared in the final version.[4]

The new Constitution retains for Bulgaria the title of "people's republic" but, unlike the 1947 Constitution, also declares the country a socialist state. Emphasis is placed on Bulgaria's membership in the "world socialist community" and the "world socialist economic system." Also unlike the former Constitution, the new one refers to the leading role of the Communist party in Bulgarian society, though no mention is made of how the party is to carry out this role.[5]

The Constitution recognizes four forms of ownership: state, cooperative, public organizational, and individual or personal. It also stipulates that the public owns the means of production.

The rights and duties of Bulgarian citizens are basically the same as those under the former Constitution. Again, most rights are negated by restrictions which render them meaningless. A new provision declares that Bulgarian youth should be "educated in the spirit of communism."

The final version of the Constitution changed the terms of office set in the original draft, as well as those set by an amendment to the 1947 Constitution. The term of office of National Assembly deputies is five years; of the people's councils, two and a half years; and of the chief prosecutor, five years. These changes resulted from a decision made at the Tenth Party Congress (held in April, after the first draft had been issued) to hold congresses every five years instead of every four, in imi-

[4] "The Draft of the New Bulgarian Constitution," *Radio Free Europe Research*, April 16, 1971, pp. 1–2; and "The New Bulgarian Constitution Goes into Effect," *ibid.*, June 2, 1971, pp. 1–2.

[5] *Radio Free Europe Research*, April 16, 1971, pp. 3, 4. Additional information on the text and meaning of the new Constitution was made public in *ibid.*, June 2 and July 15, 1971.

tation of Soviet party congresses. In both the amendment to the 1947 Constitution and the first draft of the new Constitution, the term of office for Assembly deputies had been set at four years. The modification reflected the opinion of the party's Central Committee, voiced at its July, 1968, plenum, that elections should be held after, not before, party congresses—that is, every five years, not every four.

At least on paper, the new Constitution expands the role of the National Assembly by broadening its control, through permanent commissions, over the ministries and state agencies, as well as its supervision of domestic and foreign policy. The right to initiate legislation was previously granted only to the government and to the Assembly, with the requirement that proposed legislation be signed by at least one-fifth of the deputies. Now this right is extended to the new State Council, the permanent Assembly commissions, the Supreme Court, the chief prosecutor, and a number of public organizations (such as the Komsomol, the Fatherland Front, and trade unions), and the one-fifth provision regarding legislative initiative in the Assembly has been removed. Despite the expanded role accorded the National Assembly, many of its functions can be carried out by the newly created State Council, which replaces the Presidium of the Assembly but possesses much greater power.

Most of the proposals for modification of the original draft of the new Constitution related to the State Council and were motivated by concern over the broad powers granted to the council and its chairman. Many of the suggestions for change were ignored, but the State Council's powers were slightly curtailed as a result of the criticism.

The functions of the State Council include almost all of the functions of the former Presidium, plus a few new ones. When the National Assembly is not in session, which is most of the year, the State Council exercises some of its powers. Among these are the right to promulgate decrees (unlike the Presidium, the council is not required to obtain Assembly approval later), the right to revoke decisions of the ministries, and general supervision of the government, the people's councils and the prosecutor's office. In all, the State Council is in a stronger position vis-à-vis the government than was the Presidium. All of the council members are to be Assembly deputies. Although elected by the Assembly and theoretically subordinate to it, the broadened powers of the council and the omission of provisions (such as existed in the Dimitrov Constitution regarding the Presidium) for the Assembly to change the council or dismiss members indicate that the council is also in a stronger position vis-à-vis the National Assembly. Provisions permitting the concentration of great power in the hands of the chairman of the State Council suggested that this position would be occupied by the party's first secretary, and, indeed, the chairmanship was ultimately assumed by Todor Zhivkov.

The composition and functions of the government remain basically the same as those under the old Constitution. Two new elements are the government's increased subordination to the State Council, to which it is required to give an annual accounting of its work, and the narrowing of its rights vis-à-vis the executive committees of the people's councils. The people's councils have been granted increased powers in the local administration of economic activities.

Several progressive provisions concerning the judicial system have been introduced into the Constitution. These relate to the election of judges, the independence of prosecutors, and the binding nature of legislation in imposing punishment for crimes.

Provision has also been made for the future adoption of new constitutions. The Dimitrov Constitution provided only for constitutional amendments. As previously, a two-thirds majority of the National Assembly is required for amendments, as well as for the adoption of a new constitution.

At least on paper, the new Constitution introduces several progressive features. These include the right of the electorate to recall deputies, the right of individual deputies to introduce bills, the suggestion of increased emphasis on the use of referendums, and the new provisions regarding the judicial system. All these are counterbalanced by the broad powers granted to the State Council and the apparent lack of controls on its abuse of power.

The publication of the draft constitution was timed to shortly precede the convocation of the Tenth Party Congress, which proceeded to approve the document. Zhivkov's report to the congress was delivered on April 20, 1971, the opening day.[6] The speech stressed Bulgarian-Soviet ties and gave light treatment to domestic matters. Apart from routine denunciations of imperialism, the contents of the report included even greater praise of the Soviet Union and stress on friendship with the Soviet Union than did the 1966 report before the Ninth Party Congress. Regarding Bulgaria's Balkan neighbors, Yugoslavia and Rumania received cooler treatment than in 1966: Yugoslavia because of the disputes over Macedonia; Rumania because of the deterioration of relations between the two countries, which culminated in Rumania's opposition to the invasion of Czechoslovakia. The somewhat friendly treatment of Turkey and Greece (the 1967 military coup in Athens notwithstanding) represented an expression of Bulgaria's desire for normal relations with those two Balkan states. The endeavor to harmonize Bulgaria's policies with those of the Soviet Union in this sphere was all too obvious.

Communist China was harshly condemned, in terms much stronger than those employed in 1966. Zhivkov referred to the "sins" of the Chinese Communist leaders, their "slanderous fabrications" and their "efforts to bring dissent into the ranks of socialist countries and to weaken the anti-imperialist front." Albanian leaders also were strongly attacked for their anti-sovietism, but the first secretary noted that Bulgaria would continue its efforts to improve Bulgarian-Albanian relations in the future.

Atypically, no reference was made to West German militarism. Bonn was mentioned only in connection with its treaties with the Soviet Union and Poland, which, Zhivkov stated, should be ratified. Regarding the problems between Bonn, on the one hand, and East Germany and Czechoslovakia, on the other, Zhivkov called for a "favorable solution," but he did not make the latter a condition for the establishment of Bulgarian–West German diplomatic relations as he had done in a statement in September, 1970.

The report was unenthusiastic about prospects for economic

6 The text of Zhivkov's report was reproduced in *Rabotnichesko delo*, April 21, 1971.

and trade relations with the West. This reflected Bulgaria's foreign-trade policy since the Ninth Congress, which had stressed increased trade with the Communist bloc countries and a corresponding relative decrease in trade with the developed nations of the West.

Turning to party affairs, Zhivkov repeated an old theme—the need to unite younger and older cadres and to utilize to the fullest those of all ages. His emphasis on the subject indicated that the problem of retiring old leaders remained unresolved. This was duly reflected in the party elections held at the end of the congress. Few changes were made in party posts. Todor Zhivkov was re-elected the party's first secretary. Central Committee membership was increased from 137 to 147 full members and from 87 to 110 candidate-members. The membership of the Politburo remained the same, except for the removal of Luchezar Avramov as candidate-member of the Politburo and his replacement by Venelin Kotsev. All eleven full members were re-elected. They were: Boris Velchev; Boian Bulgaranov; Zhivko Zhivkov; Ivan Mikhailov; Ivan Popov; Pencho Kubadinski; Stanko Todorov; Tano Tsolov; Todor Zhivkov; Todor Pavlov; and Tsola Dragoicheva. There were six candidate-members of the Politburo: Angel Tsanev; Venelin Kotsev; Ivan Abadzhiev; Kostadin Giaurov; Krustiu Trichkov; and Peko Takov.

The secretaries of the newly elected secretariat of the Central Committee were, in addition to Todor Zhivkov as first secretary, Stanko Todorov, Boris Velchev, Ivan Abadzhiev, Venelin Kotsev, Ivan Prumov, and Teniu Kiratsov. Vladimir Bonev and Georgi Bokov were co-opted as members of the newly elected secretariat.

The most remarkable feature of the new Politburo and Central Committee secretariat was the lack of change. Despite expectations, all previous full members of the Politburo were retained, and, most notably, the octogenarian Todor Pavlov. Like the congress itself, the preservation of the Politburo's former membership was intended to demonstrate unity within the party leadership.

General elections were held in Bulgaria on June 27, 1971. On July 7 and 8, the new National Assembly met and elected a State Council and the new government. Party First Secretary Todor Zhivkov relinquished his position as premier to become head of state as chairman of the new State Council. Politburo member Stanko Todorov replaced Zhivkov as premier. The State Council was composed of the chairman, a first deputy chairman, three deputy chairmen, a secretary, and seventeen members. Apart from Zhivkov himself, the new State Council did not include outstanding personalities. The council met on July 14 and began to establish its auxiliary agencies, which were composed mainly of technocrats and specialists in the respective areas of concern.

The new Council of Ministers, like the previous one, had twenty-nine members aside from the premier. Structural changes in the government included the decision to re-establish the Bureau of the Council of Ministers, whose decisions were to have "the same force as acts of the Council of Ministers." The bureau was headed by the premier and included the two first deputy premiers, the five deputy premiers, the minister of finance, and the minister of labor and social welfare.

The composition of the State Council and the Council of Ministers suggested that neither body would completely dominate the other. This remains a preliminary judgment, however, one to be verified or altered in the future.

The state of the economy remained a central question before, during, and after the Tenth Party Congress. Throughout the sixties, the Communist party had repeatedly re-evaluated economic policies in an endeavor to reconcile ideology and the demands of economic modernization. The result was the introduction of a degree of economic decentralization as embodied in the reform plan which was adopted by the Central Committee plenum of April, 1966. Among other features, the reform plan called for decentralization of economic decision-making and planning and greater emphasis on the profit motive in increasing productivity. The concept of "planning from below," however, proved more significant in theory than in practice. By the July, 1968, plenum the party had reverted to the concept of greater centralization. A new reform plan called for less freedom for individual enterprises and an increase in centralized planning. During the Central Committee plenums of July,

1968, and September, 1969, much emphasis was placed on science and technology.

Within the agricultural sector, two innovations had been introduced in recent years. One involved a change in the management of state farms. The second was the creation of agro-industrial complexes (AICs), which consisted of a number of state and/or collective farms. The latter concept was introduced by Zhivkov at the July, 1968, plenum, and, after a trial period, the April, 1970, plenum decided to establish such complexes throughout the country. They were to be based on "voluntary-ism"—each farm was to decide for itself whether or not to join a complex—and member farms were to retain their legal and economic independence within the complex. The aims of the AIC idea were to increase the specialization and concentration of production and to increase output while lowering costs, thereby making Bulgarian goods more competitive. Another consideration was the desire to stem the flow of people from rural areas by including industrial, construction, and trade activities within the complexes.

Statistics on AICs given in November, 1971, claimed that in the first quarter of 1971 there were 139 such complexes, and that these included 73.5 percent of all arable land and employed 75 percent of all the people permanently employed in agriculture. Articles appearing around the same time in the Bulgarian press indicated the existence of two trends of thought within the party regarding the merging of state and cooperative farms into all-national property. One line of thought emphasized the importance of retaining the cooperative system and saw its transformation into all-national property as a distant objective. The second trend favored the early abolition of cooperative farms and the subsequent transformation of agro-industrial complexes into all-national property.

On April 24, 1971, directives for the Sixth Five-Year Plan, which will cover 1971–75, were approved by the Tenth Party Congress. The new Five-Year Plan and the plan for 1972 were approved by the National Assembly at a session on December 14–16, 1971. The new directives reflected to some extent the newly adopted approach to economic planning and management. Some of the failures of the Fifth Five-Year Plan (1966–70) were perhaps the result of the economic reorganization of the past few years. In the main, the aims of the new plan resembled those of its predecessor and stipulated high growth rates in most sectors of the economy, despite the difficulties presented by the new reforms.

The stated objective of the Sixth Five-Year Plan is to increase "the social productivity of labor" through "utilization of the results of the scientific-technical revolution," and "to ensure the . . . satisfaction of the growing material and spiritual needs of the people and a raising of their socialist consciousness." The main objective is generally referred to as "care for the man," but few of the plan's targets actually promise significant improvement in the living standard. Rather, as previously, the emphasis is on industrialization: the target for total industrial production is an increase of 55–60 percent over the 1970 level; and, for the production of consumer goods, an increase of 50 percent. The projected increase in national income by 1975 is 47–50 percent above the 1970 level, and the average annual growth rate is placed at 8.5 percent. In the 1966–70 period, a 49 percent increase in national income was achieved, falling only slightly short of the planned 50 percent increase.

Despite the references to "care for the man" and the presumption of increased funds for consumption, the projected figure for accumulation for 1971–75 remains high at 26–28 percent of the national income. Likewise, about 20,000 million leva (calculated on the basis of January 1, 1971, prices) have been allotted for capital investments. The sharp rise in the figures for capital investments, from 7,500 million leva in 1961–65, to 15,000 million leva in 1966–70, to about 20,000 million leva for 1971–75, indicate the existence of inflation, for it is unlikely that such a large increase has occurred in the amount of construction work.

The aims for the agricultural sector are to increase production while lowering costs by means of specialization and utilization of industrial technology, and to increase exports and food supplies for the Bulgarian consumer. The target increase in rural production for 1971–75 is 17–20 percent above the 1966–70 production rate. The corresponding figures for 1961–65 and

1966–70 were 45–50 percent and 30 percent, respectively, and were unachieved.

The directives on foreign trade refer to economic integration within Comecon, economic cooperation with developing nations, and the continuation of trade with developed Western countries. The target increase in the total volume of foreign trade is 60–65 percent above the 1970 level. In 1966–70 the target was an increase of "not less than 65 percent" and was in fact reported to have been 70 percent. In 1971–75, 82 percent of Bulgaria's foreign trade is to be with socialist countries, as opposed to about 79 percent in 1970. The share of trade with the Soviet Union is to be about 58 percent of the total foreign trade. From the late fifties to the early sixties this figure averaged about 53 percent; it dropped to 49.2 percent in 1966, but has since risen gradually.

Despite the growth in the share of Bulgaria's exports going to socialist countries, the percentage of her imports coming from these countries declined somewhat in 1970 and in at least the first quarter of 1971. The facts thus contradict the official policy established in 1969, which, as reiterated in the Sixth Five-Year Plan, was to increase trade with Communist countries. The motives for the official policy may be partly political and partly economic (in that the Soviet Union and Comecon provide a market for Bulgarian goods). On the other hand, in order to further industrialization and to advance technological development, Bulgaria may require equipment of a quality the Comecon countries cannot provide, and this may lead her to purchase it from developed non-Communist countries.

The directives give special attention to scientific research and development, which have been allotted funds that are to reach 2.5–3.0 percent of the national income by 1975.

Among the aims relating to the standard of living is a 25–30 percent increase in the real per capita income (as compared to the 1966–70 period, when the target was 30 percent, but a 33.5 percent increase was reported).

Basically, the new Five-Year Plan may be said to resemble the previous plan, despite changes in the economic system. Like its predecessor, it gives top priority to heavy industry.

CONCLUSION

In a sense, contemporary history precludes summations of any kind. Of necessity, generalizations remain tentative, conclusions preliminary. The favorite metaphor of Traicho Kostov, the unfortunate general secretary of the Bulgarian Communist party, was to depict the socialist revolution in Bulgaria as a scaffold which temporarily concealed the perfection of the Communist society-in-the-building. A quarter of a century after his purge and execution, the new society remains hidden behind the same scaffolding which the Communists began erecting in 1944.

Communist rule in Bulgaria has endured for almost one-third of Bulgaria's entire modern history of independence. Those born on the eve of the Red Army's entry into the country have by now approached the age of thirty. The entire populace under the age of forty-five has come to political maturity under communism. Their memories of pre-Communist days are vague, at best. Only those in their late fifties can claim any degree of active participation in the pre-Communist world of politics.

These mere truisms are startling when examined in the light of the political self-perceptions of a people who for an entire generation have subsisted under a strictly modified national sovereignty. The maxims of Russia's righteousness and of Soviet superiority in all spheres of endeavor have, since 1944, taken official precedence over all national values. In the absence of an empirical sociology, it is impossible to ascertain how much

171

of the official tenets have in fact been inculcated into the minds and souls of the Bulgarians. Even though the cultural resilience —the "antibodies" of sovietism—must not be underestimated, the sustained and all-pervasive educational efforts must have had a lasting impact. Has the national ego of this small people been impaired in the process? A sanctified theology of "second-best," which states that the Bulgarians are great, but which reminds everyone from the cradle on that the Russians are even greater, continues unabated.

Indeed, this question strikes at the heart of the problem, which remains largely impenetrable. Having preserved for Bulgaria her prewar frontiers, the Communists proceeded to reduce the country to the level of yet another Soviet socialist republic, along with Armenia, Georgia, Estonia, and the remaining components of the enormous Great Russian domain. As a result, politics was converted into mere public administration, and international politics all but lost its meaning in the process. Rather than turn it into a Soviet regional subsystem, the Communists effectively integrated the land of this once unruly people into the Soviet in-system. Bulgaria's present-day statesmen—if such they be—act more like Soviet regional governors than like Russian imperial viceroys. The absurd charges brought by Stalin's secret agents against the Bulgarian Communist émigrés in the thirties, accusing them of conspiracy to annex the Ukraine to Bulgaria, have, in the reverse situation, proved not so absurd. For all practical purposes, the Soviet Union annexed Bulgaria, despite the absence of land contiguity.

In the last fifty years, Bulgarian politics has been affected most profoundly by three different men, representing three distinct types of political action. The populism of Stamboliiski, the monarchism of Boris, and the Stalinism of Chervenkov left their marks on the country, producing three clearly distinguishable political styles and socioeconomic by-products. The influence of these three styles in the realm of international politics can be more easily delineated than can their impact on the domestic scene. Of the three, Stamboliiski's answers to Bulgaria's international problems were the most original and, in many ways, the most ambitious. Intellectually or intuitively, he comprehended full well that, as long as Bulgaria's problems in

her immediate neighborhood remained unresolved, her dependence on the protection of at least one Great Power would
remain an absolute requisite. His fundamental approach, therefore, was to resolve first the regional equation. In this manner
he hoped to make possible Bulgaria's escape from entangle-
ments with any of the Great Powers. The fact that the temporary eclipse of German and Russian power helped Stamboliiski arrive at his foreign-policy formulations does not detract
from the originality of his thought or diminish the magnitude
of his political courage.

There were several reasons why his foreign-policy ideas
remained unfulfilled. Stamboliiski was a better political strate-
gist than he was a political tactician. As a result, the translation
of his ideas into a working diplomacy left much to be desired.
The intoxication of the Belgrade politicians by the new great-
ness they gained at the end of the war made them both un-
reasonable and unreceptive to Bulgarian minimalism. Most
important, however, was the brevity of Stamboliiski's tenure,
which did not last long enough for his revolutionary approaches
to be tested. Still, the basic validity of the Stamboliiski solution
and the intrinsic value of his foreign-policy ideas remain as true
today as they were fifty years ago.

Although not an original thinker by any means, Boris was,
in comparison, a better tactician than his Agrarian detractor.
To him, the optimal solution to Bulgaria's international problem was to find a place for his kingdom within the subsystem of
Nazi Germany. As long as Germany's might lasted, he was able
to secure for Bulgaria what was probably the maximum possible
freedom of action within very narrow, preset margins. By employing skillful personal diplomacy, Boris succeeded in assuring
Hitler and his entourage of his trustworthiness, and thus was
able to retain a small but meaningful degree of freedom even
while the German army was present in the country. The fatal
flaw in Boris' conception was not his diplomacy but the ultimate
destruction of the empire on which he had hinged the political
destinies of his people. Whether or not he could have mitigated
the magnitude of Bulgaria's catastrophe in the Second World
War had he not departed from the scene in the summer of 1943
remains a moot point and leaves him with the benefit of the

doubt, which he deserves.

As a political prototype, Chervenkov stands on the extreme edge of the spectrum of Bulgaria's international possibilities. Immersed as he was in the Stalinist interpretation of material determinism, he rejected independence but was not satisfied with vassalage or with servitude. He was committed to the principles of submergence under, if not fusion with, the interests, political being, and ultimate destinies of the First Land of Socialism. For him, as for his fellow doctrinaires, international politics was merely a reflection of domestic realities, and Bulgaria's particular reality constituted an inseparable part of Stalin's world. For him, total dependence led to total freedom, a postulate which has some philosophical merit for those obsessed with a totalistic view of history and the world.

The domestic solutions projected by Stamboliiski, Boris, and Chervenkov varied as greatly as did the foreign-policy models of the three regimes. Stamboliiski's populism envisaged an idyllic peasant society which was never truly attainable. The rural interests could not be allowed to dominate the interests of the urban sector without creating an intolerable anachronism. Given Bulgaria's poverty, the ever-growing pressure on the land, and the absence of a sizable foreign-capital inflow, there was no way in which the peasants' welfare could be enhanced. In effect, what Stamboliiski proposed was a reversal of the sequences which had already become inevitable. In his scheme, the village was to become a recipient of capital. The question of where this capital was to come from was never resolved. The truth of the matter was that only a postindustrial society could have produced Stamboliiski's garden-village.

Boris' economic model was that of the urban bourgeoisie. Slowly, but inevitably, the peasants were made to pay the price of urbanization. Indeed, Bulgaria's modest industrial plant continued to expand from the early thirties well into the war years. This progress was never rapid enough to become truly satisfactory, however. The formidable problem of underemployment remained untackled. Essentially, the economic problems which haunted Bulgaria during the last decade of Boris' reign are the problems which face developing countries in the contemporary world. Still, Boris' economic policy retained two significant attributes. At the very least, the economic development of the country pointed in the right direction. Furthermore, the country was spared the human dislocation brought on by the more radical economic solutions. The result was little progress at a modest price.

Under Chervenkov, Bulgaria was forced to accept the antithesis of Agrarian populism. The factory became the new object of worship. In its utter degradation, the countryside was turned into an internal colony to be exploited on behalf of the newly erected, gigantic industrial plant. An incalculable rate of human dislocation was enforced with unprecedented brutality. The end result was a miniature replica of the Stalinist pattern, which was made even more grotesque by the smallness of the land and its people.

In the course of its development, Bulgarian politics supplied ready-made alternatives to the Stamboliiski, Boris, and Chervenkov prototypes. In due time, Stamboliiski's populist idealism came to be modified by the pragmatic agrarianism of Dimitur Gichev. The small but respectable Democratic party under Nikola Mushanov spoke Boris' economic language, but did not resort to his one-man authoritarianism. Under Krustiu Pastukhov, the Social Democrats proposed to represent the interests of the urban working classes, but stopped short of the extremes of bolshevism.

Taken separately, the solutions offered by these three men were neither comprehensive nor all-embracive. None of them pretended or aspired to a single-party domination. Gichev, Mushanov, and Pastukhov—the men to whom this book is dedicated—were willing and able to work together and provide a reasonable synthesis of divergent interests. With all of its faults, the short-lived People's Bloc regime of the early thirties came close to realizing a meaningful rural-urban political alliance. On the eve of the Communists' seizure of power, the alliance once again joined the all-too-brief Muraviev government, this time with Pastukhov's personal blessing. In both cases the alliance was curtailed, at first by the intervention of militarism and later by the Red Army and the Communists. These unique constellations of forces contrasted sharply with the practical and doctrinal inability of Stamboliiski, as well as of Boris and the Communists, to maintain meaningful alliances of any kind. Stamboliiski was determined to rule alone. At most, Boris attended to his courtiers, who represented only themselves. Having refused Petkov's extended hand, the Communists had no other resort but to make use of Agrarian renegades, such as Obbov and, later, Georgi Traikov, the archcollaborationist.

What of the other Bulgarian politicians who played a role of any consequence? Tsankov was learned and able, but morally corrupt. Despite his gregariousness and political skills, Andrei Liapchev remained a captive of his Macedonian origin, with all that this implied in the context of the latter part of the twenties. Atanas Burov was a man of wisdom, but had little or no following. Old Kosturkov, the founder and leader of the Radicals, lost his previous political respectability by selling himself to the Communists when the time was opportune. Damian Velchev of the Military League was politically illiterate and relied too heavily on the presumed realism of Kimon Georgiev, whose opportunism ultimately corrupted his career. The undoubted brilliance of Kosta Todorov of the Pladne Agrarians was wasted in political exile. The political career of his younger successor, Dr. G. M. Dimitrov, was twice wrecked, first by the monarchist dictatorship and finally by the Communist dictatorship. The particular circumstances which elevated Nikola Petkov to the top were more a test of his boundless courage than a tribute to his political wisdom.

Politically, Georgi Dimitrov was as much the victim of Stalinism as were the men he helped purge while occupying the seat of the general secretary of the Comintern. His earlier courage and talents were expended on futile revolutionism and Comintern intrigues. He returned to Bulgaria an empty and broken man. Kolarov's education and intelligence were harnessed to Stalin's will as one of the Comintern's outstanding purgers. The tragic Kostov, whose life was spared by Boris, only to be taken by Stalin, possessed many of the qualities which go into the making of a statesman. Whether his courage and intellect would have found a way out from his fanaticism necessarily remains in question. Had he stayed alive, developments in the post-Stalin years might well have taken a different course. His early removal undoubtedly hastened the transfer of power from the old guard to the faceless group of men who have managed the country in the last fifteen years.

In one major way the development of communism in Bulgaria contained a built-in anomaly which differentiated it from the development of the Communist parties in the remaining East European states. The revolutionary fervor of the Bulgarian party was more powerful and more genuine at the end of the First World War than it was at the end of the Second World War. Between 1912 and 1918 the Bulgarians fought three successive wars, which strained the social fabric of the nation to the breaking point. Defeat brought misery and disillusionment, which were strengthened by the arrival of a wave of refugees from the lands beyond the new frontiers. These circumstances rendered Bulgaria of the early twenties highly receptive to radical solutions.

In the thirties and the early forties, much of the ferment died down. During those years, communism survived largely through inertia. The modest but real economic recovery, and, later, the apparent resolution of the national question, removed much of the impetus to revolution. Except for some superficial bombing by the Allies in the winter of 1943/44, Bulgaria was spared physical destruction. The army did not fight and thus suffered no defeat on the battlefield. The remarkable combination of resistance and civil war which swept Yugoslavia and Greece was not repeated in Bulgaria. The Communists organized an underground resistance, but, in view of the objective circumstances which prevailed throughout the war, they failed to harmonize their political program with popular sentiment.

The revolutionary potential after September, 1944, was meager. The few thousand partisans, most of whom were recent recruits, and the Communist cadres, newly freed from the state jails, were the only contingents determined to undertake direct action against the remnants of the old regime. They created a semblance of unsettledness which for a time the party high command encouraged and directed. The "revolutionary barricades," as it were, were set up largely by decree. The Communists who were called upon to man the newly captured positions were faced not with violence but with the stubborn, passive resistance of much of the peasantry. The one meaningful assault came from the rear—from the Belgrade Communists, who sought to consolidate their revolution by reclaiming for Macedonia the southwestern corner of Bulgaria. This was a bitter blow for the Bulgarian Communists, in terms of their nationalist sentiments and their Communist ego.

The Bulgarian Communists had patronized their Serb comrades throughout the interwar period as an insignificant contingent of the Comintern. When fate turned against them, they were insulted and enraged. Because their élan had been blunted, they once again felt compelled to turn to Moscow for consolation and protection.

The revolution in Bulgaria proceeded by administrative design. In a painstaking and methodic way, the soil was upturned and the old order was restructured. Given the Communists' unscrupulousness and determination, physical progress was indeed achieved. The price, however, was dear. Much of the small but valuable political and entreprenurial elite produced by this peasant people in the course of three generations was decimated. This was a loss which Bulgarian society could ill afford. More significantly, the egalitarian peasant society, which, although destitute, had not harbored significant class injustice, was tampered with until it was changed beyond recognition. For those expelled from their land and pushed into the towns, the transition meant a degree of material betterment which was implicit rather than immediate. For the majority left behind, rural life under collectivization was a burden and a constraint. The Bulgarian peasantry was left in oblivion and became the unknown half of society. Its voice remains unheard but for the official utterances of the bogus Agrarian Union, which has been retained to serve as the agrarian section of the Communist Central Committee. Although the future remains impenetrable, the old political aspirations of the Bulgarian peasantry have been mutilated. In a parting speech at his trial in 1948, Gichev spoke of the hopelessness of resurrection; he spoke of himself, but he meant the peasants whom he had led and their values.

The new urban working classes came to represent the face of progress. The surplus labor force which was taken off the land was pushed into the rapidly growing cities and towns. Numbering in the hundreds of thousands, the newly arrived city-dwellers formed the lowest stratum of urban Bulgaria. In a large measure, they displaced the tiny working class of the interwar years, which was propelled upward to assume the various managerial and administrative functions of the rapidly expanding socialist industrial sector. Although the level of consumption remained low, city life opened up unknown possibilities and new opportunities for the newcomers. The educational facilities on all levels, the public health services, and the various social-welfare measures broadened the prospects for advancement for those inclined to take advantage of the new offerings. Socialist construction provided new jobs, giving hope to the sons and daughters of those who in earlier years had subsisted in hopeless misery. Although a substantial degree of unemployment continues to haunt the Communist regime to this day, the stifling underemployment of the interwar years has been radically reduced. The price of progress has been charged to the peasantry and the dispossessed middle class; the fruits of progress have gone largely to the new urban Bulgaria.

Much of the energy expended during the first sixty years of Bulgaria's independence on resolving the problems of Macedonia and Thrace has been conserved under communism. Since 1948, the regime has given greater attention to revisionist rhetoric than to irredentist deeds. Yet, on balance, the saving has proved to be more apparent than real. Bulgaria borders on two NATO countries, as well as on Yugoslavia, whose trustworthiness remains in perpetual doubt in Moscow's eyes. As a result, the Bulgarians have been forced to devote a significant portion of their Gross National Product to defense. The size of Bulgaria's new army stands in striking disproportion to her economic capacity, as well as to her immediate national requirements. Rumania's special position within the Soviet bloc in the last decade has not contributed to the easing of Bulgaria's military posture. Bulgaria has continued to be cultivated as Russia's safest military position in the Balkans. Only time will show whether Bulgaria's huge investment in the building of her military establishment has in fact been devoted to protecting Soviet strategic interests or has been aimed at meeting her own legitimate defense needs.

Revolutions are better sustained by a large nation than by a

small people. Scars heal more easily on a large body. The interaction between size and rate of change remains to be better
understood. This was the major theme chosen by Pastukhov,
the socialist evolutionist, in the address he delivered to his
revolutionist prosecutors in 1946 at the end of his political trial.
Pastukhov was willing to accept the Russian October, but he
questioned the merits and possible benefits of a revolution in
Bulgaria, which, because of its smallness, might be overwhelmed, if not emasculated. Whatever the validity of his
contention, there is little doubt that the submergence of
national sovereignty, accompanied, if not caused, by Communist revolution, is a calamity the full scope of which is yet to
be assessed.

Bulgaria has come to constitute a unique category within the
cluster of East European Communist states. For a full quarter
of a century, the Yugoslavs have successfully maintained their
independence. In the main, their success represents a dividend
which was prepaid by the peoples of Yugoslavia—and above
all by the Serbs—during the Second World War. In a way,
their independence was underwritten in the course of their
outstanding revolutionary civil war fought during the German
occupation. Their attainments in 1948 and after were thus
commensurate with their limitless will to bear the brutal price
of self-sacrifice. Once the Cold War had commenced, the newly
gained Yugoslav free spirit broke loose from the Stalinist grip.
Tito's undoubted talent for playing the perpetual balancing
act was aided and augmented by the rivalry between East and
West, as well as by the fortunate circumstance that the land
of the Yugoslavs lies on the outermost periphery of the Soviet
European empire.

The belated rebelliousness of the Hungarians, Poles, and
Czechoslovaks failed to attain ultimate success. Yet, none of
those endeavors was altogether futile. The Hungarians' bargaining position vis-à-vis Moscow improved noticeably in the
aftermath of their debacle. Although Hungary remained a
Soviet satellite, her terms of servitude were renegotiated, as it
were. At the very least, Poland's new status quo, set up in 1957,
made possible the removal of the bondage of collectivization
from her countryside. Were it not for their fatal geopolitical

position, the Polish Communist reformers would undoubtedly have extracted more and better terms from their Russian overlords. The tragedy of Prague under Red Army occupation would have been complete had not the lingering myth of 1968 restored somewhat the national self-esteem of the Czechs as a people. The sensible Czechs will, no doubt, improve their terms of trade with Soviet Russia and, in so doing, will enhance their economic well-being, which is so very important for the maintenance of their high level of civilization. Even East Germany, which is not a nation-state but a mere political fragment, will find her immediate future improved because of the immense wealth of West Germany and the relative poverty of the Russian economy.

Little Albania would probably have remained content with her position as a full-fledged Soviet satellite. What the Albanians were not prepared to accept, however, was the role of a subsatellite bossed by Belgrade and overlorded by Moscow on top. Since her leaders were unwilling to remain in Moscow's imperial sub-basement and were unprepared to shed their Stalinism, they sought and found temporary shelter under China's wing.

The Rumanian formula of Stalinism at home and controlled independence in the international arena has now become firmly set. The amazement which greeted the performance of the Rumanian Communists was due to the fact that they created, rather than exploited, Rumania's margins of maneuver, which were nonexistent in the beginning.

The utter penetration of the Bulgarian state as a political entity and the stifling immobilism of her political behavior are markedly dissonant with Bulgaria's past and with her potential. On the face of it, when the Red Army pursued its assault westward in 1944, Bulgaria's objective possibilities of preserving a degree of national autonomy were fair, if not good. The Bulgarian army did not fight the Russians, and therefore the Red Army did not cross the Danube in pursuit of a fighting enemy. Yet, unlike the controlled moderation manifested by the Red Army High Command on its extreme right flank, the Russians chose maximalism on their extreme left. Finland, which fought the Soviet Union and took part in the siege of

Leningrad, escaped occupation and remained unsovietized. At the same time, the seemingly favorable conditions of Bulgaria and the guarded optimism of her statesmen withered away overnight. It is true that, unlike Finland, at Bulgaria's back stood not a neutral Sweden but a vengeful Greek government-in-exile and a timid and frightened Turkey.

These were circumstances which the Bulgarians could do little to control. Furthermore, Stalin was fully aware of Britain's utter disinterest in the ultimate fate of Bulgaria. His revived affection for the sentiments and political advantage of neo-Pan-Slavism, which he had devotedly fostered throughout the war, was yet another factor that worked against the interests of Bulgarian political sovereignty.

While the above observations pertain to historic sequences which can never be replayed, the future need not remain in permanent bondage to past events. Bulgaria's present-day apologists contend that her docility and untainted discipline as a Russian satellite have worked to Bulgaria's favor in the economic sphere. In their view, Bulgaria has remained a recipient of Soviet credits which are larger and more favorable than those allotted to all the other client-states. This contention is plausible, though its verification is not easy to achieve. If passivity has paid off, could not the dividends be increased by a policy of less than total compliance? Can a nation of nine million people remain permanently satisfied with the benefits of Soviet good will? As long as immobilism remains the sanctified doctrine of Bulgaria's diplomacy, her bargaining position vis-à-vis Moscow is bound to remain nonexistent.

The problems are not only economic but political as well. More than that, an improved bargaining posture will help repair the national ego, which has been emasculated for more than a full generation. Obviously, a measure of independence on the part of Bulgaria is in the interests of all her neighbors, who, in varying degrees, look at present-day Bulgaria as a Trojan horse left behind to lure those who have gone astray and to serve the regional designs of the Soviet leadership.

The state of exhaustion to which the Bulgarian people were brought during the period of sovietization and the height of Stalinist terror cannot last forever. The tightly knit domestic political fabric and the fixation of a country permanently nailed down and devoid of an independent role within the region and in international politics constitute intolerable constraints for a nation-state of long standing. The state of political deep freeze in which the country has been placed will have to give way sooner or later. As always, two options exist: to modify the domestic sociopolitical system while retaining the present foreign-policy orientation, or to exploit the available margins of maneuver on the international plane while preserving the domestic political status quo. The two alternatives cannot be explored simultaneously, for fear of Soviet retribution. Failure to explore either of the two may bring about an uncontrollable explosion.

BIBLIOGRAPHY

American-Bulgarian Good Neighbor League. *Bulgaria's True Record.* Detroit, Mich., 1945.

Anastasoff, Christ. *The Tragic Peninsula: A History of the Macedonian Movement for Independence Since 1878.* Saint Louis, Mo., 1938.

Angelov, D., and Andreev, M. *Istoriia na Bulgarskata durzhava i pravo* [History of the Bulgarian State and Law]. Sofia, 1955.

Angelov, V. *Zemedelskiiat vupros v Bulgariia* [The Agricultural Problem in Bulgaria]. Sofia, 1947.

Arditi, Benjamin. *Yehudei bulgariya beshnot hamishtar hanatsi* [The Bulgarian Jews during the Years of the Nazi Regime]. Holon, Israel, 1962.

Armstrong, Hamilton F. *The New Balkans.* New York, 1926.

——. *Tito and Goliath.* New York, 1951.

——. *Where the East Begins.* New York, 1929.

Atanasov, Gen. Shteriu, *et al. Bulgarskoto voenno izkustvo prez kapitalizma* [The Military Art in Bulgaria Under Capitalism]. Sofia, 1959.

——. *Kratka istoriia na Otechestvenata voina* [A Short History of the War for the Fatherland]. Sofia, 1958.

Avramov, Petur. *Bulgarskata komunisticheska partiia i formirane na sotsialisticheskata inteligentsiia* [The Bulgarian Communist Party and the Formation of the Socialist Intelligentsia]. Sofia, 1966.

Bagranov, T. S. *The American Mission's Share in the Regeneration and Defense of Bulgaria.* Pittsburgh, Pa., 1947.

Baldwin, Roger N., ed. *A New Slavery.* Dobbs Ferry, N.Y., 1953.

Barker, Elisabeth. *Macedonia: Its Place in Balkan Power Politics.* London, 1950.

——. *Truce in the Balkans.* London, 1948.

Barov, Nikola St. *BKP v noviia podem na antifashistkoto dvizhenie, 1929–1935* [The Bulgarian Communist Party in the New Advance of the Antifascist Movement]. Sofia, 1968.

Bartlett, Vernon. *East of the Iron Curtain*. New York, 1950.

Beamish, Tufton. *Must Night Fall?* London, 1950.

Bekhar, Alfred. *Germanskiiat imperializm i otrazhenieto mu v Bulgariia* [The German Imperialism and Its Reflection in Bulgaria]. Sofia, 1949.

Belev, Krustiu. *Pesen na svobodata* [A Song of Freedom]. Sofia, 1945.

Berov, L. *Polozhenieto na rabotnicheskata klasa v Bulgariia pri kapitalizma* [The State of the Working Class in Bulgaria under Capitalism]. Sofia, 1968.

Betts, R. R., ed. *Central and South East Europe, 1945–1948*. London, 1950.

Biriuzov, S. S. *Sovetskii soldat na Balkanakh* [Soviet Soldier in the Balkans]. Moscow, 1963.

Black, C. E. *The Establishment of Constitutional Government in Bulgaria*. Princeton, N.J., 1943.

————, ed. *Challenge in Eastern Europe*. New Brunswick, N.J., 1954.

Blagoev, Dimitur. *Suchineniia* [Works]. 5 vols. Sofia, 1957–58.

Blagoeva, Stela. *Georgi Dimitrov: Biografichen ocherk* [Georgi Dimitrov: A Biographic Outline]. 6th ed. Sofia, 1953.

Boiadzhiev, Asen. *Istoriia na sindikalnoto dvizhenie v Bulgariia* [History of the Syndicalist Movement in Bulgaria]. Sofia, 1948.

Bojkoff, Liuben. *Bulgaria Is Not the Land of Roses Only*. Sofia, 1946.

Borkenau, Franz. *European Communism*. New York, 1953.

————. *The New German Empire*. New York, 1939.

————. *World Communism: A History of the Communist International*. New York, 1939.

Borov, T., ed. *Vasil Kolarov: Bio-bibliografiia* [Vasil Kolarov: Bio-Bibliography]. Sofia, 1947.

Bozhinov, Voin. *Politicheskata kriza v Bulgariia prez 1943–1944* [The Political Crisis in Bulgaria during 1943–44]. Sofia, 1957.

————. *Zashtitata na natsionalnata nezavisimost na Bulgariia, 1944–1947* [The Defense of the National Independence of Bulgaria, 1944–1947]. Sofia, 1962.

Brown, J. F. *Bulgaria under Communist Rule*. New York, 1970.

Bulgaria, Ministry of Information. *The Two Year Economic Plan*. Sofia, 1947.

Bulgarian Atrocities in Greek Macedonia and Thrace, 1941–1944. Athens, 1945.

Bulgarian National Committee. *Nicola Petkov: In Memoriam*. Washington, D.C., 1952.

Burks, R. V. *The Dynamics of Communism in Eastern Europe*. Princeton, N.J., 1961.

Byrnes, James F. *Speaking Frankly*. New York, 1947.

Carlton, Richard K., ed. *Forced Labor in the People's Democracies*. New York, 1955.

Chakalov, A. *Formi, razmer, i deinost na chuzhdiia kapital v Bulgariia, 1878–1944* [Forms, Size, and Activity of the Foreign Capital in Bulgaria, 1878–1944]. Sofia, 1962.

———. *Natsionalniiat dokhod i razkhod na Bulgariia, 1924–1945* [The National Income and Expenditure of Bulgaria, 1924–1945]. Sofia, 1946.

Charukchiev, Asen T. *Kharakter i dvizheshti sili na narodnodemokrati-cheskata revoliutsiia v Bulgariia* [Character and the Moving Forces of the People's Democratic Revolution in Bulgaria]. Sofia, 1956.

Chary, Frederick B. "Bulgaria and the Jews: 'The Final Solution,' 1940 to 1944." Ph.D. diss., University of Pittsburgh, 1968.

Chervenkov, Vulko. *Bio-bibliografiia, 1900–1950* [Bio-Bibliography, 1900–1950]. Sofia, 1950.

———. *Po putiia na Georgi Dimitrov: Izbrani dokladi i rechi, 1948–1950* [In the Footsteps of Georgi Dimitrov: Selected Reports and Speeches, 1948–1950]. Sofia, 1950.

———. *Report of the Central Committee of the Bulgarian Communist Party to the Sixth Congress of the Party.* Sofia, 1954.

———. *Tasks of the Cooperative Farms.* Sofia, 1950.

———. *Za naukata, izkustvoto, i kulturata* [On Science, Art, and Culture]. Sofia, 1953.

———. *Za rabotata na komunisticheskata partiia v selo* [On the Work of the Communist Party in the Village]. Sofia, 1951.

Christopoulos, George. *Bulgaria's Record.* Chicago, Ill., 1944.

Clissold, Stephen. *Whirlwind.* New York, 1949.

Damianov, Georgi. *Izbrani proizvedeniia, 1892–1958* [Selected Works, 1892–1958]. Sofia, 1966.

Daskalov, Raiko. *Borba za zemia* [Struggle for Land]. 3rd ed. Sofia, 1945.

Dedijer, Vladimir. *Tito Speaks.* London, 1953.

Dellin, L. A. D., ed. *Bulgaria.* New York, 1957.

Dennett, R., and Johnson, J. E., eds. *Negotiating with the Russians.* Boston, Mass., 1951.

Dewar, Margaret. *Soviet Trade with Eastern Europe, 1945–1949.* London, 1951.

Dicey, Edward. *The Peasant State: An Account on Bulgaria in 1894.* London, 1894.

Dimitrov, Georgi. *Political Report Delivered to the Fifth Congress of the BKP.* Sofia, 1949.

———. *Suchineniia* [Works]. 15 vols. Sofia, 1951–55.

Dimitrov, Ilcho. *Burzhoaznata opozitsiia v Bulgariia, 1939–1944* [The Bourgeois Opposition in Bulgaria, 1939–1944]. Sofia, 1969.

———. *Godini na prelom* [Years of Change]. Sofia, 1969.

———. *Izgrazhdane na edinen mladezhki suiuz v Bulgariia, 1944–1947* [Establishment of a United Youth Union in Bulgaria, 1944–1947]. Sofia, 1964.

Dimitrov, Mircho. *Petiiat kongres na BKP* [The Fifth Congress of the Bulgarian Communist Party]. Sofia, 1965.

Djilas, Milovan. *Conversations with Stalin.* New York, 1962.

Dragoicheva, Tsola. *Politicheska, organizatsionna, i stopanska deinost na . . . Otechestvenofrontovskite komiteti . . .* [Political, Organizational, and Economic Activity of the . . . Fatherland Front Committees . . .]. Sofia, 1945.

Dramaliev, Kiril. *Istoriia na Otechestveniia front* [History of the Fatherland Front]. Sofia, 1947.

Feis, Herbert. *Between War and Peace: The Potsdam Conference.* Princeton, N.J., 1960.

————. *Churchill, Roosevelt, Stalin.* Princeton, N.J., 1957.

————. *From Trust to Terror.* New York, 1970.

Ganev, Ivan. *Agrarna reforma v chuzhbina i u nas* [Agrarian Reform Abroad and at Home]. Sofia, 1946.

Ganev, Venelin. *Demokratsiia* [Democracy]. Sofia, 1946.

Genovski, Mikhail, *et al. Osnovi na durzhavata i pravoto na NRB* [Foundations of the State and the Law of the People's Republic of Bulgaria]. 3rd rev. ed. 2 vols. Sofia, 1957–58.

Georgiev, Ivan. *Dobrudzha v borbata za svoboda, 1913–1940* [Dobruja in the Struggle for Freedom, 1913–1940]. Sofia, 1962.

Geshkoff, T. I. *Balkan Union.* New York, 1940.

Gialistras, Gen. Serge A. *Hellenism and Its Balkan Neighbours.* Athens, 1945.

Gindev, Panaiot. *Kum vuprosa za kharaktera na narodnodemokraticheskata revoliutsiia v Bulgariia* [On the Question of the Character of the People's Democratic Revolution in Bulgaria]. Sofia, 1956.

Girginov, Aleksandur. *Bulgariia pred Velikata voina* [Bulgaria before the Great War]. Sofia, 1932.

————. *Izpitaniata v voinata, 1915–1918* [The Trials in the War, 1915–1918]. Sofia, 1936.

————. *Narodnata katastrofa: Voinite, 1912–1913* [The National Catastrophe: The Wars, 1912–1913]. Sofia, 1926.

————. *Ot voinata kum mir* [From War to Peace]. Sofia, 1937.

Gornenski, Nikifor. *Vuoruzhenata borba . . . 1941–1944* [The Armed Struggle . . . 1941–1944]. Sofia, 1958.

Grigoroff, Georges. *Reforme Agraire et Collectivisation de l'Agriculture en Bulgarie.* Paris, 1956.

Grigorov, K. I. *Razvitie na burzhoaznata ikonomicheska misul v Bulgariia mezhdu dvete Svetovni voini* [Development of Bourgeois Economic Thought in Bulgaria in the Interwar Period]. Sofia, 1960.

Grinberg, Natan. *Khitleristkiiat natisk za unishtozhavane na evreite ot Bulgariia* [The Hitlerite Pressure for the Extermination of the Jews of Bulgaria]. Tel-Aviv, 1961.

————, ed. *Dokumenti* [Documents]. Sofia, 1945.

Gross, Feliks, ed. *European Ideologies.* New York, 1948.

————. *The Seizure of Political Power in a Century of Revolutions.* New York, 1958.

Gyorgy, Andrew. *Governments of Danubian Europe.* New York, 1949.

Ianev, Ianko G. *Funktsiite na durzhavata v NRB* [The Functions of State in the People's Republic of Bulgaria]. Sofia, 1957.

Istoriia na BKP [History of the Bulgarian Communist Party]. Sofia, 1969.

Istoriia na Bulgariia [History of Bulgaria]. Vol. 2. Sofia, 1955.

Istoriia na Bulgariia [History of Bulgaria]. 2nd ed. Vol. 3. Sofia, 1964.

Istorijski arhiv KPJ [Historic Archive of the Communist Party of Yugoslavia]. Vol. 7. Belgrade, 1951.

Isusov, Mito. *Rabotnicheskata klasa v Bulgariia, 1944–1947* [The Working Class in Bulgaria, 1944–1947]. Sofia, 1971.

Ivanov, K. *Chlenstvoto v partiiata i reguliraneto na neiniia sustav* [The Membership of the Party and the Regulation of Its Composition]. Sofia, 1956.

Ivanov, Vasil. *Sotsialisticheskata revoliutsiia i rabotnicheskata klasa v Bulgariia* [The Socialist Revolution and the Working Class in Bulgaria]. Sofia, 1969.

Izvestiia na Instituta po Istoriia na BKP [Announcements of the Institute for History of the Bulgarian Communist Party]. 21 vols. Sofia, 1957–69.

Jouvenel, Renaud de. *L'Internationale des Traitres*. Paris, 1948.

The Just Cause of the Fatherland Front Prevails. Sofia, 1955.

Kamenov, Evgenii G. *Ikonomicheskata pomosht na Suvetskiia suiuz* [The Economic Aid of the Soviet Union]. Sofia, 1955.

Karadzhov, Kiril. *Suiuzut na rabotnicheskata klasa i selianite* [The Alliance of the Working Class and the Peasants]. Sofia, 1957.

Kazasov, Dimo. *Bez put i bez idei* [Without Direction and Ideas]. Sofia, 1926.

———. *Burni godini, 1918–1944* [Stormy Years, 1918–1944]. Sofia, 1949.

———. *Political Bulgaria between 1913–1944*. Sofia, 1945.

———. *Vidiano i prezhiviano* [Seen and Outlived]. Sofia, 1969.

———. *Zveno bez grim* [Zveno Unmasked]. Sofia, 1936.

Kertész, Stephen D., ed. *East Central Europe and the World: Developments in the Post-Stalin Era*. Notre Dame, Ind., 1962.

———, ed. *The Fate of East Central Europe*. Notre Dame, Ind., 1956.

Khadzhiiliev, I. *Natrupvaneto i potreblenieto v ikonomikata na Bulgariia pri kapitalizma* [Accumulation and Consumption in the Bulgarian Economy under Capitalism]. Sofia, 1957.

Khadzhinikolov, Veselin. *Stopanski otnosheniia i vruzki mezhdu Bulgariia i Suvetskiia suiuz do deveti septemvrii, 1917–1944* [Economic Relations between Bulgaria and the Soviet Union until September 9, 1944, 1917–1944]. Sofia, 1956.

Khristov, Filiu. *Voenno-revoliutsionnata deinost na BKP, 1912–1944* [The Military-Revolutionary Activities of the Bulgarian Communist Party, 1912–1944]. Sofia, 1959.

Khristov, Khristo. *Revoliutsionnata kriza v Bulgariia prez 1918–1919* [The Revolutionary Crisis in Bulgaria during 1918–1919]. Sofia, 1957.

———, et al. *Sotsialisticheskata revoliutsiia v Bulgariia* [The Socialist Revolution in Bulgaria]. Sofia, 1965.

Kiosev, Dino G. *Istoriia na Makedonskoto natsionalno revoliutsionno dvizhenie* [History of the Macedonian National Revolutionary Movement]. Sofia, 1954.

Kirchev, Ivan. *Otechestvenata voina, 1944–1945* [The War for the Fatherland, 1944–1945]. Sofia, 1946.

Kiselinchev, Asen, *et al. Vuprosi na razvitieto na Bulgariia po putia na sotsializma* [Problems on the Development of Bulgaria on the Way to Socialism]. Sofia, 1954.

Kishales, Haim. *Korot yehudei bulgariya* [History of the Bulgarian Jews]. Vols. 1, 3, 4. Tel-Aviv, 1969–71.

Klincharov, I. G. *Istoriia na rabotnicheskoto dvizhenie v Bulgariia, 1882–1903* [History of the Labor Movement in Bulgaria, 1882–1903]. 2 vols. Sofia, 1926–28.

Klugman, James. *From Trotsky to Tito.* London, 1951.

Kodzheikov, Dragoi. *Materiali po sindikalnoto dvizhenie v Bulgariia* [Materials on the Syndicalist Movement in Bulgaria]. Sofia, 1948.

————, *et al. Revoliutsionnoto profsuiuzno dvizhenie v Bulgariia* [The Revolutionary Trade-Union Movement in Bulgaria]. Sofia, 1957.

Kofos, Evangelos. *Nationalism and Communism in Macedonia.* Salonika, 1964.

Kolarov, Vasil. *Antisuvetskata i antipartiina deinost na Tr. Kostov* [The Anti-Soviet and Antiparty Activities of Traicho Kostov]. Sofia, 1949.

————. *Izbrani proizvedeniia* [Selected Works]. 3 vols. Sofia, 1954–55.

————. *Protiv liiavoto sektantstvo i trotskizma v Bulgariia* [Against Left Sectarianism and Trotskyism in Bulgaria]. Sofia, 1949.

Kolev, Stoiko. *Borbata na BKP za Naroden front, 1935–1939* [The Struggle of the Bulgarian Communist Party for the Popular Front, 1935–1939]. Sofia, 1959.

Konstitutsiia na NRB [Constitution of the People's Republic of Bulgaria]. Sofia, 1947.

Kosev, Dimitur. *Kum istoriiata na revoliutsionnoto dvizhenie v Bulgariia prez 1867–1871* [Toward the History of the Revolutionary Movement in Bulgaria during 1867–1871]. Sofia, 1958.

————. *Septemvriiskoto vustanie v 1923 godina* [The September 1923 Uprising]. Sofia, 1954.

Kostanick, H. L. *Turkish Resettlement of Bulgarian Turks, 1950–1953.* Berkeley, Calif., 1957.

Kostov, Traicho. *Izbrani statii, dokladi, rechi* [Selected Articles, Reports, Speeches]. Sofia, 1964.

————. *Politicheskoto polozhenie i zadachite na partiiata* [The Political Situation and the Tasks of the Party]. Sofia, 1945.

Kozhukharov, K. *Aleksandur Stamboliiski: Biograficheski ocherk* [A. Stamboliiski: A Biographic Outline]. Sofia, 1956.

————. *BZNS v minaloto i dneshnite zadachi* [The Bulgarian Agrarian National Union in the Past and in the Contemporary Tasks]. Sofia, 1956.

————. *Kum sotsialistichesko preustroistvo na nasheto zemedelsko sto-*

panstvo [Toward a Socialist Reconstruction of Our Agricultural Economy]. Sofia, 1948.

KPJ i makedonskoto natsionalno prashanye [The Communist Party of Yugoslavia and the Macedonian National Problem]. Skoplje, 1949.

Krapchev, Danail. *Izminut put, 1906–1936* [The Road Behind, 1906–1936]. Sofia, 1936.

Krizata v Yugoslavskata komunisticheska partiia [The Crisis in the Yugoslav Communist Party]. Sofia, 1948.

Kuncheva, Pavlina, ed. *Septemvriiskoto vustanie, 1923* [The September Uprising, 1923]. Sofia, 1948.

Kunev, Trifon. *Sitni-drebni . . . kato kamilcheta* [Small and Tiny . . . Like the Camels]. Sofia, 1946.

Lambrev, Kiril. *Makedonskiiat vupros i balkanskoto edinstvo* [The Macedonian Problem and Balkan Unity]. Sofia, 1938.

————. *Polozhenieto na rabotnicheskata klasa ot Osvobozhdenieto do nachaloto na XX vek* [The Condition of the Working Class from the Liberation until the Beginning of the Twentieth Century]. Sofia, 1954.

Leites, N., and Bernaut, E. *Ritual of Liquidation: The Case of the Moscow Trials.* Glencoe, Ill., 1954.

Logio, George C. *Bulgaria, Past and Present.* Manchester, 1936.

————. *Bulgaria, Problems and Politics.* London, 1919.

Lukacs, John A. *The Great Powers and Eastern Europe.* New York, 1953.

Macartney, C. A., and Palmer, A. W. *Independent Eastern Europe.* London, 1962.

Malinov, A. *Pod znaka na ostrasteni i opasni politicheski borbi* [Under the Sign of Passionate and Dangerous Political Struggles]. Sofia, 1934.

————. *Stranichki ot nashata nova politicheska istoriia: Spomeni* [Pages from Our New Political History: Memoirs]. Sofia, 1938.

Manning, C. A., and Smal-Stocki, R. *The History of Modern Bulgarian Literature.* New York, 1960.

Markham, R. H. *Communists Crush Churches in Eastern Europe.* Boston, 1949.

————. *Meet Bulgaria.* Sofia, 1931.

————. *Tito's Imperial Communism.* Chapel Hill, N.C., 1947.

Markov, Marko. *Kum vuprosa za klasovite izmeneniia v NRB* [On the Question of Class Changes in the People's Republic of Bulgaria]. Sofia, 1960.

Materiali po istoriia na BKP, 9 septemvrii 1944–1960 g. [Materials on the History of the Bulgarian Communist Party, September 9, 1944–1960]. Sofia, 1961.

Materiali po istoriia na BKP, 1925–1962 [Materials on the History of the Bulgarian Communist Party, 1925–1962]. Sofia, 1965.

Memorandum: Bulgaria and Her Peace Problems. Sofia, 1946.

Meyer, Peter, *et al. The Jews in the Soviet Satellites.* Syracuse, N.Y., 1953.

Mihailoff, Ivan. *Macedonia: A Switzerland of the Balkans.* Saint Louis, Mo., 1950.

[————]. *Stalin and the Macedonian Question*. Saint Louis, Mo., 1948.

Mitev, I. *Fashistkiiat prevrat na Deveti iuni 1923 godina* [The Fascist *Putsch* of June 9, 1923]. Sofia, 1956.

Mitev, I. *Kratka istoriia na bulgarskiia narod* [A Short History of the Bulgarian People]. Sofia, 1951.

Mitrany, David. *Marx against the Peasant*. Chapel Hill, N.C., 1951.

Mitrev, Dimitar. *Pirinska Makedonija vo borba za natsionalno osvobo-duvanje* [Pirin Macedonia in the Struggle for National Liberation]. Skoplje, 1950.

Mizov, Nikolai. *Islamut v Bulgariia* [Islam in Bulgaria]. Sofia, 1965.

Mojsov, Lazo. *Bulgarskata rabotnichka partija (komunisti) i makedonskoto natsionalno prashanye* [The Bulgarian Workers Party (Communists) and the Macedonian National Question]. Skoplje, 1948.

Molho M., and Nehama, J. *Shoat yehudei yavan* [The Holocaust of the Greek Jews]. Jerusalem, 1965.

Moshanov, Stoicho. *Vunshnata politika na demokraticheskata partiia* [The Foreign Policy of the Democratic Party]. Sofia, 1946.

Natan, Zhak. *Bulgarskoto vuzrazhdane* [The Bulgarian Awakening]. 4th ed. Sofia, 1949.

————. *Ikonomicheska istoriia na Bulgariia* [Economic History of Bulgaria]. Sofia, 1957.

Natan, Zhak, and Berov, L. *Monopolisticheskiiat kapitalizum v Bulgariia* [Monopoly Capitalism in Bulgaria]. Sofia, 1958.

Natsionalna konferentsiia na Narodniia suiuz Zveno [National Conference of the People's Union Zveno]. Sofia, 1948.

Newman, Bernard. *Bulgarian Background*. London, 1961.

Nikolaev, N. P. *Le Règne et la Mort de Boris III*. Uppsala, Sweden, 1952.

Nollau, G. *International Communism and World Revolution*. New York, 1961.

Omarchevski, Stoian. *Bulgarskite upravnitsi prez Svetovnata voina: Fakti i dokumenti* [The Bulgarian Rulers during the World War: Facts and Documents]. Sofia, 1921.

Oren, Nissan. *Bulgarian Communism: The Road to Power, 1934–1944*. New York, 1971.

Ormandzhiev, Ivan P. *Federatsiia na balkanskite narodi* [A Federation of the Balkan People]. Sofia, 1947.

Ostoich, Petur Dragoliubov. *BKP i izgrazhdaneto na narodnodemokrati-cheskata durzhava* [The Bulgarian Communist Party and the Establishment of the People's Democratic State]. Sofia, 1967.

Otechestvenata voina na Bulgariia, 1944–1945 [Bulgaria's War for the Fatherland, 1944–1945]. 3 vols. Sofia, 1961–66.

Padev, Michael. *Dimitrov Wastes No Bullets: Nikola Petkov, the Test Case*. London, 1948.

Pashev, Boris. *Ideologiiata na zamedelskoto dvizhenie* [The Ideology of the Agrarian Movement]. Sofia, 1945.

Pavlov, Boris. *Osnovni nachala na Demokraticheskata partiia* [Basic Rules of the Democratic Party]. Sofia, 1946.

Pavlov, Todor. *Teoriia na otrazhenieto* [The Theory of Reflection]. 3rd ed. Sofia, 1947.

Peti kongres na BKP [Fifth Congress of the Bulgarian Communist Party]. Vol. 1. Sofia, 1949.

Petkov, Nikola D. *Aleksandur Stamboliiski: Lichnost i idei* [A. Stamboliiski: The Man and His Ideas]. Sofia, 1930.

Petrova, Dimitrina V. *BZNS i narodniiat front, 1934–1939* [The Bulgarian Agrarian Union and the Popular Front, 1934–1939]. Sofia, 1967.

―――. *BZNS v kraia na burzhoaznoto gospodstvo v Bulgariia, 1939–1944* [The Bulgarian Agrarian Union at the End of the Bourgeois Domination in Bulgaria, 1939–1944]. Sofia, 1970.

Piti, Buko. *Te, spasitelite* [They, the Saviors]. Tel-Aviv, 1969.

Popisakov, Grigor A. *Ikonomicheski otnosheniia mezhdu NRB i SSSR* [Economic Relations between the People's Republic of Bulgaria and the Soviet Union]. Sofia, 1968.

Popov, Petur. *Ustanoviavane, razvitie, i sistema na proletarskata diktatura u nas* [Establishment, Development, and System of the Proletarian Dictatorship in Our Country]. Sofia, 1956.

Pundeff, Marin V. "Bulgaria's Place in Axis Policy, 1936–1944," Ph.D. diss., University of Southern California, 1958.

Rothschild, Joseph. *The Communist Party of Bulgaria: Origins and Development, 1883–1936*. New York, 1959.

Royal Institute of International Affairs. *The Soviet-Yugoslav Dispute: Text of the Published Correspondence*. London, 1948.

Rusev, Dimitur. *Borbata na BKP za sotsialisticheska industrializatsiia na Bulgariia, 1949–1953* [The Struggle of the Bulgarian Communist Party for the Socialist Industrialization of Bulgaria, 1949–1953]. Sofia, 1964.

Sakuzov, Ianko. *Bulgariia v svoiata istoriia* [Bulgaria in Her History]. 2nd ed. Sofia, 1918.

Sedmi kongres na BKP. [Seventh Congress of the Bulgarian Communist Party]. Sofia, 1958.

Seton-Watson, Hugh. *Eastern Europe Between the Wars, 1918–1941*. London, 1945.

―――. *The East European Revolution*. 3rd ed. New York, 1956.

Sharlanov, D., and Damianova, P. *Miastoto i roliata na Otechestveniia front v sistemata na narodnata demokratsiia* [The Place and Role of the Fatherland Front in the System of the People's Democracy]. Sofia, 1968.

Sharp, Samuel L. *New Constitutions in the Soviet Sphere*. Washington, D.C., 1950.

Shesti kongres na BKP [Sixth Congress of the Bulgarian Communist Party]. Sofia, 1954.

Shterev, Pantelei. *Obshti borbi na bulgarskiia i grutskiia narod sreshtu khitlerofashistakata okupatsiia* [Common Struggles of the Bulgarian and Greek Peoples against the Hitlerite-Fascist Occupation]. Sofia, 1966.

Shuster, George N. *Religion behind the Iron Curtain.* New York, 1954.

Sipkov, Ivan. *Legal Sources and Bibliography of Bulgaria.* New York, 1956.

Soviet Foreign Policy during the Patriotic War: Documents and Materials. 2 vols. London, 1946.

The Soviet-Yugoslav Controversy, 1948–1958: A Documentary Record. New York, 1959.

Spisarevski, Kosta D. *Zemedelskoto dvizhenie v Bulgariia: Poteklo i razvitie* [The Agrarian Movement in Bulgaria: Origins and Development]. Sofia, 1923.

Spulber, N. *The Economics of Communist Eastern Europe.* New York, 1957.

Stainov, P., and Angelov, A. *Administrativno pravo na NRB* [Public Law of the People's Republic of Bulgaria]. 2 vols. Sofia, 1957–60.

Stamboliiski, A. *Politicheski partii ili suslovni organizatsii?* [Political Parties or Estatist Organizations?]. 3rd ed. Sofia, 1945.

Stanev, Nikola. *Istoriia na nova Bulgariia, 1878–1928* [History of Contemporary Bulgaria, 1878–1928]. Sofia, 1929.

Statisticheski godishnik na NRB: Sukrateno izdanie, 1956 [Statistical Yearbook of the People's Republic of Bulgaria: Abbreviated Edition, 1956]. Sofia, 1957.

Statisticheski godishnik na tsarstvo Bulgariia [Statistical Yearbook of the Kingdom of Bulgaria]. Sofia, 1940.

Stavrianos, L. S. *Balkan Federation: A History of the Movement toward Balkan Unity in Modern Times.* Northhampton, Mass., 1944.

Stefan I, Ekzarkh, and Shavelski, G. *Sotsialniiat problem v svetlinata na Evangielieto* [The Social Problem in the Light of the New Testament]. Sofia, 1947.

Stoianov, D. *Istoriia na kooperativnoto dvizhenie v Bulgariia: Chast I, 1863–1910* [History of the Cooperative Movement in Bulgaria: Part I, 1863–1910]. Sofia, 1937.

The Struggle of the Bulgarian People against Fascism. Sofia, 1946.

Sweet-Escott, Bickham. *Baker Street Irregular.* London, 1965.

Swire, Joseph. *Bulgarian Conspiracy.* London, 1939.

Tadzher, Zh. *Nova Bulgariia* [New Bulgaria]. Sofia, 1922.

Tchitchovski, T. *The Socialist Movement in Bulgaria.* London, 1931.

Titovata banda, orudie na imperialistite: Dokumenti i materiali, 1948–1951 [Tito's Gang, a Weapon of Imperialism: Documents and Materials, 1948–1951]. Sofia, 1951.

Todorov, Kosta. *Balkan Firebrand.* New York, 1943.

Topencharov, Vladimir. *Istoriiata shte mine pokrai tiakh* [History Will By-Pass Them]. Sofia, 1947.

Traikov, Georgi. *Za narodna vlast* [For a People's Rule]. Sofia, 1951.

Treta konferentsiia na BKP [Third Conference of the Bulgarian Communist Party]. Sofia, 1950.

The Trial of Nikola D. Petkov, August 5–15, 1947: Record of the Judicial Proceedings. Sofia, 1947.

The Trial of the Fifteen Pastor-Spies. Sofia, 1949.

The Trial of Traicho Kostov and His Group. Sofia, 1949.

Trunski, Slavcho. *Bulgarskata narodna armiia: Istoricheski ocherk* [The Bulgarian People's Army: A Historical Outline]. Sofia, 1969.

Tsankov, A. *Posledstvie ot voinata* [An Aftermath of the War]. Sofia, 1919.

———. *Trite stopanski sistemi* [The Three Economic Systems]. Sofia, 1942.

The Turkish Minority in the People's Republic of Bulgaria. Sofia, 1951.

Ulam, Adam. *Titoism and the Cominform.* Cambridge, Mass., 1952.

Union of Bulgarian Jurists. *Inquiry into the Legality of Communist Rule in Bulgaria.* New York, 1955.

U.S., Department of State. *Foreign Relations of the United States: Diplomatic Papers.* Selected vols. Washington, D.C.

———. *Macedonian Nationalism and the Communist Party of Yugoslavia.* Washington, D.C., 1954.

Ustanoviavane i ukrepvane na narodnodemokraticheskata vlast, Septemvrii, 1944–Mai, 1945: Sbornik dokumenti [Establishment and Strengthening of the People's Democratic Regime, September, 1944–May, 1945: A Collection of Documents]. Sofia, 1969.

Vasev, Slavcho, and Khristov, Krum. *Bulgariia na mirnata konferentsiia, Parizh, 1946* [Bulgaria at the Peace Conference, Paris, 1946]. Sofia, 1947.

Vasilev, Orlin. *Vuoruzhenata suprotiva* [The Armed Resistance]. Sofia, 1946.

Velchev, Damian. *Statii, rechi, i zapovedi . . .* [Articles, Speeches, and Orders . . .]. Sofia, 1946.

Vergnet, Paul, and Bernard-Derosne, Jean. *L'affaire Petkov.* Paris, 1948.

Vladikin, Liubomir. *Istoriia na Turnovskata konstitutsiia* [History of the Turnovo Constitution]. Sofia, 1936.

Vlahov, D. *Govori i statii, 1945–1947* [Speeches and Articles, 1945–1947]. Skoplje, 1947.

———. *Svobodna Makedoniia i federalna Yugoslaviia* [Free Macedonia and Federal Yugoslavia]. Sofia, 1945.

Vtoriiat kongres na Otechestveniiat front [The Second Congress of the Fatherland Front]. Sofia, 1948.

Vutov, Petur. *Amerikano-angliiskite imperialisti: Nai zli vragove na bulgarskiia narod* [The Anglo-American Imperialists: The Bulgarian People's Worst Enemies]. Sofia, 1953.

Warriner, D. *Revolution in Eastern Europe.* London, 1950.

Wolff, Robert Lee. *The Balkans in Our Time.* Cambridge, Mass., 1956.

Woodhouse, C. M. *Apple of Discord: A Survey of Recent Greek Politics in Their International Setting.* London, 1948.

Xydis, S. G. *Greece and the Great Powers, 1944–47.* Salonika, 1963.

Zagoroff, S. D. *The Economy of Bulgaria.* Council for Economic and Industrial Research, Inc., Report no. A-19. Washington, D.C., 1955.

————, et al. *The Agricultural Economy of the Danubian Countries, 1935–45.* Stanford, Calif., 1955.

Zhivkov, Todor. *Eighth Congress of the Bulgarian Communist Party.* Sofia, 1963.

————. *Po niakoi osnovni vuprosi na nashata partiina i obshtestvena rabota* [On Some Basic Questions pertaining to Our Party Work and the Public]. Sofia, 1960.

————. *Za uskoriavane razvitieto na narodnoto stopanstvo . . .* [On Hastening the Development of the People's Economy . . .]. Sofia, 1959.

INDEX

Abadzhiev, I., 166
Academy of Sciences, Bulgarian, 154–57
Agrarianism, 12, 15
Agrarian Union, Bulgarian: in Agrarian era, 5–6, 8–11; in People's Bloc government, 6, 13–17; and elections of March, 1938, 42; foreign policy of under Stamboliiski, 46–50; and Fatherland Front, 81, 84; in anti-Communist opposition, 91–92, 100; bogus, 96, 114, 131, 149, 178; reunification of Pladne and Gichev wings of, 100; domestic policy of, 114, 116
—Pladne Agrarians: split from Gichev Agrarians, 16; and Communists, 42; and Yugoslavia, 49; opposition of to Germans, 66; and Fatherland Front, 73, 84
—Gichev Agrarians: in Iron Bloc, 22; and Communists, 42; and Fatherland Front, 84
Agriculture, in Bulgaria, 115–16, 143, 145, 152–53, 168, 169–70
AIC (agroindustrial complexes), 168
Albania, 82, 143, 148, 165, 181
Alexander, king of Yugoslavia, 52
Allied Control Commission (ACC), 79, 99
Allied Mediterranean Command, 72
Allies, Western: Bulgaria declares war on, 65; and regency council, 74; and Allied Control Commission, 79
Anarchist movement, Bulgarian, 38n
"Anna, the Comrade of the District" (Toromanski), 138
Anti-Stamboliiski coup. *See* Coups d'état: anti-Stamboliiski

Army, Bulgarian: and First World War, 1; and Second World War, 1, 77, 85–87; purge of, 62, 86, 87, 113; in the present day, 179
Austria, and Bulgaria, 55, 86
Austro-Hungary, relations of with Bulgaria, 155
Authoritarianism, 17, 19
Avramov, L., 166

Bagrianov, I., 73, 89
Balkan Pact: of February, 1934, 53; of February, 1953, 127
Balkan wars, 8n, 156
Barnes, M., 99
Batolov, K., 54
Benefactors (Nesnakomov), 138
Berlin Treaty, 155
Biriuzov, General S. S., 79–80, 91, 99
Blagoev, D.: leader of "narrow" Socialists, 23; origin of, 30; and Macedonian issue, 155–56
Bled Agreement, 119n
Bokov, G., 166
Bolshevism, 19, 23, 24
Bonev, V., 166
Boris III, king of Bulgaria: accedes to throne, 8; regime of in interwar period, 35–36, 40–41, 61; foreign policy of, 44, 50, 52–53, 63–64, 67–68, 74, 173; during Second World War, 62, 65, 77; death of, 74; economic policy of, 117, 174–75
Bourgeoisie, Bulgarian, 60
Brezhnev, L., 158
"Broad" Socialists, 22, 23
Bukharin, N., 115

THE JOHNS HOPKINS UNIVERSITY PRESS

This book was composed in Baskerville text and Baskerville and Albertus
display by Port City Press, Inc. It was printed on S. D. Warren's 55-lb Sebago paper,
in an antique shade, and bound by Port City Press, Inc. The cloth edition
was bound in Roxite cloth, vellum finish.

Library of Congress Cataloging in Publication Data

Oren, Nissan.
 Revolution administered.

 (Integration and community building in Eastern Europe, EE8)
 Bibliography: p.
 1. Bulgaria—Politics and government. 2. Bulgaria—Politics and government—
1944– 3. Communism—Bulgaria. I. Title. II. Series.
DR89.068   320.9'4977'03   72-8831
ISBN 0-8018-1209-7
ISBN 0-8018-1210-0 (pbk)